D0547674

BRITAIN'S FAVOURITE
PUB WALKS
AND
CYCLE RIDES

© Automobile Association Developments Limited 2005

All rights reserved. No part of this publication may be reproduced, stored in a retrieval system, or transmitted in any form by any means – electronic, mechanical, photocopying, recording or otherwise – unless the written permission of the publisher has been given beforehand. This book may not be lent, resold, hired out or otherwise disposed of by way of trade in any form or binding or cover other than that in which it is published, without the prior consent of the publisher.

The contents of this book are believed to be correct at the time of printing. Nevertherless, the publisher cannot be held responsible for any errors or omissions or for any changes in the details given in this book or for the consequences of any reliance on the information provided by the same. This does not affect your statutory rights. We have tried to ensure accuracy in this book, but things do change. Please advise us of any inaccuracies you may find.

Produced by AA Publishing

The views expressed in this book are those of the author but they are general views only and readers are urged to consult a relevant and qualified specialist for individual advice in particular situations. Marks and Spencer plc and Automobile Association Developments Limited hereby exclude all liability to the extent permitted by law for any errors or omissions in this book and for any loss, damage or expense (whether direct or indirect) suffered by a third party relying on any information contained in the book.

Printed and bound by Graficas Estella, S.A., Navarra, Spain

Published by AA Publishing, which is a trading name of Automobile Association Developments Limited. Registered number 1878835.

A CIP catalogue record for this book is available from the British Library.

A02791

Ordnance Survey This product includes mapping data licensed from Ordnance Survey® with the permission of the Controller of Her Majesty's Stationery Office.
© Crown copyright 2005. All rights reserved. Licence number 399221

ISBN-10: 0-7495-4452-X
ISBN-13: 978-0-7495-4846-9

Cover Picture Credits
Top left AA/Clive Sawyer; top centre left AA/Roger Moss; top centre right AA/Clive Sawyer; top right AA; bottom left AA/Mike Haywood; bottom centre left AA/Tom Mackie; bottom centre right AA/Jonathan Welsh; bottom right AA/Jeff Beazley.
Back Cover Picture Credits
Left AA/Clive Sawyer; centre left AA/Clive Sawyer; centre right AA/John Morrison; right AA.

BRITAIN'S FAVOURITE
PUB WALKS
AND
CYCLE RIDES

AA

Locator map

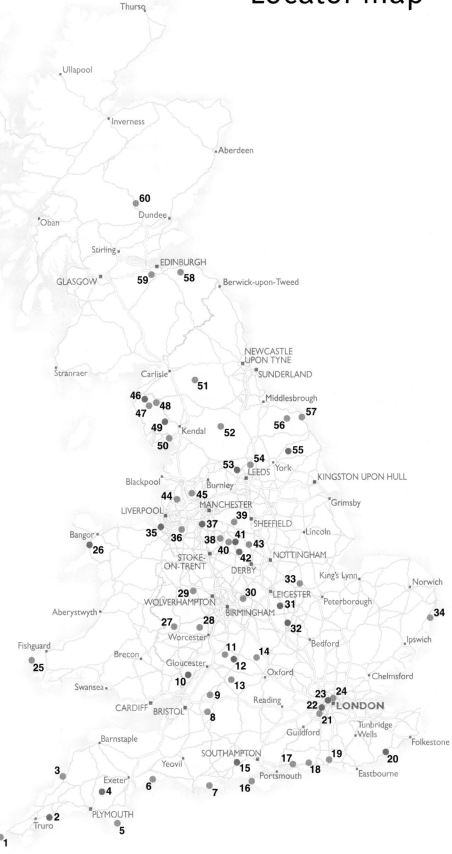

Thurso

Ullapool

Inverness

Aberdeen

Oban

60
Dundee

Stirling

EDINBURGH
59   58
GLASGOW   Berwick-upon-Tweed

NEWCASTLE
UPON TYNE
Stranraer   Carlisle   SUNDERLAND

51   Middlesbrough
46   57
47 48   56
49   Kendal
50   55
53 54   York
LEEDS   KINGSTON UPON HULL
Blackpool   Burnley
44 45   Grimsby
LIVERPOOL MANCHESTER
Bangor   35 36 38 39 SHEFFIELD
26   37 41 43 Lincoln
40 42 NOTTINGHAM
STOKE-
ON-TRENT DERBY
33   King's Lynn   Norwich
29 30 LEICESTER Peterborough
WOLVERHAMPTON 31
Aberystwyth   BIRMINGHAM 32 34
27 28   Ipswich
Worcester Bedford
11 14
Fishguard   Brecon   12 Oxford   Chelmsford
25   Gloucester   13 Reading
10   9   23 24
Swansea   23 22 LONDON
CARDIFF BRISTOL   8 21 Tunbridge
Barnstaple   Guildford Wells Folkestone
19
SOUTHAMPTON 17 18 20
3   Yeovil   15   Eastbourne
Exeter 6 Portsmouth
4   16
2   7
Truro   PLYMOUTH
5
1

Contents

Contents

Walking and cycling around Britain

Southwest England
Surrounded by the Southwest Coast Path National Trail, the maritime influence is great here, but there are plenty of routes away from the coast. In the downlands and valleys of Dorset and Wiltshire, discover pastoral farmland and picturesque villages while the moorlands of Devon and Somerset offer excellent routes away from the crowds.

Southeast England
Here, London's urban sprawl is counter-balanced by superb parkland in the capital; chalk downland ridges that stretch away to the west; deep beech woods that shelter roe deer and muntjac; towering white cliffs along the coast, and thatched houses that huddle around a village green.

Wales
The Welsh landscape can compete with the best in the British Isles. Its high, jagged mountains in the north are like naive impressions of what mountains should look like. Its quiet valleys feel remote and undiscovered. The Pembrokeshire coastline. in the south, juts its rugged cliffs into a foaming sea and the crests of the Brecon Beacons soar above the wooded vales.

Central England
This is Shakespeare country, land of warm stone and fine cathdral cities. Apart from the canals, you may be surprised at how much hill country you'll find here. In the east the Chilterns form a natural beech-wood boundary to Oxfordshire's farming country.

In the west the Black Mountains carry summits over 2,000ft (610m). Staffordshire claws its way into the Peak District while the Wrekin and the Shropshire Hills secure plenty of upland challenge.

Eastern England

This area extends from the ancient oaks of Sherwood Forest, across the Fens to the Norfolk Broads and the North Sea coast, and up to the Lincolnshire Wolds. The only appreciable heights are the Lincolnshire Wolds, Bedfordshire's Dunstable Downs and Charnwood Forest in Leicestershire but there is plenty of scenic landscape to explore.

Northwest England

This is a region of great industrial towns and cities, high moors and the sands of Morecambe Bay. This is 'outdoor' country. From the Peak District National Park to the Lake District and the Scottish Borders, northwest England has mountains, lakes and dales to discover.

Northeast England

The hills dominate here. The gritstone Pennines form a western boundary, only broken where the Tyne breaks through against the Scottish border. Yorkshire's heritage coastline and the wild Northumbrian shore offer plenty of opportunites for walking and cycling. There's plenty of history too, from the industry that shaped the region to great monasteries and castles to explore.

Scotland

Scotland is a country of huge spaces and mountains on a grand scale. The western seaboard is littered with islands and vast fjord-like lochs. The rounded hilltops and deep valleys characterise the Borders, while the central belt, including Edinburgh and Glasgow, is where most people live. But it is the Highlands that define Scotland – freshwater lochs surrounded by silver birch and Scots pine. Here, and in the wilder reaches of the Southern uplands, you'll find wildlife to spot and routes to discover.

Using this book

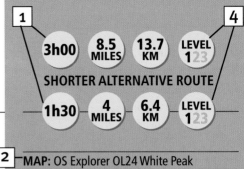

Each walk and cycle ride has a coloured panel giving essential information for the walker and cyclist, including the distance, terrain, nature of the paths, and where to park your car.

[1] **MINIMUM TIME:** The time stated for completing each route is the estimated minimum time that a reasonably fit family group of walkers or cyclists would take to complete the circuit. This does not allow for rest or refreshment stops.

[2] **MAPS:** Each route is shown on a detailed map. However, some detail is lost because of the restrictions imposed by scale, so for this reason, we recommend that you use the maps in conjunction with a more detailed Ordnance Survey map. The relevant Ordnance Survey Explorer map appropriate for each walk or cycle is listed.

[3] **START/FINISH:** Here we indicate the start location and parking area. There is a six-figure grid reference prefixed by two letters showing which 100km square of the National Grid it refers to. You'll find more information on grid references on most Ordnance Survey maps.

[4] **LEVEL OF DIFFICULTY:** The walks and cycle rides have been graded simply (1 to 3) to give an indication of their relative difficulty. Easier routes, such as those with little total ascent, on easy footpaths or level trails, or those covering shorter distances are graded 1. The hardest routes, either because they include a lot of ascent, greater

---

3h00 · **8.5 MILES** · **13.7 KM** · **LEVEL 1**23

SHORTER ALTERNATIVE ROUTE

1h30 · **4 MILES** · **6.4 KM** · **LEVEL 1**23

[2] **MAP:** OS Explorer OL24 White Peak

START/FINISH: Rudyard Old Station, grid ref
[3] SJ 955579

TRAILS/TRACKS: old railway trackbed

LANDSCAPE: wooded lake shore, peaceful pastures and meadows

PUBLIC TOILETS: Rudyard village

[5] **TOURIST INFORMATION:** Leek, tel 01538 483741

[6] **CYCLE HIRE:** none near by

THE PUB: The Abbey Inn, Leek, see Directions to the pub, page 27

[7] ❶ Take care along the banks of the lake – keep well away from the shore line

---

distances, or are in hilly, more demanding terrains, are graded 3.

[5] **TOURIST INFORMATION:** The nearest tourist information office and contact number is given for further local information, in particular opening details for the attractions listed in the 'Where to go from here' section.

[6] **CYCLE HIRE:** We list, within reason, the nearest cycle hire shop/centre.

[7] ❶Here we highlight any potential difficulties or dangers along the route. At a glance you will know if the walk is steep or crosses difficult terrain, or if a cycle route is hilly, encounters a main road, or whether a mountain bike is essential for the off-road trails. If a particular route is suitable for older, fitter children we say so here.

About the pub

Generally, all the pubs featured are on the walk or cycle route. Some are close to the start/finish point, others are at the midway point, and occasionally, the recommended pub is a short drive from the start/finish point. We have included a cross-section of pubs, from homely village locals and isolated rural gems to traditional inns and upmarket country pubs which specialise in food. What they all have in common is that they serve food and welcome children.

The description of the pub is intended to convey its history and character and in the 'food' section we list a selection of dishes, which indicate the style of food available. Under 'family facilities', we say if the pub offers a children's menu or smaller portions of adult dishes, and whether the pub has a family room, highchairs, baby-changing facilities, or toys. There is detail on the garden, terrace, and any play area.

DIRECTIONS: If the pub is very close to the start point we state see Getting to the Start. If the pub is on the route the relevant direction/map location number is given, in addition to general directions. In some cases the pub is a short drive away from the finish point, so we give detailed directions to the pub from the end of the route.

PARKING: The number of parking spaces is given. All but a few of the walks and rides start away from the pub. If the pub car park is the parking/start point, then we have been given permission by the landlord to print the fact. You should always let the landlord or a member of staff know that you are using the car park before setting off.

OPEN: If the pub is open all week we state 'daily' and if it's open throughout the day we say 'all day', otherwise we just give the days/sessions the pub is closed.

FOOD: If the pub serves food all week we state 'daily' and if food is served throughout the day we say 'all day', otherwise we just give the days/sessions when food is not served.

BREWERY/COMPANY: This is the name of the brewery to which the pub is tied or the pub company that owns it. 'Free house' means that the pub is independently owned and run.

REAL ALE: We list the regular real ales available on handpump. 'Guest beers' indicates that the pub rotates beers from a number of microbreweries.

DOGS: We say if dogs are allowed in pubs on walk routes and detail any restrictions.

ROOMS: We list the number of bedrooms and how many are en suite. For prices please call the pub.

Please note that pubs change hands frequently and new chefs are employed, so menu details and facilities may change at short notice. Not all the pubs featured in this guide are listed in the AA Pub Guide. For information on those that are, including AA-rated accommodation, and for a comprehensive selection of pubs across Britain, please refer to the AA Pub Guide or see the AA's website www.theAA.com

Alternative refreshment stops

At a glance you will see if there are other pubs or cafés along the route. If there are no other places on the route, we list the nearest village or town where you can find somewhere else to eat and drink.

☛ Where to go from here

Many of the routes are short and may only take a few hours. You may wish to explore the surrounding area after lunch or before tackling the route, so we have selected a few attractions with children in mind.

Walking and cycling in safety

WALKING

All the walks are suitable for families, but less experienced family groups, especially those with younger children, should try the shorter or easier walks first. Route finding is usually straightforward, but the maps are for guidance only and we recommend that you always take the suggested Ordnance Survey map with you.

Risks

Although each walk has been researched with a view to minimising any risks, no walk in the countryside can be considered to be completely free from risk. Walking in the outdoors will always require a degree of common sense and judgement to ensure that it is as safe as possible, especially for young children.

- Be particularly careful on cliff paths and in upland terrain, where the consequences of a slip can be serious.
- Remember to check tidal conditions before walking on the seashore.
- Some sections of route are by, or cross, busy roads. Remember traffic is a danger even on minor country lanes.
- Be careful around farmyard machinery and livestock.
- Be aware of the consequences of changes in the weather and check the forecast before you set out. Ensure the whole family is properly equipped, wearing warm clothing and a good pair of boots or sturdy walking shoes. Take waterproof clothing with you and carry spare clothing and a torch if you are walking in the winter months. Remember the weather can change quickly at any time of the year, and in moorland and heathland areas, mist and fog can make route finding much harder. In summer, take account of the heat and sun by wearing a hat and carrying enough water.

- On walks away from centres of population you should carry a whistle and survival bag. If you do have an accident requiring emergency services, make a note of your position as accurately as possible and dial 999.

CYCLING

Cycling is a fun activity which children love, and teaching your child to ride a bike, and going on family cycling trips, are rewarding experiences. Not only is cycling a great way to travel, but as a regular form of exercise it can make an invaluable contribution to a child's health and fitness, and increase their confidence and sense of independence.

The growth of motor traffic has made Britain's roads increasingly dangerous and unattractive to cyclists. Cycling with children is an added responsibility and, as with everything, there is a risk when taking them out for a day's cycling. However, in recent years many measures have been taken to address this, including the on-going development of the National Cycle Network (8,000 miles utilising quiet lanes and traffic-free paths) and local designated off-road routes for families, such as converted railway lines, canal towpaths and forest tracks.

In devising the cycle rides in this guide, every effort has been made to use these designated cycle paths, or to link them with quiet country lanes and waymarked byways and bridleways. Unavoidably, in a few cases, some relatively busy B-roads have been used to link the quieter, more attractive routes.

Rules of the road
- Ride in single file on narrow and busy roads.
- Be alert, look and listen for traffic, especially on narrow lanes and blind bends and be extra careful when descending steep hills, as loose gravel can lead to an accident.
- In wet weather make sure you keep a good distance between you and other riders.
- Make sure you indicate your intentions clearly.
- Brush up on *The Highway Code* before venturing out on to the road.

Off-road safety code of conduct
- Only ride where you know it is legal to do so. It is forbidden to cycle on public footpaths, marked in yellow. The only 'rights of way' open to cyclists are bridleways (blue markers) and unsurfaced tracks, known as byways, which are open to all traffic and waymarked in red.
- Canal towpaths: you need a permit to cycle on some stretches of towpath (www.waterscape.com). Remember that access paths can be steep and slippery and always get off and push your bike under low bridges and by locks.
- Always yield to walkers and horses, giving adequate warning of your approach.

- Don't expect to cycle at high speeds.
- Keep to the main trail to avoid any unnecessary erosion to the area beside the trail and to prevent skidding, especially if it is wet.
- Remember the Country Code.

Cycling with children

Children can use a child seat from the age of eight months, or from the time they can hold themselves upright. There are a number of child seats available which fit on the front or rear of a bike and towable two-seat trailers are worth investigating. 'Trailer bicycles', suitable for five- to ten-year-olds, can be attached to the rear of an adult's bike, so that the adult has control, allowing the child to pedal if he/she wishes. Family cycling can be made easier by using a tandem, as it can carry a child seat and tow trailers. 'Kiddy-cranks' for shorter legs can be fitted to the rear seat tube, enabling either parent to take their child out cycling. With older children it is better to purchase the right size bike rather than one that is too big, as an oversized bike will be difficult to control, and potentially dangerous.

Preparing your bicycle

A basic routine includes checking the wheels for broken spokes or excess play in the bearings, and checking the tyres for punctures, undue wear and the correct tyre pressures. Ensure that the brake blocks are firmly in place and not worn, and that cables are not frayed or too slack. Lubricate hubs, pedals, gear mechanisms and cables. Make sure you have a pump, a bell, a rear rack to carry panniers and, if cycling at night, a set of working lights.

Preparing yourself

Equipping the family with quality cycling clothing need not be an expensive exercise. Comfort is the key when considering what to wear. Essential items for well-being on a bike are padded cycling shorts, warm stretch leggings (avoid tight-fitting and seamed trousers like jeans or baggy tracksuit trousers that may become caught in the chain), stiff-soled training shoes, and a wind and waterproof jacket. Fingerless gloves will add to your comfort.

A cycling helmet provides essential protection if you fall off your bike, so they are essential for young children learning to cycle.

Wrap your child up with several layers in colder weather. Make sure you and those with you are easily visible by car drivers and other road users, by wearing light-coloured or luminous clothing in daylight and reflective strips or sashes in failing light and when it is dark.

What to take with you

Invest in a pair of medium-sized panniers (rucksacks are unwieldy and can affect balance) to carry the necessary gear for you and your family for the day. Take extra clothes with you, the amount depending on the season, and always pack a light wind/waterproof jacket. Carry a basic tool kit (tyre levers, adjustable spanner, a small screwdriver, puncture repair kit, a set of Allen keys) and practical spares, such as an inner tube, a universal brake/gear cable, and a selection of nuts and bolts. Also, always take a pump and a strong lock.

Cycling, especially in hilly terrain and off-road, saps energy, so take enough food and drink for your outing. Always carry plenty of water, especially in hot and humid weather conditions. Consume high-energy snacks like cereal bars, cake or fruits, eating little and often to combat feeling weak and tired. Remember that children get thirsty (and hungry) much more quickly than adults so always have food and diluted juices available for them.

USEFUL CYCLING WEBSITES

NATIONAL CYCLE NETWORK
A comprehensive network of safe and attractive cycle routes throughout the UK.
It is co-ordinated by the route construction charity Sustrans with the support of more than 450 local authorities and partners across Britain. For maps, leaflets and more information on the designated off-road cycle trails across the country contact
www.sustrans.org.uk
www.nationalcyclenetwork.org.uk

LONDON CYCLING CAMPAIGN
Pressure group that lobbies MPs, organises campaigns and petitions in order to improve cycling conditions in the capital. It provides maps, leaflets and information on cycle routes across London.
www.lcc.org.uk

BRITISH WATERWAYS
For information on towpath cycling, visit
www.waterscape.com

FORESTRY COMMISSION
For information on cycling in Forestry Commission woodland see
www.forestry.gov.uk/recreation

CYCLISTS TOURING CLUB
The largest cycling club in Britain, provides information on cycle touring, and legal and technical matters
www.ctc.org.uk

Prussia Cove coastal walk

WALK

Prussia Cove CORNWALL

A stroll through the coastal domain of one of Cornwall's most famous smugglers.

Prussia Cove

Smuggling clings to the image of Cornwall: old time 'freetraders' stole ashore with their cargoes of tea, spirits, tobacco and silk. Modern smuggling, chiefly of drugs, has no such romantic sheen yet we attach an image of honest adventure to old-time smuggling.

Such 'honest adventuring' seems personified by the famous Carter family which lived at Prussia Cove. The cove is really more of a series of rocky inlets close to the magnificent St Michael's Mount, the castle-crowned island that so enhances the inner corner of Mount's Bay. John and Henry (Harry) Carter were the best known members of the family and ran their late 18th-century smuggling enterprise with great flair and efficiency. John Carter was the more flamboyant, styling himself in early childhood games as 'the King of Prussia'. The name stuck and the original Porth Leah Cove became known as the 'King of Prussia's Cove'. Fame indeed. John Carter had integrity. He once broke in to an excise store in Penzance to recover smuggled goods confiscated from Prussia Cove in his absence.

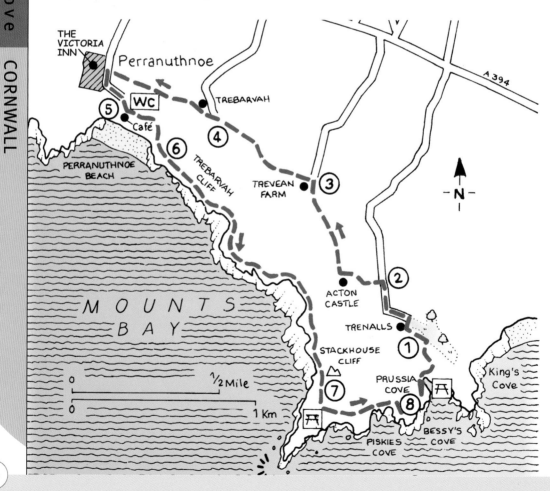

The authorities knew it must have been Carter because he was 'an upright man' and took only his own goods. His brother Harry became a Methodist preacher and forbade swearing on all his vessels.

As you follow this walk inland, you sense the remoteness of hamlets, the secretiveness of the lanes and paths. At Perranuthnoe, the beach resounds with the sound of the sea where surfers and holidaymakers now enjoy themselves. From here the coastal footpath leads back across the rocky headland of Cudden Point.

the walk

1 From the car park entrance walk back along the approach road, past the large house. Watch for traffic. After the second bend, look for a **stile** on the left, just past a field gate.

2 Cross the stile and follow the left-hand field edge, bearing off to the right, where it bends left, to reach a stile in the hedge opposite. Walk down the edge of the next field, behind Acton Castle (private dwellings), then turn right along field edges to a stile into the adjacent **rough lane**. Turn right.

3 Pass a house called **Acton Barns** and turn left along a rough track at a junction in front of a bungalow entrance at **Trevean Farm**. At a left-hand bend go onto a stony track for just a few paces, then look out for the **public footpath sign**, ascend to the right, up some narrow steps, then turn left along the edge of the field.

Prussia Cove, once the haunt of smugglers

2h00 · **4 MILES** · **6.4 KM** · **LEVEL 123**

MAP: OS Explorer 102 Land's End
START/FINISH: Trenalls, Prussia Cove. Small, privately-owned car park; grid ref: SW 554283. Alternatively, park at Perranuthnoe, from where the walk can be started at Point **5**
PATHS: good field paths and coastal paths, 18 stiles
LANDSCAPE: quiet coast and countryside
PUBLIC TOILETS: Perranuthnoe
TOURIST INFORMATION: Penzance, tel 01736 362207
THE PUB: Victoria Inn, Perranuthnoe
❶ Care to be taken on the cliff path near Prussia Cove

Getting to the start
Prussia Cove is signposted off the A394 at Rosudgeon between Penzance and Helston, 6 miles (9.7km) east of Penzance. Follow the narrow lane to its end at Trenalls. The parking area is just past the farm at the end of the tarmac road.

7 At the National Trust property of **Cudden Point**, follow the path steeply uphill and then across the inner slope of the headland above **Piskies Cove**.

8 Go through a gate and pass some ancient fishing huts. Follow the path round the edge of the **Bessy's Cove** inlet of Prussia Cove, to reach a track by a thatched cottage. The cove can be reached down a path on the right just before this junction. Turn right and follow the track. Ignore the track left by the postbox and take the second left (**green sign**) to return to the car park at the start of the walk.

4 At Trebarvah, cross the farm lane, pass in front of some barns, (there's a view of St Michael's Mount ahead), then follow the right-hand field edge to a hedged-in path. Follow the path ahead through fields, then pass in front of some houses to reach the main road opposite the **Victoria Inn**. Go left and follow the road to the car park above **Perranuthnoe Beach**.

5 For the beach and Cabin Café keep straight ahead. On the main route of the walk, go left, just beyond the car park, and along a lane. Bear right at a fork, then bear right again just past a house at a junction.

6 Go down a track towards the sea and follow it round left. Then, at a field entrance, go down right (signposted), turn sharp left through a gap and follow the **coast path** along the edge of Trebarvah and **Stackhouse Cliffs**.

what to look for

Along the sandy paths and fields east of Perranuthnoe, the feathery-leafed tamaraisk (Tamarix anglica), lends an exotic Mediterranean atmosphere to the Cornish scene. The tamarisk was introduced to Britain from the Mediterranean and is often used at coastal locations as a windbreak because of its resilience and its ability to survive the battering of salt-laden winds. Take time midway in the walk to enjoy Perranuthnoe Beach, known as Perran Sands, a fine little beach, which is south-facing and catches the sun all day. It's also worth exploring Prussia Cove itself and its individual rocky inlets. This is a good place for a swim at low tide in the crystal clear water.

Victoria Inn

Situated on a peaceful lane leading up to the parish church, this 12th-century inn was built to accommodate the masons constructing the church and is reputed to be one of the oldest in Cornwall. The pretty, pink-washed exterior is adorned with hanging baskets and the inn sign shows a very young Queen Victoria. Inside, the large, L-shaped bar has a beamed ceiling, some exposed stone walls, an open log fire, and a snug alcove for intimate dining. Local coastal and wreck photographs and various maritime memorabilia decorate the bar. In summer you can sit outside in the sheltered, Mediterranean-style patio garden.

Food

Expect daily fresh fish and seafood like Dover sole, scallops and crevettes in garlic and monkfish with basil sauce, as well as wild boar steak with cider sauce, slow roasted lamb, and lunchtime snacks – baguettes, ploughman's and filled jacket potatoes.

Family facilities

Young children are welcome in the dining areas. There are high chairs available as well as a children's menu and smaller portions of adult dishes.

Alternative refreshment stops

On the approach to Perranuthnoe Beach is the busy little Cabin Café, open all summer and at weekends in winter.

☛ Where to go from here

Reached on foot by a causeway at low tide, or by ferry at high tide in the summer only, St Michael's Mount rises dramatically from the sea, with its medieval castle, to which a magnificent east wing was added in the 1870s (www.nationaltrust.org.uk). Nearby Godolphin House at Godolphin Cross is a romantic Tudor and Stuart mansion that is being beautifully restored by English Heritage (www.goldolphinhouse.com). Children will enjoy visiting the Paradise Park Wildlife Sanctuary at Hayle, where they can see rare and beautiful tropical birds, otters and red squirrels, and explore the Fun Farm and play areas (www.paradisepark.org.uk).

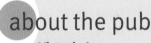

about the pub

Victoria Inn
Perranuthnoe, Penzance
Cornwall TR20 9NP
Tel 01736 710309
www.victoriainn-penzance.co.uk

DIRECTIONS: village signposted off the A394 0.5 mile (800m) east of the junction with the B3280. Point **4** on the walk

PARKING: 10

OPEN: daily

FOOD: daily

BREWERY/COMPANY: Innspired

REAL ALE: Bass, Sharp's Doom Bar, Greene King Abbot Ale

DOGS: allowed in the bar

ROOMS: 3 en suite

Through the Pentewan Valley

A gentle ride along the banks of the St Austell River, with an optional extension to Heligan Gardens.

The Lost Gardens and Pentewan

Even if you don't get as far as the Lost Gardens of Heligan on your bike, you should somehow include it in your itinerary. Home of the Tremayne family for over 400 years, the story of the 'uncovering' of the gardens during the 1990s by Tim Smit (latterly of Eden Project fame) and his team is well known. But this is so much more than just a 'garden' – for a start it covers 200 acres – there's also a subtropical jungle, farm walks, fabulous vegetable gardens, various wildlife projects, and the romantic 'Lost Valley', as well as a farm shop, attractive restaurant, plants sales and shop.

It's worth taking some time to have a look around Pentewan village, with its narrow streets and attractive square. The glorious sandy beach, popular with holidaymakers, is featured in the Lloyds Bank 'Black Horse' advertisements. The old harbour opposite the Ship Inn is now silted up, a recurring problem during the life of the railway due to clay waste being washed downriver from the mines. This, and the growing importance of the ports at Par and Fowey, contributed to the closure of the Pentewan railway, which never reached the Cornwall Railway's main line, in 1918.

the ride

1 From the village car park return towards the B3273 and pass through the **parking area** for Pentewan Valley Cycle Hire, and round a staggered barrier onto the trail, which initially runs levelly through marshy woodland. The trail emerges from woodland onto the banks of the **St Austell River**, with a caravan site opposite.

2 Turn right and follow the trail along the riverbank. Watch out for pedestrians as this is a popular stretch. Along part of the trail walkers have the option of taking a narrow parallel route on a bank.

3 Note the turn-off left across the river to the Lost Gardens of Heligan. Pass round the edge of a small parking area into **King's**

Top right: The Lost Gardens of Heligan
Left: Millennium signpost

Wood (owned by the Woodland Trust), and follow the trail as signed left back onto the riverbank. Dip into woodland again, then bear right, away from the river onto a **lane**, with a small parking area a little uphill to the right.

4 Turn left; pass a small parking area to meet a tarmac lane on a bend. Bear right as signed. Turn left opposite **'Brooklea'** and continue on a narrow wooded path, with a caravan site left. The track bears left at **Molingey** – with the London Apprentice on the other side of the river – then right to run along the right bank of the river again. Follow this tarmac way as it bears right through fields, then left along the edge of the **water treatment works**. Turn left for 50yds (46m) to meet the B3273. Turn right along the pavement.

5 Cross the lane to **Tregorrick,** and take the **second lane** on the left (Sawles Road – unsigned). Follow this quiet country lane to its end. For St Austell (and a possible extension to the Eden Project) turn left uphill to cross the A390. For Pentewan either turn around here, or for a more pleasant alternative, turn right and cycle steeply uphill through pleasant countryside. Drop to a T-junction and turn right, steeply downhill, through Tregorrick. On meeting the B3273 turn left to return to **Pentewan**.

6 **Heligan extension:** just after passing Point 2 above, turn right to cross the river on the **footbridge** (you must dismount). On reaching the B3273, turn left. Pass the touring park left, then turn right to cross the road as signed. Turn left with the pavement, then continue on a track. This bears right,

2h30	10 MILES	16.1 KM	LEVEL 1**2**3

SHORTER ALTERNATIVE ROUTE

1h30	7 MILES	11.3 KM	LEVEL **1**23

MAP: OS Explorer 105 Falmouth & Mevagissey

START/FINISH: Pentewan Valley Cycle Hire; grid ref: SX 017473

TRAILS/TRACKS: mainly well-surfaced track, some woodland paths, little roadwork

LANDSCAPE: woodland and fields, riverside, roadwork on extension

PUBLIC TOILETS: in centre of Pentewan

TOURIST INFORMATION: St Austell, tel 01726 879500

CYCLE HIRE: Pentewan Valley Cycle Hire, tel 01726 844242

THE PUB: The Ship, Pentewan

⚠ Busy roads (in season) and steep ascent/descent on Heligan extension

Getting to the start

Pentewan lies just off the B3273, about 1.5 miles (2.4km) north of Mevagissey. Lane-side parking in Pentewan is limited, but there is a free car park. Start at the cycle hire shop.

Why do this cycle ride?

This pleasant route, which opened in 1995, follows the line of the old Pentewan railway along the tranquil St Austell river. A loop through quiet lanes provides a convenient 'turnaround', and an optional, steep extension to the Lost Gardens of Heligan for those seeking more strenuous exercise.

away from the road into **Tremayne Estate woodland**. Climb steadily uphill for 0.75 mile (1.2km), levelling off as the track passes beneath a road. Bear left to a fork; Mevagissey may be found via the right fork. Keep left to meet the road (note that this can be busy); turn left for 0.5 mile (0.8km) to find **Heligan** on the left.

7 On leaving Heligan, turn right along the road. Cycle gently downhill, with great views over St Austell Bay. Turn left on the **first narrow lane**, steeply downhill. On meeting the next minor road, turn left, even more steeply, to meet the B3273 opposite **Pentewan Sands Holiday Park**. Turn left towards the Esso garage, then right into Pentewan village.

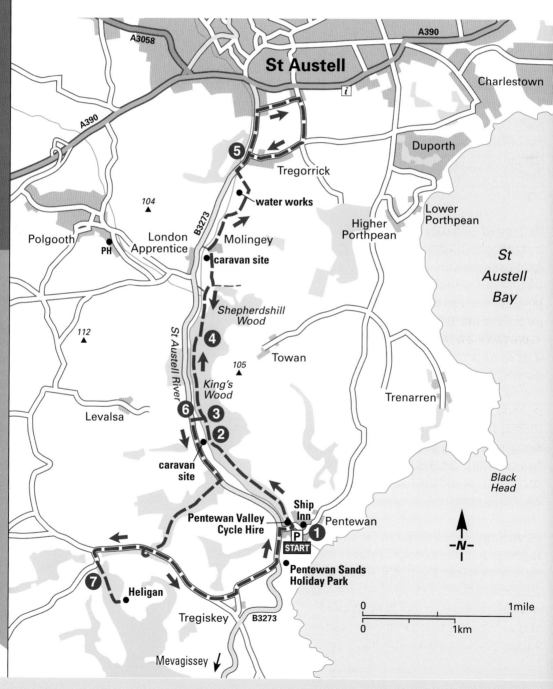

The Ship

about the pub

The Ship
West End, Pentewan
St Austell, Cornwall PL26 6BX
Tel: 01726 842855
www.staustellbrewery.co.uk

DIRECTIONS: see Getting to the start; pub on the main village street
PARKING: none
OPEN: daily; all day May to October
FOOD: daily
BREWERY/COMPANY: St Austell Brewery
REAL ALE: St Austell Tinner's Ale, Tribute and HSD

Festooned with colourful hanging baskets, the attractive Ship Inn fronts on to the main village street and is a real picture in summer, drawing in passing visitors, coast path walkers and cyclists fresh from the Pentewan Valley Trail. Tables fill early in the garden on fine days as they make the most of the pub's view across the village and the old harbour. The interior is equally appealing, with beams, shipwreck and maritime memorabilia, comfortable furnishings and a welcoming atmosphere filling the two bars, and there's the added attraction of the full complement of St Austell ales on hand-pump.

Food

Expect a traditional choice of pub meals that includes sandwiches, crusty baguettes, fisherman's lunch (smoked mackerel), steak and kidney pudding, and ham, egg and chips at lunch. Evening additions take in various grills and fresh local fish.

Family facilities

Children are allowed in the lounge bar where under 11s have a children's menu to choose from. Food is not served outside due to pestering crows and seagulls.

Alternative refreshment stops

There are cafés at the Lost Gardens of Heligan and a choice of pubs and cafés in Pentewan.

☛ Where to go from here

For an unforgettable experience in a breathtaking location, visit the Eden Project (www.edenproject.com) north of St Austell. It is the gateway into a fascinating world of plants and human society – space age technology meets the lost world in the biggest greenhouse ever built. There are two gigantic geodesic conservatories: the Humid Tropics Biome and the Warm Temperate Biome. To view the largest display of shipwreck artefacts in Britain, head for the Charlestown Shipwreck and Heritage Centre (www.shipwreckcharlestown.com), and for more information on the Lost Gardens of Heligan visit www.heligan.com.

A coastal route from Crackington Haven

A coastal and inland walk with views of the spectacular north Cornish coast.

Crackington's cliffs

Crackington Haven has given its name to a geological phenomenon, the Crackington Formation, a fractured shale that has been shaped into contorted forms. On the sheared-off cliff faces, you can see the great swirls and folds of this sedimentary rock that was 'metamorphosised' by volcanic heat and contorted by geological storms of millions of years ago. The name Crackington derives from the Cornish word for sandstone, crak.

During the 18th and 19th centuries, Crackington Haven was a small port, landing coal and limestone, and shipping out local agricultural produce and slate. Plans to expand Crackington into a major

port were made in the 19th century. The scheme did not materialise, otherwise the Crackington Haven of today might have been a dramatically different place.

Along the open cliff south from Crackington, the remarkable geology unfolds. Looking back from Bray's Point, you see the massive contortions in the high cliff face of Pencannow Point on the north side of Crackington. Soon the path leads above Tremoutha Haven and up to the cliff edge beyond the domed headland of Cambeak. From here there is a breathtaking view of the folded strata and quartzite bands of Cambeak's cliffs. A path leads out to the tip, but it is precarious and isn't recommended.

A short distance further on you arrive above Strangles Beach where again you look back to such fantastic features as Northern Door. Where the route of the walk turns inland there are low cliffs set back from the main cliff edge. These represent the old

Left: Crackington Haven
Below: The headland beyond Strangles beach

wounds of a land slip where the cliff has slumped towards the sea. From here the second part of the walk turns inland and descends into East Wood and the peaceful Trevigue Valley, once a 'fjord' filled by the sea. Today much of the valley is a nature reserve and wandering down its leafy length is an antidote to the coastal drama of the Crackington cliffs.

the walk

1 From the Crackington Haven car park entrance go left across a bridge, then turn right at a **telephone kiosk**. Follow a broad track round to the left, between a signpost and an old wooden seat, then go through a kissing gate onto the coast path. At a fork follow the coast path right, signed **'Cambeak'**.

2 Cross a footbridge then, at a fork of paths, follow white arrow left and a path up a sheltered valley on the inland side of the steep hill. Continue on the **cliff path**.

3 Where a stretch of low inland cliffs begins, at a junction of paths and marker post, go left (signed **'Trevigue'**) following the path to reach a road by a National Trust sign for **The Strangles**.

4 Go left, walking past the farm entrance to Trevigue, then, in just a few paces, turn right down a drive by the **Trevigue sign**. Then bear off to the left across the grass to go through a gate by a signpost.

MAP: OS Explorer 111 Bude, Boscastle & Tintagel

START/FINISH: Crackington Haven car park (can be busy in summer) or Burden Trust car park, along B3263 road to Wainhouse; grid ref: SX 145968

PATHS: good coastal footpath and woodland tracks, can be very wet and muddy, 9 stiles

LANDSCAPE: open coast and wooded valley

PUBLIC TOILETS: Crackington Haven

TOURIST INFORMATION: Bude, tel 01288 354240

THE PUB: Coombe Barton Inn, Crackington Haven

❶ Coast path is steep in places and close to the cliff edge

Getting to the start

Crackington Haven is signposted off the A39 Bude to Wadebridge road at Wainhouse Corner, 7 miles (11.3km) south of Bude. It can also be reached from the B3263 north of Boscastle.

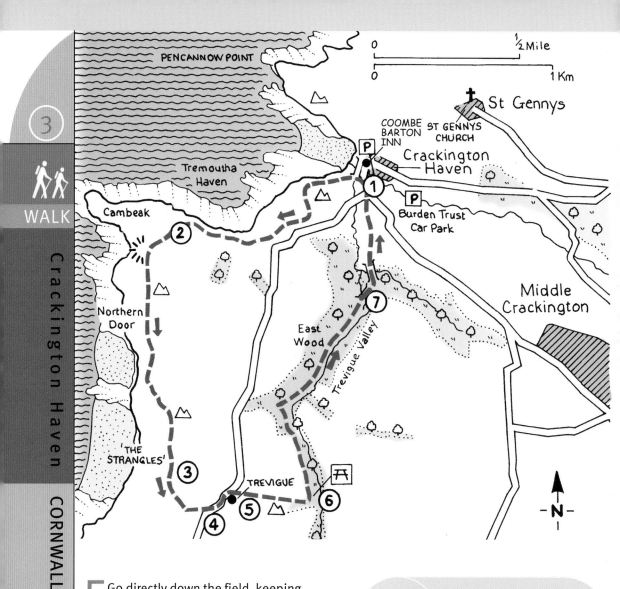

5 Go directly down the field, keeping left of a **telegraph pole**, to reach a stile. Continue downhill to the edge of a wood. Go down a tree-shaded path to a junction of paths in a shady dell by the river.

6 Turn sharp left here, following the signpost towards **Haven**, and continue on the obvious path down the wooded river valley.

7 Cross a footbridge, then turn left at a junction with a track. Cross another **footbridge** and continue to a gate by some houses. Follow a track and then a surfaced lane to the main road, then turn left to the **car park**.

what to look for

The field and woodland section of this walk supports a very different flora to that found on the heathery, windswept cliffland. Some of the most profuse fieldedge and woodland plants belong to the carrot family, the Umbelliferae. They may seem hard to distinguish, but the commonest is cow parsley, identifiable by its reddish stalk, feathery leaves and clustered white flower heads. Hogweed is a much larger umbellifer often standing head and shoulders above surrounding plants; it has hairy stalks and broad toothed leaves and can cause an unpleasant rash if it comes in contact with your skin. A third common umbellifer is the alexander, prolific in spring and early summer. It has broad, lime green leaves and clustered yellow florets.

Coombe Barton Inn

about the pub

Coombe Barton Inn
Crackington Haven, Bude
Cornwall EX23 0JG
Tel 01840 230345
www.combebartoninn.com

DIRECTIONS: see Getting to the start; pub beside car park
PARKING: 25
OPEN: daily; all day in summer
FOOD: daily
BREWERY/COMPANY: free house
REAL ALE: St Austell Dartmoor Best and HSD, Sharp's Doom Bar
DOGS: allowed in the bar
ROOMS: 6 bedrooms, 3 en suite

Originally built for the 'Captain' of the local slate quarry, the Coombe Barton (it means 'valley farm' in Cornish) is over 200 years old and sits in a small cove, opposite the beach and surrounded by spectacular rock formations. Much extended and modernised, it features a big, open-plan bar with local pictures on the walls and a surfboard hanging from the wood-planked ceiling – the pub is very popular with surfers from the beach. There's a screened off games area, a huge family dining area, and a summer terrace for alfresco eating and drinking. Bedrooms are comfortable and one suite is suitable for families.

Food

Local seafood is a feature of the menu and includes sea bass, lemon sole, plaice and halibut. Good range of daily specials, lunchtime sandwiches (try the local crab), vegetarian meals and Sunday roast carvery lunches.

Family facilities

Very popular with families seeking refreshment away from the beach, the pub welcomes children and offers a family dining area, high chairs, a children's menu and smaller portions.

Alternative refreshment stops

There are two cafés either side of the car park in Crackington Haven.

☛ Where to go from here

Head down the coast to Tintagel and explore the ruins of Tintagel Castle, one of the most spectacular spots in the country associated with King Arthur and Merlin (www.english-heritage.org). On the way, visit the renowned and attractive National Trust fishing village of Boscastle with its narrow, cliff-hung harbour entrance, small quay, Heritage Coast Visitor Centre, and walks through the beautiful Valency Valley and St Nectan's Glen.

The Princetown railway

A tough ride through the wilds of Dartmoor, along the old route of the Princetown to Yelverton railway.

Quarrying round Princetown

There's a long history of quarrying granite on Dartmoor. Quarrying began around 1820 at both Haytor Quarry, under George Templer, and (in direct competition) at Swelltor and Foggintor, under Thomas Trywhitt (who also built roads and many buildings in the Princetown area, including the Plume of Feathers Inn in 1785). Foggintor (originally known as Royal Oak) ceased working around 1900, and Swelltor in 1921.

Both reopened for a while in 1937, in response to an increase in demand for roadstone. Foggintor supplied granite for Dartmoor Prison, and local granite was also used in Nelson's Column in Trafalgar Square, London. Look towards Foggintor (Point 3) and you'll see various ruined buildings: as well as cottages, there was also a chapel used as a school. The old quarry workings are now flooded and provide a peaceful picnic spot.

Merrivale Quarry (originally Tor Quarry), a little further along the route, was the last working quarry on Dartmoor, operating from 1875 to 1997. Granite blocks from the old London Bridge were re-dressed here when

the bridge was sold to the USA, and stone was also used in the war memorial in the Falklands after the war in 1982.

the ride

1 Turn left out of the car park along the rough road. Just past the **fire station** (left) bear left as signed (disused railway/Tyrwhitt Trail) on a narrow fenced path, which bears right. Go through a gate. The path widens to a gritty track, and passes a **coniferous plantation** (right).

2 Suddenly you're out in the open on a long embankment, looking towards the forests around **Burrator Reservoir** ahead right, below **Sheeps Tor** (left) and **Sharpitor** (right). Continue along the contours of the hill – it's quite rough – as you progress look ahead left to the railway winding its way towards **Ingra Tor**. This is the old Plymouth and Dartmoor railway line, brainchild of Sir Thomas Tyrwhitt, friend of and private secretary to the Prince Regent. Originally a tramway with horse-drawn wagons, it opened in 1823. It was part of Tyrwhitt's plans to exploit the area's natural resources (granite), at the same time enabling materials such as coal and lime to be brought to Princetown more easily. The Princetown Railway Company (a subsidiary of the GWR) took it over in 1881; it reopened as a steam railway in 1883, but was never profitable and closed in 1956. However, it's a great footpath and cycle track.

Above: The Dartmoor Inn at Merrivale Bridge
Left: Walkers on the trail

MAP: OS Explorer OL28 Dartmoor

START/FINISH: Princetown car park (contributions), grid ref: SX 588735

TRAILS/TRACKS: rocky former railway track and one particularly steep and rough section

LANDSCAPE: open moorland

PUBLIC TOILETS: at start

TOURIST INFORMATION: High Moorland Visitor Centre, Princetown, tel 01822 890414

CYCLE HIRE: Runnage Farm, Postbridge (plus camping barn), tel 01822 880222

THE PUB: Dartmoor Inn, near Princetown

🛈 Only suitable for older children with mountain bikes

Getting to the start

Princetown lies on the B3212 between Two Bridges and Yelverton, on Dartmoor. From Two Bridges, turn right in the middle of the town; from Yelverton, turn left (High Moorland Visitor Centre on the corner), following signs for the car park.

Why do this cycle ride?

This is a rather different sort of ride, and one that will test both your bike and your concentration! It follows the line of the old Princetown to Yelverton railway, but has not been surfaced. It's suitable for families with older children and those who have mountain bikes, and you'll have to push your bikes up one particularly rough section. But for a taste of Dartmoor 'proper', it's hard to beat.

3 Reach the edge of **Foggintor Quarry** (left), with Swelltor Quarry on the hill ahead; a track crosses the trail. The site of King Tor Halt (1928), from where a siding led to Foggintor, is near by. Keep straight ahead, almost immediately taking the left fork (the track becomes grassier). Look right towards the spoil heaps of Foggintor Quarry. Follow the track on – look left towards Merrivale Quarry (the Dartmoor Inn is just out of sight below) – try to spot the Bronze Age **Merrivale stone rows**. Follow the track as it bears left round the hill (below King's Tor Quarry), to enjoy views right over **Vixen Tor**, almost 100ft (30m) high, home to one of the moor's most evil characters, the witch Vixana. Pass through a cutting – another branch joins right – and keep on to another fork.

4 Keep right along the lower track; views change again, with the wooded **Walkham Valley** below right and – on a

good day – the sparkling waters of Plymouth Sound in the distance. About 50yds (46m) beyond the fork look left to see a pile of dressed stone on the upper track: 12 granite corbels, cut in 1903 for work on London Bridge, but excess to requirements. Pass the spoil heaps of **Swelltor Quarry**; the track is now fenced on the right, with views ahead to the bridge en route for **Ingra Tor**.

5 Where the track starts to curve sharp right, turn left opposite an old gate. Push your bike up a rough, rocky track to regain the outward route near **Foggintor Quarry**.

6 Turn right and make your way bumpily back to **Princetown**. The building of the infamous prison in 1806 – originally for French prisoners from the Napoleonic wars – was also down to Trywhitt. Since 1850 it has been a civilian establishment.

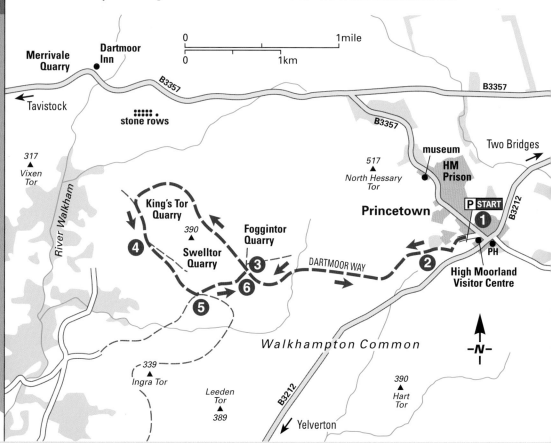

Dartmoor Inn

Situated at 1,000ft (305m) above sea level, this whitewashed old inn enjoys sweeping views across moorland and the Walkham Valley, and on a clear evening the lights of Plymouth and the Eddystone Lighthouse can be seen. Originally quarrymen's cottages built in the 17th century, the pub was once part of the Walreddon Manor Estate and has been a pub since at least 1852. A roaring log fire in a big stone fireplace is a welcome sight in the largely open-plan and partly carpeted main bar. On fine summer days soak up the view with a pint at one of the picnic benches on the grassy area to the front of the pub.

Food
Traditional bar meals range from salads, ploughman's and filled baps, to chicken, ham and mushroom pie, gammon steak and jam sponge and custard. Evening dishes take in grills, pasta meals and specialities like rack of lamb and steak au poivre.

Family facilities
Although there are no special facilities for children, families are made very welcome at the pub.

Alternative refreshment stops
Pubs and tea rooms in Princetown.

about the pub

Dartmoor Inn
Merrivale Bridge, Princetown
Devon PL20 6ST
Tel: 01822 890340

DIRECTIONS: load up bikes, turn left out of the car park, pass the prison and turn left again at the T-junction with the B3357, the pub is on the right in 1.5 miles (3km)
PARKING: 25
OPEN: closed Sunday evening, Monday and Tuesday between November and Easter
FOOD: daily
BREWERY/COMPANY: free house
REAL ALE: Marston's Pedigree, Bass, guest beer
ROOMS: 3 bedrooms, 2 en suite

☛ Where to go from here
To discover more about the history of Dartmoor, and what to see and do in the area, visit the High Moorland Visitor Centre in Princetown (www.dartmoor-npa.gov.uk). Young children will enjoy a visit to Dartmoor's Miniature Pony and Animal Farm near Moretonhampstead, where they can see ponies, donkeys, pigs and lambs at close quarters, and there are nature trails and indoor and outdoor play areas (www.miniatureponycentre.com). Discover the rugged beauty of the Bovey Valley at the Becky Falls Woodland Park (www.beckyfalls-dartmoor.com), and the world of otters and butterflies at the fascinating Buckfast Butterfly Farm and Dartmoor Otter Sanctuary (www.ottersandbutterflies.co.uk).

East Portlemouth to Limebury Point

Salcombe

DEVON

Only a short ferry trip apart, the contrasts across the Kingsbridge Estuary could not be greater.

Salcombe

A delightful place, Salcombe is nevertheless very busy. To avoid the crowds you can follow this walk from East Portlemouth, opposite the town, from where you get some of the best views in the area. Once the haunt of smugglers and pirates, Salcombe has a civilised, prosperous, and, as a result of its sheltered position and deep blue waters, an almost Mediterranean feel. It's smaller and gentler than Dartmouth, and popular with the sailing fraternity. The estuary is a marvellous place for young families, too.

At low tide there is a run of sandy beaches all along the East Portlemouth side, enabling those staying in Salcombe simply to hop on the ferry for a day on the beach. (Note: Many of these sandy coves are cut off at high tide – take care.)

From Limebury Point you can see across the estuary to Overbecks (National Trust), an elegant Edwardian house in a magnificent setting above South Sands.

East Portlemouth has a totally different feel from Salcombe. It is small, quiet and unspoilt. During the 19th century half the population was evicted by the absentee landlord as a result of their preference for fishing and wrecking.

the walk

1 Park on the verge near the phone box at East Portlemouth (or in the parking area – contributions to village hall fund). Walk through the parking area and steeply downhill on a narrow tarmac footpath signposted 'Salcombe', which gives way to **steep steps**.

Below: Salcombe and its harbour
Below right: The sandy beach at Mill Bay

2h00	4 MILES	6.4 KM	LEVEL 1 2 3

MAP: OS Explorer OL20 South Devon

START/FINISH: near phone box in East Portlemouth or in small parking bay, grid ref: SX 746385

PATHS: good coast path, field paths and tracks, no stiles

LANDSCAPE: river estuary, rocky coast and coves, farmland

PUBLIC TOILETS: at Mill Bay, passed on Points 3 and 7

TOURIST INFORMATION: Salcombe, tel 01548 843927

THE PUB: Victoria Inn, Salcombe

 Undulating, sometimes steep and rocky, coastal path

Getting to the start

East Portlemouth is about 9 miles south east of Kingsbridge on very narrow and winding roads. From Kingsbridge take the A379 towards Dartmouth. In 4 miles (6.4km), turn right at Frogmore following signs for East Portlemouth for 5 miles (8km). Park on the roadside next to the telephone box, opposite a row of cottages. Alternatively park in the village car park straight ahead, with wonderful views over the Kingsbridge Estuary.

2 When you reach the lane at the bottom of the steps, turn right if you want to visit the Venus Café and catch the ferry to Salcombe. If you want to get on with the walk, turn left along the lane as it follows the edge of the estuary. This is the official route of the **coast path** and it passes some very exclusive residences in almost sub-tropical surroundings.

3 The lane leads to the pretty, sandy beach at **Mill Bay**. Follow the coast path signs for **Gara Rock** along the edge of a sycamore wood, with lovely views across the estuary, and glimpses of inviting little coves.

4 At **Limebury Point** you reach open cliff, with great views to South Sands and Overbecks opposite and craggy Bolt Head. The coast path now veers eastwards below **Portlemouth Down**, which was divided into strip fields in the late 19th century.

5 The path along this stretch undulates steeply, and is rocky in places. Keep going until you reach the bench and viewpoint over the beach at **Rickham Sands**. Just beyond this, as the coast path continues right along the cliffs (there is reasonable access to the beach), take the left fork and climb steeply up below the lookout to reach the wall in front of **Gara Rock Hotel**.

6 Turn left to reach the hotel drive and walk straight on up the lane. After 100yds (91m) turn left through a gate in the hedge signposted '**Mill Bay**'. Walk straight across the field (the roped-off area indicates a car park for the beach) with lovely views to Salcombe and Malborough church beyond. Go through a **small copse**, then a gate and across the farm track. Go through a gate.

7 This leads down a beautiful **bridle path**, running gradually downhill beneath huge, ancient pollarded lime trees, with a

grassy combe to the right. The path leads past the car park to reach **Mill Bay**.

8 Turn right along the lane. If you want to avoid the steps, look out for a **footpath sign** pointing right, up a narrow, steep, path to regain **East Portlemouth** and your car; if not, continue along the lane and retrace your steps up the steep tarmac path.

what to look for

Many stretches of the coast path in Devon and Cornwall are resplendent with wild flowers virtually all the year round, and during the summer months the path below Portlemouth Down is incredible. There are banks of purple wild thyme, heather, gorse, red campion, bladder campion, tiny yellow tormentil and pretty blue scabious. Look out too for the common dodder, a parasitic plant with pretty clusters of pink flowers. It draws the life out of its host plant, often heather or gorse, via suckers.

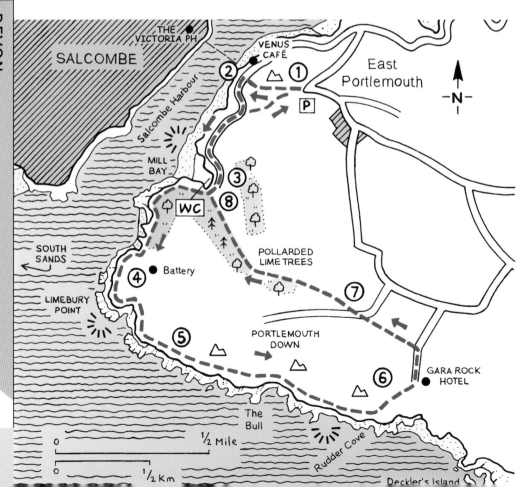

Victoria Inn

Standing on Salcombe's main street, with stunning views across Salcombe Estuary from the smartly refurbished lounge and dining areas, the Victoria is not a typical seaside town pub. Beyond the plain exterior is a super flagstoned bar area, filled with chunky wooden tables and chairs. You'll also find a log fire, attractive pictures of old Salcombe, and stairs leading up to the civilised lounge bar and restaurant. A great place to end up after this coastal stroll, for a refreshing pint of St Austell ale and a relaxing meal.

Food

Meals are freshly prepared from Devon produce and include fresh fish, local butcher meats and locally made cheeses. Expect decent sandwiches (served with chips), hot leek tart with smoked bacon, smoked haddock mornay, honey-roast ham, eggs and chips, shellfish chowder, and scallops with garlic and parsley butter.

Family facilities

Children are welcome throughout the bars. There's a children's menu in the bar, baby-changing facilities and a play area in the large sheltered terraced garden.

Alternative refreshment stops

Salcombe has pubs, cafés and restaurants, but if you want to stay on the other side try the Venus Café. It's by the ferry slipway, with a pretty garden looking across the water (open March to October).

☞ Where to go from here

Once you've caught the ferry to the other side, you can explore the pretty little town of Salcombe. The ferry runs every day from 8am–7pm on weekdays and from 8.30am–7pm on weekends and bank holidays. You can see chocolates being made at the Salcombe Chocolate Factory (www.salcombe.co.uk) and enjoy a visit to an exotic coastal garden and a house displaying toys, dolls and a natural history collection – Overbecks Museum and Garden at Sharpitor.

about the pub

Victoria Inn
Fore Street, Salcombe
Devon TQ8 8BU
Tel 01548 842604
www.victoriasalcombe.com

DIRECTIONS:	on Salcombe's main street
PARKING:	none (public car park opposite)
OPEN:	daily; all day
FOOD:	daily
BREWERY/COMPANY:	St Austell Brewery
REAL ALE:	St Austell Tinners Ale, Dartmoor Best, HSD and Tribute Ale
DOGS:	allowed in the bar

The cliffs of East Devon

Branscombe DEVON

Along the coast near Branscombe, one of the longest villages in Devon.

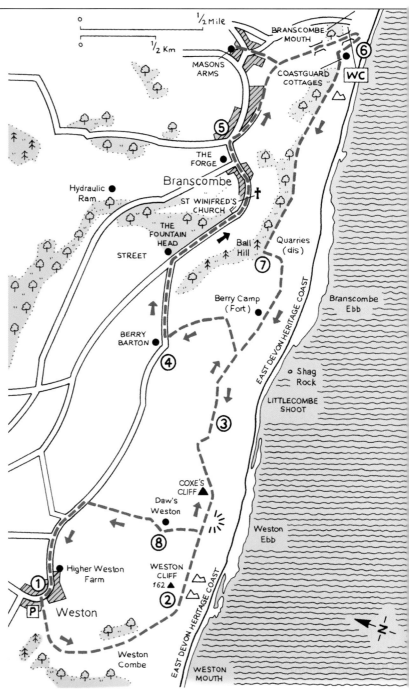

Branscombe

Picturesque Branscombe is one of the most secluded and peaceful villages in this corner of East Devon. Groups of pretty flower-decked cottages sit either side of a long narrow lane that runs gradually down the valley from Street.

This walk takes you to the village along the coast path from Weston. There are extensive views all along the path. The sloping grassy area on the cliff above Littlecombe Shoot is a popular spot for paragliders. At the footpath marker post you'll see a sign leading right that appears to direct you straight over the edge of the cliff. This steep, narrow, zig-zag path will take you to the pretty pebbly beach down below.

St Winifred's Church nestles halfway down the valley from Street, and is one of Branscombe's treasures. Dedicated to an obscure Welsh saint, it dates from the

3h30	**6.25 MILES**	**10 KM**	**LEVEL 1 2** 3

11th century and reveals evidence of continuous development up to the 16th century. The squat tower dates from Norman times and inside are remnants of medieval paintings that once adorned the walls, and an Elizabethan gallery.

Near the village hall, many buildings are owned by the National Trust: the Old Bakery (the last traditional working bakery in Devon until 1987 – now a tea room), Manor Mill (a watermill), and the Forge, complete with working blacksmith.

The beach at Branscombe Mouth gets busy in summer. This is the halfway point of the walk and you can always wander a little way to east or west to escape the crowds.

MAP: OS Explorer 115 Exeter & Sidmouth
START/FINISH: unsurfaced car park at Weston, grid ref: SY 167890
PATHS: coast path, country lanes, 6 stiles
LANDSCAPE: undulating cliffs, farmland and woodland
PUBLIC TOILETS: behind Branscombe village hall, also in car park at Branscombe Mouth
TOURIST INFORMATION: Seaton, tel 01297 21660
THE PUB: The Masons Arms, Branscombe
❶ This is an undulating walk with two steep ascents and cliff-edge paths. Suitable for older, more experienced children

the walk

1 From the car park take the flinty track over the stile onto the **East Devon Heritage Coast path** signposted 'Weston Mouth'. After 0.5 mile (800m) the sea comes into view at a stile and gate. Go straight on, then veer left across the field to join the coast path at a kissing gate.

2 Go left, steeply uphill (wooden steps) to reach the grassy top of **Weston Cliff**. A kissing gate leads onto Coxe's Cliff and, after a stile, the path runs diagonally away from the coast via a deep combe towards another kissing gate in the top left corner of the field. Cross the next field and through the kissing gate onto grassland above **Littlecombe Shoot**.

3 Go past the **coast path marker** ahead to pass two stands of gorse (left). Turn diagonally left, away from the cliff, towards a banked gap in a scrubby gorse

Getting to the start
Weston is 4 miles (6.4km) east of Sidmouth off the A3052 towards Lyme Regis. Following signs for Weston and Branscombe, pass the Donkey Sanctuary and turn right following signs for Weston. In the centre of Weston, where the road bends sharply left at a little green, turn right into the informal car park.

hedge. Aim for a metal gate in the top left corner of the next field, then turn left down the track to join the lane at **Berry Barton**.

4 Turn right down the lane to the **Fountain Head** pub. Turn right again down the valley, passing groups of thatched cottages and **St Winifred's Church** (right). Continue downhill past the post office and the Forge to St Branoc's Well and the **village hall**.

5 Turn right opposite Parkfield Terrace down the lane signposted '**Branscombe Mouth**'. After 200yds (183m) a farm gate leads to a well-signposted path through the field to a footbridge and gate (go left here for **The Masons Arms**). Go through the next meadow and gate. Turn right over a wooden bridge and gate to reach **Branscombe Mouth**.

Previous page: Branscombe's thatched cottages
Below: It's easy to get to the beach
from Branscombe

6 Turn immediately right through a kissing gate to join coast path signs uphill beneath the **coastguard cottages** (now a private house). Go through an open gateway and left into the woods via a kissing gate. The path splits here and you can take the cliff top or woodland route. After they rejoin, ignore all paths to the left and right until, after two stiles and 0.5 mile (800m), a signpost points left between grassy hummocks towards the cliffs.

7 Follow the coastal footpath signs to the cliff edge onto **Littlecombe Shoot**. Retrace your steps to Coxe's Cliff, then a stile and kissing gate onto **Weston Cliff**. Turn right into a **wildflower meadow**.

8 Pass the cottage and outbuildings (on the right) through two gateways and onto a track leading to a **tarmac lane**. Go left and in a short while you'll reach **Weston** and your car.

The Masons Arms

Charming 14th-century, thatched and creeper-clad inn, formerly a cider house and well-documented smugglers' haunt. It stands in the centre of picturesque Branscombe, which lies in a steep valley, in National Trust land and only a ten-minute stroll from the sea. Beyond the pretty front terrace is the rustic bar with stone walls, ancient beams, slate floors and an open fireplace, used for spit-roasts on a weekly basis and Sunday lunch. You'll find local Otter ales on handpump, local farm cider and a dozen wines by the glass. The attractive bedrooms are split between the main building and neighbouring terraces of cottages. The walled front terrace is a real sun-trap and very popular in summer.

Food

Popular bar food utilises locally sourced produce, including lobster and crab, and ranges from specials like venison casserole, steak and kidney pudding, local estate steaks, shellfish stew, and oven-roasted sea bass with a black bean sauce, to a tried-and-tested selection of sandwiches, ploughman's lunches and hot filled baguettes. Separate fixed-price menu in the Waterfall Restaurant.

Family facilities

Families are welcome inside the pub and you'll find high chairs for younger family members and smaller portions of adult dishes are readily available.

Alternative refreshment stops

The 14th-century Fountain Head at Street brews its own beer, has great food and a local feel. The National Trust Old Bakery Tearoom can be found near Branscombe village hall and the Sea Shanty café is at the beach at Branscombe Mouth.

☞ Where to go from here

The Donkey Sanctuary (founded in 1969) at Slade House Farm (signposted off the A3052) is a charity that cares for donkeys and is the largest such sanctuary in the world (www.thedonkeysanctuary.org.uk). At the Pecorama Pleasure Gardens in Beer ride on a miniature steam and diesel line and enjoy stunning views across Lyme Bay.

about the pub

The Masons Arms
Branscombe, Seaton
Devon EX12 3DJ
Tel 01297 680300
www.masonsarms.co.uk

DIRECTIONS:	village signposted off the A3052 between Seaton and Sidmouth; pub in village centre close to Point **5** on walk
PARKING:	40
OPEN:	daily; all day
FOOD:	daily
BREWERY/COMPANY:	free house
REAL ALE:	Bass, Otter Ale, Masons Ale, guest beers
DOGS:	allowed in the bar
ROOMS:	22 bedrooms, 20 en suite

Durdle Door and Lulworth Cove

An exhilarating walk on a spectacular piece of coastline.

Lulworth Cove

Lulworth Cove is an almost perfectly circular bay on Dorset's southern coast. Its pristine condition and geological importance earned it World Heritage status in 2002. The cove provides a secure anchorage for small fishing boats and pleasure craft, and a sun-trap of safe water for summer bathers. The cliffs around the eastern side of the bay are crumbly soft and brightly coloured in some places. The geology is intriguing and a visit to the Heritage Centre will help you to sort it out.

The oldest layer, easily identified here, is the gleaming white Portland stone. It is a fine-grained oolite, around 140 million years old. It consists of tightly compressed, fossilised shells – the flat-coiled ones are ammonites. Occasional giant ammonites, called titanites, may be seen incorporated

Durdle Door on the Lulworth coast

into house walls across Purbeck. Like the rock of Bat's Head, it may contain speckled bands of flinty chert. Above this is a layer of Purbeck marble, a limestone rich in the fossils of vertebrates. This is where dinosaur, fish and reptile fossils are usually found. The soft layer above this consists of Wealden beds, a belt of colourful clays, silts and sands, that are unstable and prone to landslips when exposed. Crumbly, white chalk overlays the Wealden beds. The chalk consists of the remains of microscopic sea creatures and

what to look for

Don't miss the baby-blue painted Dolls House on the way down to the harbour in Lulworth Cove. It's a fisherman's cottage dating from 1861. You may find it difficult to believe that 11 children were raised in this tiny house. Contrast its cramped simplicity with the dwelling opposite, with diamond-pane windows and a cosy thatched roof, built in a decorative style known as 'cottage orné'.

Boats moored in the bay at West Lulworth

shells deposited over a long period of time when a deep sea covered much of Dorset, some 75 million years ago.

This is the chalk that underlies Dorset's famous downland and is seen in the exposed soft, eroded cliffs at White Nothe. Hard nodules and bands of flint appear in the chalk – it's a purer type of chert – and in its gravel beach form it protects long stretches of this fragile coast.

the walk

1 From the corner of the car park at Durdle Door Caravan Park take the path down to **Durdle Door**. Return the same way but before steeply ascending fork right, signed to **Lulworth Cove**. Follow the path along the coast and down to the cove (the Heritage Centre and Stair Hole on the right are worth visiting).

2 Turn sharp left up steps, signed to **Bindon Hill**. Walk through a wooded area to a stile, then turn sharp right to skirt the rim of the cove. Near the top take the path left to Bindon Hill and on the brow, at a junction with a wider path, turn right. Walk across **ancient earthworks** and by the entrance to **Lulworth Army Ranges**, then turn left down towards the village of **West Lulworth**. Cross a stile and bear half-left across a field, crossing the stile on the left just before the bottom.

3 Continue along a fenced path at the back of the village. The path swings left up some **steps** (steps right lead down to the

2h00 | **3.25 MILES** | **5.3 KM** | **LEVEL 123**

MAP: OS Explorer OL 15 Purbeck & South Dorset

START/FINISH: car park (fee) above Durdle Door; grid ref: SY 811804

PATHS: stone path, grassy tracks, tarmac, 8 stiles

LANDSCAPE: steeply rolling cliffs beside sea, green inland

PUBLIC TOILETS: by Heritage Centre in Lulworth, and just above Lulworth Cove

TOURIST INFORMATION: Weymouth, tel: 01305 785747

THE PUB: The Castle Inn, West Lulworth

❶ Take heed of warning signs – steep paths (up and down) and cliff edges. A short walk but really for fitter, older children.

Getting to the start

From the A352 west of Wareham take the B3070 south for East Lulworth and continue to West Lulworth. Pass the Castle Inn and turn first right, passing the church. After 0.75 mile (1.2km) turn left, down past Durdle Door Caravan Park, to the car park.

Main Street where you turn right for the Castle Inn), then along to an unmade road. At the junction with **Bindon Road** turn left, and in 25yds (23m) turn right over a stile, signed to Lulworth Cove. In 10yds (9m) fork right through a **gate** and keep to the right edge of the field. At the **waymarker**, turn right over a stile, signed Durdle Door. Descend the fenced path to the road.

4 Turn right, and in 50yds (46m) turn left to **Durdle Door**. Cross the stile and walk along the left hand edge of a field. After the next stile ascend steps through a small wood to a stile and turn right along a chalk path, signed to **Durdle Door Camp Site**. Ignore the parallel track, and continue across fields. After four stiles return to the corner of the car park.

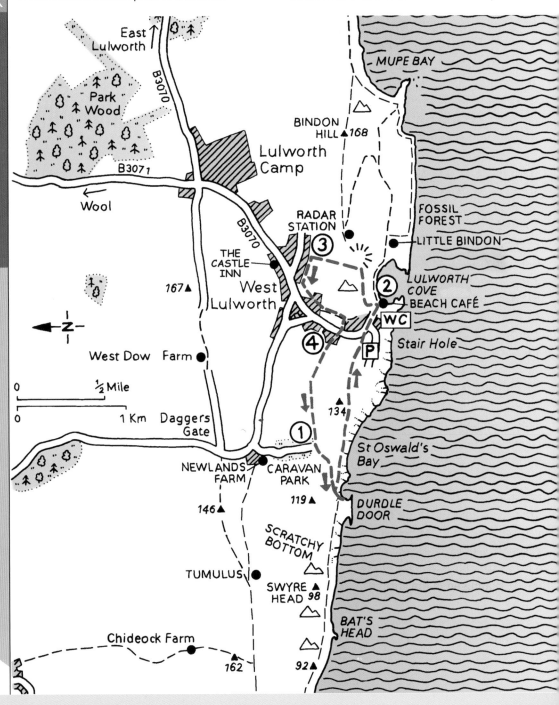

The Castle inn

This is a picturesque thatched and beamed inn, hidden away in a lovely spot near Lulworth Cove, close to great coastal walks and popular attractions. It was built in the 17th century, and is named after a castle that once existed nearby.
It was originally called the Jolly Sailor, before being destroyed by fire in 1929. Restoration over the years has resulted in two main bars, one with flagstones and an open fire, and a cosy, more modern lounge and dining room. The draw in summer among the hordes of visitors that flock to this beautiful coastline are the prize-winning terraced gardens. These are packed with plants, garden furniture, a water feature, barbecue, boules pitch and giant chess board. Comfortable, well-equipped bedrooms are tucked beneath the heavy thatch.

Food
The wide-ranging menu offers a choice of some 50 dishes, from chicken and ham pie, sirloin steak, or liver and bacon and seafood stew, to exotic cuts like crocodile, ostrich or kangaroo, plus a variety of flambé dishes cooked at the table. Lighter lunchtime snacks and Sunday roast lunches.

Family facilities
Children are welcome inside the pub. High chairs, baby-changing facilities, small portions, children's menu and small cutlery are all available. There's plenty to keep children amused in the garden.

Alternative refreshment stops
In Lulworth the Heritage Centre café includes family meals and baguettes.

Just down the hill, the Lulworth Cove Hotel is open all year and serves a multitude of fresh, locally caught fish.

☛ Where to go from here
Lulworth Castle is set in glorious parkland, just inland at East Lulworth (www.lulworth.com). It has a restored kitchen, and there are great views from the top of its tower. You'll also find an animal farm for children, an indoor activity room and pitch and putt to enjoy in the grounds.

about the pub
The Castle Inn
West Lulworth, Wareham
Dorset BH20 5RN
Tel: 01929 400311
www.thecastleinn-lulworthcove.co.uk

DIRECTIONS: on the main street	
PARKING: 20	
OPEN: daily	
FOOD: daily	
BREWERY/COMPANY: free house	
REAL ALE: Ringwood Best, Gales HSB	
DOGS: welcome in the bar	
ROOMS: 11 en suite	

A walk around Box Hill

A hilly walk around Box Hill, famous for its stone and Brunel's greatest engineering achievement.

Brunel's famous tunnel

Box is a large straggling village that sits astride the busy A4 half-way between Bath and Chippenham. Stone has been quarried here since the 9th century, but Box found fame during the 18th century when the local stone was used for Bath's magnificent buildings. Construction of Box Tunnel uncovered immense deposits of stone and by 1900 Box stone quarries were among the world's most productive. Little trace remains above ground, except for some fine stone-built houses in the village and a few reminders of the industry on Box Hill.

In 1833, the newly created Great Western Railway appointed Isambard Kingdom Brunel (1806–59) as engineer. His task was to build a railway covering the 118 miles (190km) from London to Bristol. The problems and projects he encountered on the way would help to make him the most famous engineer of the Victorian age. After a relatively straightforward and level start through the Home Counties, which earned the nickname 'Brunel's Billiard Table', he came to the hilly Cotswolds.

The solution at Box would be a tunnel, and at nearly 2 miles (3.2km) long and with a gradient of 1:100 it would be the longest and steepest in the world at the time. It would also be very wide. Already controversial, Brunel ignored the gauge of other companies, preferring the 7ft (2.1m) used by tramways and roads. He also made the tunnel dead straight.

All was on a grand scale: a ton of gunpowder and candles was used every week, 3 million bricks were fired to line the soft Cotswold limestone and 100 workers lost their lives. Although Brunel would ultimately lose the battle of the gauges, his magnificent line meant that Bristol was then a mere two hours from the capital.

the walk

1 Facing the recreation ground, walk to the far left-hand corner of the playing field, leaving by a track close to the railway line. When you reach the lane, turn left, pass beneath the railway, cross a bridge and take the arrowed **footpath**, to the right, before the second bridge.

A shaded walk near Box Hill

1h15 — 3.25 MILES — 5.3 KM — LEVEL 1 2 3

*A cricket match on Box Common –
a typical village scene*

2 Walk beside the river, cross a footbridge and turn right. Cross a further footbridge and continue to a stile. Walk through **water meadows** close to the river, go through a squeeze stile and maintain direction. Towards the far end, bear left to a squeeze stile in the field corner. Follow the right-hand field-edge to a stile and lane.

3 Turn right, then right again at the junction. Cross the river, pass **Drewett's Mill** and steeply ascend the lane. At a bend, just past **Mills Platt Farm**, take the left-most of the two arrowed footpaths ahead across a stile. Continue steeply uphill to a stile and, with care, cross the A4. Ascend steps to a lane and proceed straight on up **Barnetts Hill**. Keep right at the fork, then right again and pass the Quarryman's Arms.

4 Keep left at the fork and continue beside **Box Hill Common** to a triangle junction. Bear right and cross to take the path straight ahead into woodland. Almost immediately, fork left and follow the path close to the woodland edge. Later, as it curves right
into the beech wood, keep ahead and then bear left, leaving the trees through a gap in the wall. Immediately go right at the junction of paths.

5 Follow the bridle path, eventually reaching a fork. Keep ahead, then after a few paces turn right at a T-junction. At once, take a path left to a stile. Cross a further stile and descend into **Thorn Wood**, following the stepped path to a stile at the bottom.

MAP: OS Explorer 156 Chippenham & Bradford-on-Avon

START/FINISH: Box: village car park near Selwyn Hall; grid ref: ST 823686

PATHS: field and woodland paths, bridleways, lanes, 18 stiles

LANDSCAPE: river valley and wooded hillsides

PUBLIC TOILETS: opposite Queens Head in Box

TOURIST INFORMATION: Bath, tel 01225 477101

THE PUB: The Quarryman's Arms, Box Hill

Getting to the start

Box is 5.5 miles (8.9km) east of Bath where the A361 meets the A4. However, if approaching from the south along the A361, note there is no right turn onto the A4; you must go right at an earlier sign to Chippenham (A4) and then left along the A4. Parking is beside Selwyn Hall playing fields, signed off the main road.

what to look for

Explore Box and locate the Blind House on the main street, one of a dozen in Wiltshire for disturbers of the peace. Look for Coleridge House, named after the poet who often broke his journey here on his way to Nether Stowey. Also look for the former candle factory on the Rudloe road, which once produced the candles used during the building of Box Tunnel, and head east along the A4 for the best view of the tunnel's entrance.

6 Continue through scrub to a stile and turn right beside the fence to a wall stile. Bear right to a further stile, then bear left uphill to a stile and the A361. Cross over and follow the drive ahead. Where it curves left by stables, keep ahead along the arrowed

path to a house. Ignore the stepped garden path and go to the rear corner of the house, there swinging right up a contained path that leads to a lane at the top.

7 Turn left, then just before the houses of **Henley**, take a path right, across a stile. Follow the field-edge to a stile and descend to an allotment and stile. Continue to a stile and gate.

8 Walk on towards the buildings in front, looking for a contained path dropping between them, a little to the left. Cross the A361 to another alley opposite, taking care at the bottom as you emerge directly onto the busy A4. Turn right, then left down the access road back to **Selwyn Hall**.

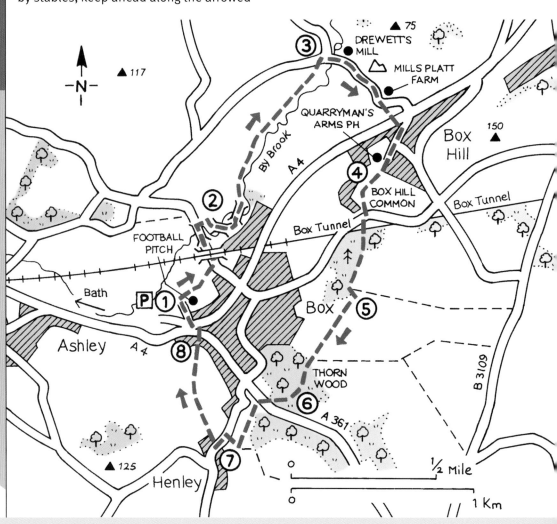

46

The Quarryman's Arms

Time your walk according to opening time at The Quarryman's Arms, a 300-year-old pub tucked away up a narrow hillside lane with quite splendid views over the Colerne Valley. This rustic rural local is also on the Macmillan Way long-distance footpath, providing accommodation and luggage transfer, and has long been a favoured watering-hole with walkers, cavers, potholers and local cyclists. The pleasantly modernised bar is packed with mining-related memorabilia and photographs as it was the local ale house of the Bath stone miners, and you can hear and feel the trains taking trips down the old stone mines. So why not enjoy the views across Box from the dining room with a hearty lunch and a pint of locally brewed ale, just like the stone miners once did.

Food

From the extensive snack menu tuck into ham, egg and chips, thick-cut sandwiches, fish and chips or a Quarryman's platter (ham, cheddar, Stilton with home-made pickle, salad and farmhouse bread). From the main menu try the Stilton and asparagus pancake, the ever-popular steak and ale pie, poached salmon, or lamb shank with mint and rosemary sauce.

Family facilities

Children are very welcome inside the pub. There's a family room, a children's menu, small portions of adult dishes, high chairs and baby-changing facilities. Supervision is required in the small garden.

Alternative refreshment stops

In Box, you will find both the Queen's Head and The Bear offer good food and ale in convivial surroundings.

☛ Where to go from here

Visit Haselbury Manor at Wadswick for its restored landscaped gardens. Learn more about the Bath stone quarrying industry through a visit to the heritage centre in nearby Corsham. In the centre of town is Corsham Court, an Elizabethan manor that was home to the Methuen family, which contains fine furniture and paintings.

about the pub

The Quarryman's Arms

Box Hill, Box, Corsham
Wiltshire SN13 8HN
Tel: 01225 743569
www.quarrymans-arms.co.uk

DIRECTIONS: A4 east of Box, turn right into Bargates before railway bridge, then at T-junction turn left up Quarry Hill. Left again at junction by grassy area, left after hotel into Beech Road, then third left into Barnetts Hill. At top of hill turn right to reach the pub

PARKING: 25

OPEN: daily; all day Friday, Saturday & Sunday

FOOD: daily

BREWERY/COMPANY: free house

REAL ALE: Butcombe Bitter, Wadworth 6X, Moles Bitter

DOGS: welcome in the pub

ROOMS: 3 bedrooms (2 en suite)

Sherston and Easton Grey

Sherston WILTSHIRE

The infant Bristol Avon links attractive stone villages on this pastoral ramble on the fringes of the Cotswolds.

Legend of a local hero

The Bristol Avon is little more than a wide, shallow stream as it flows through the rolling countryside west of Malmesbury. This peaceful river enhances the little stone villages in this unspoilt area. Between Colerne and Malmesbury, 18 villages are officially part of the Cotswold Area of Outstanding Natural Beauty. Sherston must rank among the most attractive, with its wide High Street lined with interesting 17th- and 18th-century buildings. It has been suggested that Sherston is Sceorstan where in 1016 Edmund Ironside won a battle against the Danes led by King Canute. The legend of John Rattlebone, a local yeoman promised land by Ironside in return for service against the Danes, is deep rooted. Sadly, this brave knight was wounded in battle and although he staunched his bleeding with a stone tile and continued fighting, he reputedly died as Canute's army withdrew. Other traditions say Rattlebone survived to claim his reward.

Later traditions tell us that the stone effigy on the south side of the porch of the parish church is that of Rattlebone, and that an ancient timber chest in the church, marked with the initials R B, is where he kept his armour. The Rattlebone Inn keeps his name alive.

Peaceful riverside paths lead you downstream to Easton Grey. Set around a 16th-century stone bridge and climbing a short, curving street is an intimate huddle of ancient stone houses, with mullioned windows, steep roofs and flower-filled gardens along the river bank. Set back on a rise above the river is Easton Grey House, a handsome 18th-century manor, surrounded by elegant gardens and lovely valley views.

the walk

1 On Sherston's High Street, walk towards the village stores, pass The Rattlebone

Inn and turn right into **Noble Street**. Pass Grove Road and take the footpath left up a flight of steps. Cross a cul-de-sac and follow a metalled footpath to a gate. Continue at the rear of houses to a further gate.

2 Bear diagonally right across a field to a gate and go forward in a second paddock to a kissing gate onto a lane. Turn right, cross the river and turn left, signed 'Foxley'. At the end of woodland on your left, take the footpath left through a gate. Follow the track across **Pinkney Park** to a gate.

3 Remain on the track, bearing left beside the wall and continuing ahead through a second gate towards **farm buildings**. Where it then curves left, turn right into the farmyard. Cross to join a concrete path in the far right corner and walk on to a stile. Go forward, joining the left-hand boundary, sticking with it in the next field.

4 In the third field, climb right to a gate and then bear half left along the field to a stile at the far side. Over a bridge and further stile, walk on past **game bird pens** and then beside a ranch fence, where there is a view to **Easton Grey House**. Drop through a gate at the far end onto a lane.

5 Turn left into **Easton Grey**. Cross the river and immediately turn right. Approaching entrance gates at the top, go left on a footpath past a **barn** into a gravel yard. Cross to a gate and keep ahead to a stile, just right of the field corner.

Left: The Avon passes through Easton Grey
Right: Sherston church where you will see the effigy of Rattlebone on the south of the porch

3h00 · **6.75 MILES** · **10.9 KM** · **LEVEL 1 2 3**

MAP: OS Explorer 168 Stroud, Tetbury & Malmesbury
START/FINISH: Sherston High Street; plenty of roadside parking; grid ref: ST 853858
PATHS: field and parkland paths, tracks, metalled lanes, 10 stiles
LANDSCAPE: river valley and gently rolling farmland
PUBLIC TOILETS: none on route
TOURIST INFORMATION: Malmesbury, tel 01666 823748
THE PUB: The Rattlebone Inn, Sherston

GETTING TO THE START
Sherston stands midway between Bath and Cirencester on the B4040, 5 miles (8km) west of Malmesbury. There is parking beside the wide High Street.

Keep ahead across the next field and gently descend to follow a track into the next field.

6 Turn right along the field-edge to the next corner and bear off right downhill through scrub to a **footbridge**. Keep ahead beside a ruin to a gate. Cross a stile and continue at the edge of a field to another stile by a gate. Follow a track downhill through trees to meet the **Fosse Way** beside a bridge. Turn right along the track and continue for 0.5 mile (800m) to a road.

7 Cross straight over and keep to the byway to another road. Bear left, but then keep ahead where the lane veers sharp left. Follow the track for another 0.5 mile (800m), passing a stile and later, the access to **Ladyswood Polo Ground**. Shortly beyond that, leave over a stile hidden in the right-hand hedge. Bear left, crossing to a small gate in the set-back portion of the

what to look for

The wide, hedged and dead-straight track which you follow on your return route to Sherston is the Fosse Way. This is the ancient Roman road which ran from Lincoln to Exeter and is so named because it was bordered on both sides by a 'fosse' or ditch.

opposite hedge, also not obvious. Now head diagonally right across a large paddock, joining a track to a gate.

8 It leads through to a **racecourse training gallop**. Keep ahead, passing left beside the barrier to a gate beyond. Walk through scrub to another gate and follow a track out to a lane. Turn left and continue past a crossroads and then a junction, remaining with the main lane beyond as it winds back into **Sherston**.

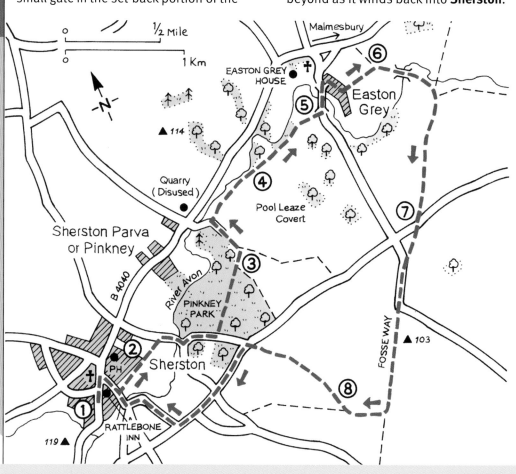

The Rattlebone Inn

This lively 16th-century village inn takes its name from the local hero John Rattlebone who, according to legend, died fighting King Canute in the Battle of Sherston in 1016. Inside, you'll find a rambling series of beamed rooms with old pews and settles, jugs and bottles hanging from the low beams, a mix of sturdy country furnishings, numerous cuttings and memorabilia relating to the pub's long and eventful history, and a good pubby atmosphere. The separate public bar has traditional and modern pub games including alley skittles. The food is good, the handpumped beer from Young's first-class and there's a decent range of wines by the glass. An annual boules championship is held on the Saturday closest to Bastille Day and features 132 teams from across Europe – the largest one-day boules event in the country. Pretty rear garden with flowerbeds, a gravel terrace and, naturally, four boules pitches.

Food

Enjoyable 'rattles snacks' include filled paninis, crusty sandwiches and ploughman's lunches. Regular lunchtime favourites take in smoked haddock fishcakes with leek sauce, home-made beef burger on foccacia bread with salad, and 'rattlebangers' with mash. The separate evening menu is more extensive.

Family facilities

Families are welcome in the pub. There are high chairs for toddlers and children can order small portions of main menu dishes.

Alternative refreshment stops

Sherston's other pub is the Carpenters Arms on the Malmesbury road out of the village.

☛ Where to go from here

Head north into Gloucestershire to visit Westonbirt Arboretum (www.forestry.gov.uk /westonbirt), one of the finest and most important collections of trees and shrubs in the country.

about the pub

The Rattlebone Inn
Church Street, Sherston
Malmesbury, Wiltshire SN16 0LR
Tel: 01666 840871

DIRECTIONS: on the High Street, opposite the church

PARKING: use High Street

OPEN: daily; all day

FOOD: daily

BREWERY/COMPANY: Young's Brewery

REAL ALE: Young's Bitter, Special & Triple A, Smiles Best

DOGS: welcome in the public bar only

CYCLE

Forest of Dean family trail

Meander through an ancient forest, where Nelson ordered the planting of oaks to build British man-of-war ships.

Forest of Dean

In 1938, the Forest of Dean was designated England's first National Forest Park, and notwithstanding its wonderfully peaceful and unspoiled setting, it is a working forest from which hundreds of tonnes of timber are harvested annually. It has also been a source of coal, and almost everywhere within the forest bears some evidence of its industrial past.

The criss-crossing leisure paths often follow the network of rail- and tramways that serviced the collieries, while heaps of spoil mark the site of the deeper workings. Contrasting with the luxuriant growth of the surrounding forest, many of these are still uncolonised except by the hardiest plants, the barren shales providing little nutrient despite the weathering of 50 years or more since they were last worked. At one time there were more than ten large pits, with countless small drift and bell mines being worked from antiquity. Although large-scale mining came to an end in 1965, anyone born within the Hundred of St Briavels, over the age of 21, and who has worked for a year and a day in a mine is still entitled to work a 'gale' in the forest as a Free Miner. The privilege was bestowed by Edward I, after forest miners helped ensure his victory at the Siege of Berwick by undermining the castle walls.

the ride

1 The cycleway is signed from beside the hire shop along a track that drops steeply to the B4234. Opposite, there is a brief but steep pull to a junction. Go left and left again to join the cycleway in the direction of Drybrook Road Station, gently rising along the course of a disused mineral railway. At **Whitegates Junction**, fork left, dropping with the main track to another obvious junction at which, turn sharp right. Where the track then divides, bear right, still following signs for Drybrook Road Station. Keep going, passing beneath a graceful horseshoe-shaped bridge before shortly encountering a tarmac track at **Drybrook Road Station**.

2 Cross and carry on along the cycleway, which is now signed to **Dilke Bridge**, the earlier gradual climb rewarded with a gentle descent. Soon, the forest clears and the scars of former coal workings become evident. Hazard signs warn of a crossing track hidden in a dip, the way continuing beyond the former **Foxes Bridge Colliery**. After a moderate descent (watch for a bend at the bottom), carry on past a junction for Cinderford Linear Park and then the

2h30 — 9.25 MILES — 14.9 KM — LEVEL 2̶1̶3̶

MAP: OS Explorer OL14 Wye Valley & Forest of Dean

START/FINISH: Car park, Pedalabikeaway Cycle Centre; grid ref: SO 606124

TRAILS/TRACKS: good surfaced cycle trails

LANDSCAPE: forest and woodland

PUBLIC TOILETS: at Pedalabikeaway Centre (also showers & changing rooms)

TOURIST INFORMATION: Coleford, tel 01594 812388

CYCLE HIRE: Pedalabikeaway Cycle Centre, New Road, Forest of Dean, tel 01594 860065; www.pedalabikeaway.com

THE PUB: The Speech House Hotel, Coleford

🛈 Gradual climbs and descents, one steep descent, 4 road crossings, overhanging twigs; route shared with pedestrians

Getting to the start
Pedalabikeaway Cycle Centre is in the Forest of Dean, 3 miles (4.8km) north east of Coleford beside the B4234.

Why do this cycle ride?
Decreed a royal hunting forest by King Canute in 1016, the Forest of Dean is steeped in a long history. Iron was smelted here before the Romans arrived and they valued not only the timber but also the abundant mineral reserves here – good-quality building stone, coal and iron ore – and began industries that continue to the present day.

outbuildings of Dilke Hospital to arrive at **Dilke Bridge**.

3 Beyond, more hazard signs announce a junction where a broad track joins from the left signed to Cannop Wharf. After a traffic barrier and the former **Lightmore Colliery**, a gate forces you to dismount. There follows a short but stiff pull, the track then bending sharply left before dropping once more past a couple of warned junctions, at the second of which, Spruce Ride to the right, offers a short-cut back via **Speech House**.

4 Otherwise, carry on to Central Bridge across **Blackpool Brook**, later reaching a crossing of tracks where Cannop Wharf and the Cycle Centre are signed right. After a turning to New Fancy picnic site, the track swings to a gate, a little distance beyond which is a road crossing.

5 Through another gate at Burnt Log, the track winds down to a fork. Keep ahead, before long coming to a notice warning of a steep descent. The main track drops through a sharply twisting 'S' bend, passing a massive ancient oak, the last survivor of The Three Brothers, where men from the nearby collieries gathered on a Sunday morning for their union meetings. Beyond, the descent continues more easily, eventually ending at a T-junction beside **Cannop Wharf**.

6 The **Cycle Centre** is signed to the right beside a couple of **artificial lakes**, at the top of which a car park and picnic area are laid out. As the metalled drive bends towards a road, branch off right to a

crossing point over the B4226. Speech House lies 0.5 mile (800m) to the right, although you may wish to return later in the car, whilst the way back is with the continuing track. Fork left when you reach a split, gently losing height to a second junction. There go left again, dropping steeply to the road. Go slowly for there is a sharp bend at the bottom. The **car park** is then at the top of the rise opposite.

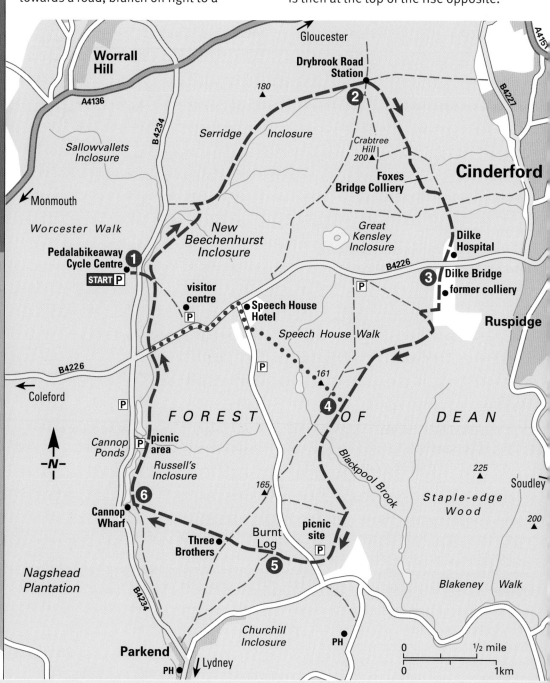

The Speech House Hotel

In the heart of Forest of Dean, close to miles of woodland trails, The Speech House was built in 1676 as a hunting lodge for Charles II. Later it became the administrative centre of the forest. The largest room was the Verderer's Court where people went to talk or make a speech, hence the name of what is now a substantial hotel. The Verderer's Court still meets four times a year in what is Britain's oldest functioning courtroom and it retains much of its original decoration. Despite its hotel status, there's a good bar area with real ale on tap, notably a beer from Whittington's brewery in nearby Newent, a traditional bar menu, and a warm welcome for walkers and cyclists. To the rear there are extensive lawns and gardens for all to use.

Food

Hearty snacks in the bar include sandwiches (beef and horseradish) served with chips, various salads and traditional dishes such as ham, egg and chips, sausages and mash, and battered cod and chips. Separate restaurant menu and Sunday roast lunches.

Family facilities

Children are genuinely welcomed (extra beds and cots are provided if staying), and the welcome extends into the bar and dining area. Here there are high chairs and young children have a standard menu to choose from.

Alternative refreshment stops

Café at the Cycle Hire Centre at start and picnic areas in the forest.

☛ Where to go from here

Learn about the history and culture of the Forest of Dean at the Dean Heritage Centre at Soudley (www.deanheritagemuseum.com) where attractions include a forester's cottage, agricultural displays, blacksmiths and craft units. At Puzzlewood in Coleford, an unusual maze takes you through 24.5ha (14 acres) of pathways, deep ravines and passageways within pre-Roman open-cast iron ore mines.

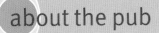

about the pub

The Speech House Hotel
Coleford, Forest of Dean
Gloucestershire GL16 7EL
Tel: 01594 822607
www.thespeechhouse.co.uk

DIRECTIONS: beside the B4226 between Coleford and Cinderford, at the junction with a minor road for Lydney

PARKING: 60

OPEN: daily; all day

FOOD: daily

BREWERY/COMPANY: free house

REAL ALE: Bass, Whittington's Cat Whiskers

ROOMS: 37 en suite

Winchcombe and Sudeley Castle

A rewarding walk above a thriving Cotswold village and the burial place of Henry's sixth queen, Catherine Parr.

Sudeley Castle

At the end of a long drive just outside Winchcombe is Sudeley Castle. The first castle was built here in 1140 and fragments dating from its earlier, more martial days are still much in evidence. Originally little more than a fortified manor house, by the mid-15th century it had acquired a keep and several courtyards. It became a royal castle after the Wars of the Roses, before being given to Thomas Seymour, Edward VI's Lord High Admiral. Seymour lived at Sudeley with his wife, Catherine Parr – he was her fourth husband. After Seymour was executed for treason the castle passed to Catherine's brother, William, but he was executed too. Queen Mary then gave the property to Sir John Brydges. Sudeley Castle was a Royalist stronghold in the Civil War but was disarmed by the Parliamentarians and left to decay until its purchase by the wealthy Dent brothers in 1863.

Catherine Parr, sixth wife of Henry VIII, is buried in Sudeley's chapel. She was born in 1512, educated in Henry's court and was first married at nine years of age, but widowed six years later. Back at court, she used her influence with the king to protect her second husband, Lord Latimer, from the machinations of courtly politics. When Latimer died in 1543, Catherine, wealthy and well-connected, was an obvious choice of wife for Henry. She looked after him until his death in 1547. She married Seymour and moved to Sudeley, where she died in 1548.

The village of Winchcombe has a considerable history. In Anglo-Saxon times it was a seat of the Mercian kings and the capital of Winchcombshire until the shire's incorporation into Gloucestershire in the 11th century. It became a significant place of pilgrimage due to the abbey established in 798 and dedicated to St Kenelm, the son of its founder, King Kenulf.

The abbey was razed in the Dissolution, but the village's parish church survived and is a fine example of a 'wool church', financed through income from the medieval wool trade. Of particular interest are the amusing gargoyles that decorate its exterior. They are said to be modelled on real local people. Winchcombe also boasts two stimulating small museums: the Folk Museum on the corner of North Street and the Railway Museum on Gloucester Street.

the walk

1 Leave the long stay car park behind the library by a pedestrian access at its far-left corner and turn right along Cowl Lane into the town centre. Turn left onto High Street and then go right in front of **The White Hart** down Castle Street. Soon after crossing a bridge at the bottom, turn left beside **Briar Cottage** along a narrow alley to a field behind. Strike half right across a meadow, still bearing the ridges and furrows of medieval ploughing.

Sudeley Castle is a largely 15th-century reconstruction of the original building

2h00 — 3.75 MILES — 6 KM — LEVEL 1 23

2 Emerging onto a lane, turn right. At the end of a high stone wall on your right, leave into a field on the left and stride out half right to a gap, about two-thirds the way along the right-hand hedge. Over a **bridge and stile**, bear left to another stile by a gate. Maintain your diagonal course through a break in the middle of the right-hand hedge until you reach a protruding corner and then turn with the fence up the hill to a stile in the overgrown corner.

3 Now climbing more steeply up **Dunn's Hill**, strike a bee-line across the curve of the left-hand fence to a stile beside a gate at the top of the field. Carry on up by the fence and into the next field then bear half right to a stile in the top corner. Keep ahead over more stiles, until the fence on your left turns away.

The Knot Garden at Sudeley Castle

MAP: OS Explorer OL45 The Cotswolds

START/FINISH: Winchcombe: long stay car park on Back Lane; grid ref: SP 023284

PATHS: fields and lanes, 13 stiles

LANDSCAPE: woodland, hills and villages

PUBLIC TOILETS: at car park and on corner of Vine Street

TOURIST INFORMATION: Winchcombe, tel 01242 602925

THE PUB: The White Hart Inn, Winchcombe

Getting to the start

Situated at the junction of the B4632 and B4078, Winchcombe is 6 miles (9.7km) north east of Cheltenham. Park in the long stay car and coach park in Back Lane, which you will find signed from High Street.

4 At that point, swing right down the hill to a stile beside a gate, about half-way along the boundary. A field track leads past a small building protected within a fenced enclosure, marking **St Kenelm's Well**.

5 Passing into the next field, leave the track, bearing right to cross the field to a stile and gate, some two-thirds of the way down the opposite hedge. Keep going downhill, aiming left of **Sudeley Hill Farm** at the bottom to emerge at a road. Turn left and then go right along a lane signed to **Sudeley Lodge** and **Parks Farm**.

6 Opposite a **cottage**, leave right on a footpath falling at the edge of a field. Over a stile, turn right and then left to remain within the field, but leave at the bottom corner. Go forward to a stile on the right and, guided by obvious waymarkers, walk half left, eventually joining a fence to pass **Sudeley Castle** on your right.

7 Passing through two kissing gates into the park, carry on along a contained path to the main drive. Cross to a gate beyond the lawn opposite and bear half right over open grazing, later crossing another track to leave through a kissing gate in the farthest corner. Back in **Castle Street**, turn left and retrace your outward steps past **The White Hart** to the car park.

what to look for

If you go into the church at Winchcombe, note the embroidery behind a screen, said to be the work of Catherine of Aragon, the first wife of Henry VIII. As you descend the hill on the approach to Sudeley Hill Farm, look out for St Kenelm's Well. This is a 19th-century version of a holy well connected with the martyred prince, patron saint of the vanished Winchcombe Abbey.

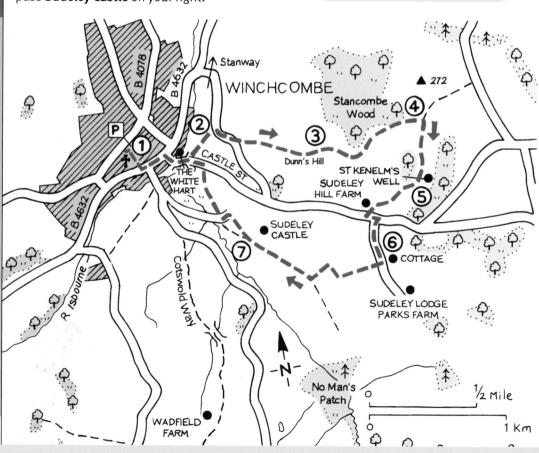

The White Hart Inn

Standing in the heart of this pretty Cotswold town, the black-and-white painted White Hart looks every inch the traditional 16th-century coaching inn it once was. Step inside and the rustic front bar with its wood floor, dark wood pub tables and row of handpumps on the bar maintain the illusion that this is a classic English pub, but throughout the rear dining room and the eight stylishly decorated bedrooms there's a distinct Scandinavian feel. The Swedish owners have brought a cool elegance and minimalist style that permeates the place. The chefs and staff are also from Sweden and Swedish flavours influence the contemporary menu. However, you can still sup local ale, tuck into a rare roast beef baguette, or a home-made pizza in the Stable Bar.

Food
Adventurous diners can enjoy Swedish meatballs, Scandinavian open sandwiches and the speciality smorgasbord platter (cold meats, seafood and salads). Alternatives include crusty baguettes, Gloucestershire pork sausages with mustard mash and onion gravy, and ploughman's platters with home-made chutney. Separate evening restaurant menu. English or Scandinavian breakfast menu served to non-residents.

Family facilities
The pub has a children's licence and they are welcome inside until 9pm. There's a good children's menu and family bedrooms.

Alternative refreshment stops
A large number of possibilities range from pubs to tea rooms and restaurants. If you visit Sudeley Castle, there's a good café.

☞ Where to go from here
Spend some time at Sudeley Castle (www.sudeleycastle.co.uk) or visit the atmospheric ruins of 13th-century Hailes Abbey (www.english-heritage.org.uk). Children will love the Cotswold Farm Park (www.cotswoldfarmpark.co.uk) for the animals, farm safari and pets corner.

about the pub

The White Hart Inn
High Street, Winchcombe
Gloucestershire GL54 5LJ
Tel: 01242 602359
www.the-white-hart-inn.com

DIRECTIONS: town centre, at the junction of High Street and Castle Street

PARKING: 12

OPEN: daily; all day

FOOD: daily; all day

BREWERY/COMPANY: Enterprise Inns

REAL ALE: Goffs White Knight, Wadworth 6X, Greene King IPA & Old Speckled Hen, Bass

DOGS: welcome in the bar and some bedrooms

ROOMS: 8 en suite

The Upper Windrush Valley and the Slaughters

CYCLE

Explore the countryside around two of the Cotswolds most famous villages.

The Slaughters

Bubbling from a spring in a secluded fold of the Cotswold hills, the River Eye embarks on a short but pretty journey past the Slaughters before becoming lost in the River Windrush, just a couple of miles further on below Bourton-on-the-Water.

But for their unashamed loveliness, the two tiny villages would probably have escaped the notice of the modern world. Despite their popularity, they have remained unspoiled, resisting large car parks and commercial gift shops. At Lower Slaughter, you can visit a corn mill, which, although dating only from the 19th century, continues the tradition of a succession of earlier
mills that have occupied the site since the Normans arrived on these shores. It houses a small shop, tea room, and museum which shows how grist milling has been carried out over the centuries.

Despite the proximity of the two villages, Upper Slaughter displays a completely different character to its neighbour. The cottages around The Square were reconstructed in 1906 by the great architect

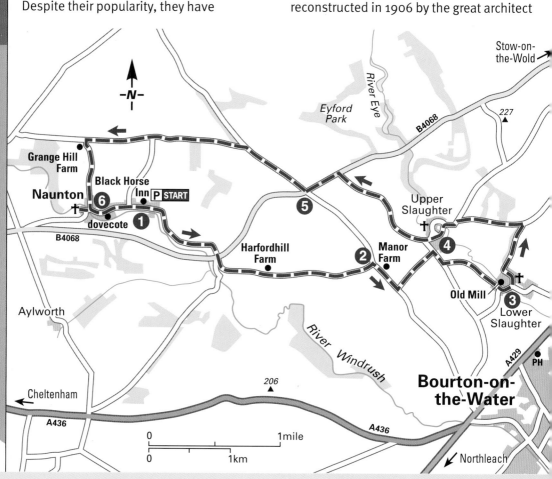

The River Eye passing through Upper Slaughter

Sir Edward Lutyens, the designer of New Delhi, while a little earlier, the Victorian vicar of the Norman church, the Reverend Francis E Witts wrote *The Diary of a Cotswold Parson*.

Back in Naunton, the impressive dovecote is a rare survivor of its type, the roof sporting four gables and topped by a louvre to permit access by the birds. It is thought to date from around 1600 and was built to provide the lord of the manor with fresh meat during the winter months.

the ride

1 Starting with the pub on your left, follow the lane out of the village, as yet pedalling easily along the bottom of the **Windrush valley**. At a crossroads with the B4068, the honeymoon comes to an end as you take the leftmost of the two lanes opposite. Tunnelled in trees it climbs steeply away, but before long you can start changing up through the gears as the gradient levels past **Harfordhill Farm**. Your exertion is rewarded by a fine view across the wolds as you continue to a junction.

2 Go right past **Manor Farm**, and then left at the next turning, signed to Upper and Lower Slaughter. Free-wheeling down, watch your speed, for there is a T-junction at the bottom where you should go right to **Lower Slaughter**. Keep with the main lane as it shortly bends left in front of a junction and sweeps around beside the River Eye into the centre of the village.

3h00 · **9 MILES** · **14.5 KM** · **LEVEL 123**

CYCLE

MAP: OS Explorer OL 45 The Cotswolds
START/FINISH: The Black Horse Inn, Naunton (ask permission first); grid ref: SP 234119
TRAILS/TRACKS: country lanes
LANDSCAPE: rolling Cotswold countryside between the valleys of Windrush and Eye
PUBLIC TOILETS: none on route
TOURIST INFORMATION: Stow-on-the-Wold, tel 01451 831082
CYCLE HIRE: none locally
THE PUB: The Black Horse Inn, Naunton
❶ Several stiff and one steep ascent, and a long downhill stretch. Suitable for fitter, older family groups.

Getting to the start
Naunton is located just off the B4068, 4.5 miles (7.2km) west of Stow-on-the-Wold. Leaving the main road, follow a narrow lane through the village to find The Black Horse Inn, from which the ride begins.

Why do this cycle ride?
The twin villages of the Slaughters are the epitome of the Cotswold village, and although both can become unbearably crowded on a fine weekend during the summer, they display nothing but charm on a quieter day. Inevitably, the ride encounters a succession of hills, but take your time, and you will discover scenic beauty in this pastoral countryside that is often missed when travelling by car.

The Slaughters

GLOUCESTERSHIRE

The Slaughters

GLOUCESTERSHIRE

3 At a junction in front of **St Mary's Church**, go left, passing through the more recent part of the village and the

5 Turn right on a lane, signed to **Cotswold Farm Park**, enjoying a much easier 0.5 mile (800m). At a fork, bear left to

cricket green before climbing steadily away. After 0.33 mile (500m) at a bend, turn sharp left to **Upper Slaughter**, pedalling over a gentle rise before dropping to a junction. To the left the lane falls more steeply, winding sharply to a bridge at the bottom of the hill. Climb away on the far side to a small raised green at the heart of the village, above which to the right stands the **church**. Don't leave without having a look at the **ford**, which lies over the hill behind the church. The high ground opposite was once the site of an early Norman stronghold.

4 The route continues with the main lane through the village to a junction. Go right towards Cheltenham. There follows a prolonged pull out of the valley, which eventually eases to a junction with the **B4068**. To the left the climb resumes for another 0.25 mile (400m) to a crossroads.

Guiting Power and Winchcombe, the gently undulating road offering more expansive views to the south. Go past the first turning off left, signed to Naunton, continuing for a further 0.5 mile (800m) to a second turning, also on the left by **Grange Hill Farm**. An unmarked narrow lane, it drops steeply into the valley. Go carefully as it winds sharply to a junction at the edge of Naunton.

6 The way back to The Black Horse Inn is to the left, but first have a look at the **church**, which lies a short distance along to the right. As you return to the pub, another deviation is merited, this time, turning right just after the **Baptist church** to see Naunton's historic **dovecote**.

A cyclist passes through Lower Slaughter village without encountering other traffic

The Black Horse Inn

The setting is a typical Cotswold village sunk deep in the beautiful Windrush Valley, much beloved of ramblers, cyclists and locals alike. Original flagstones, blackened beams, open log fires, simple tables and chairs and fine oak pews exude rural charm in the main bar while the lounge offers a smaller, snugger retreat. Built of honey-coloured stone and dating from the 1870s, the pub is renowned for its home-cooked food, Donnington real ales and utterly peaceful bed and breakfast.

Food

Dishes range from ploughman's, filled baguettes and jacket potatoes to some accomplished main dishes: steak and kidney pudding, grilled trout, chicken breast with Stilton and bacon, salmon fillet in saffron sauce, and local game in season. There's also the day's selection of 'sinful sweets'!

Family facilities

Families are welcome inside the pub. There's a children's menu, smaller portions of adult meals and high chairs are available.

Alternative refreshment stops

Hotels for lunches and cream teas in both the Slaughters; café at The Mill in Lower Slaughter.

☛ Where to go from here

Spend some time in Bourton-on-the-Water. Children will enjoy the fabulous toy collection and the cars at the Cotswold Motoring Museum and Toy Collection (www.cotswold-motor-museum.com), the perfect replica of a Cotswold village at the Model Village, and a visit to Birdland Park and Gardens, a natural setting of woodland, river and gardens inhabited by more than 500 birds.

about the pub

The Black Horse Inn
Naunton, Stow-on-the-Wold
Gloucestershire GL54 3AD
Tel: 01451 850565
www.blackhorsenaunton.com

DIRECTIONS:	see Getting to the Start
PARKING:	12
OPEN:	daily; all day Saturday & Sunday
FOOD:	no food Monday evening
BREWERY/COMPANY:	Donnington Brewery
REAL ALE:	Donnington BB & SBA
ROOMS:	1 en suite

A circuit from Bibury

(13)

WALK

Bibury

GLOUCESTERSHIRE

The outer charm of a weavers' village conceals miserable former working conditions.

Weaving industry

Arlington Row is the picturesque terrace of cottages that led William Morris to refer to Bibury as the most beautiful village in England. It was originally built, it is thought, in the late 14th century, to house sheep belonging to Osney Abbey in Oxford. Following the Dissolution the land was sold off and the sheep houses converted to weavers' cottages. Before mechanisation transformed the wool weaving industry, most weaving took place in the houses of the poor. Firstly, women and children spun the wool either at home or at the workhouse. Then it was transferred to the houses of the weavers, who worked on handlooms at home at low rates.

Strictly speaking, much of what is considered picturesque in Bibury is in the neighbouring village of Arlington, but they are now indistinguishable. Apart from Arlington Row, there is plenty to enjoy in the village, especially the church, which has Saxon origins and is set in pretty gardens. Across the bridge is the old mill, open to the public. Nearby Ablington has an enchanting group of cottages, threaded by the River Coln. A minor classic, *A Cotswold Village* (1898), which describes local life in the late 19th century, was written by J Arthur Gibbs, the squire who lived at Ablington Manor. You pass the walls of the manor on the walk. Close by, further into the village, are a couple of beautiful 18th-century barns.

the walk

1 From the parking area opposite **Arlington Mill**, walk along the main road in the direction of Cirencester. Some 50yds (46m) after **The Catherine Wheel**, and opposite a telephone box, turn right along a narrow lane towards **Arlington Farm**. Through gates, keep left at a fork, pass the farmhouse and walk on at the edge of a field. Over a drive, maintain the same line across successive fields, eventually passing a house to emerge onto a lane.

2 Turn right and walk down to a junction, there going right into **Ablington**. Some 30yds (27m) after crossing a bridge, double back sharp left onto a minor lane, following a mill leat past cottages. Degenerating to a track beyond a gate, it meanders pleasantly for 0.5 mile (800m) before reaching a second gate.

3 Entering a field, curve right to follow a sinuous route along the base of a valley, passing through occasional gates and eventually going by **Downs Barn**.

Arlington Row in Bibury was where weavers once lived and worked

2h45 — **6.25 MILES** — **10.1 KM** — **LEVEL 1 2 3**

MAP: OS Explorer OL45 The Cotswolds

START/FINISH: Bibury: opposite Arlington Mill; grid ref: SP 114068

PATHS: field tracks and a lane, may be muddy in places, 6 stiles

LANDSCAPE: exposed wolds, valley, villages and streams

PUBLIC TOILETS: opposite river on main street, close to Arlington Row

TOURIST INFORMATION: Cirencester, tel 01285 654180

THE PUB: The Catherine Wheel, Bibury

Getting to the start

Bibury is on the B4425, almost midway between Cirencester – 7 miles (11.3km) and Burford – 10 miles (16.1km). There is a roadside car park in the centre of the village by the bridge opposite Arlington Mill on the southern bank of the river.

Bibury

GLOUCESTERSHIRE

4 A track now develops, bearing right and ascending towards the head of a side valley. When the main track subsequently veers right, keep ahead on a lesser track that winds left to a **gate**. Follow it out to a lane.

5 Turn right, but after 300yds (274m) at a right-hand bend, leave onto a track ahead, the **Salt Way**, and follow it for 0.5 mile (800m) to **Saltway Barn**.

6 Through a gate just before the scatter of buildings, keep left where the track splits. Walk past sheds on the left and go through an opening into the corner of a field. A track to the right continues at the edge of successive fields for almost 0.75 mile (1.2km) before meeting a junction.

7 Turn right through a gate, remaining with the new track past **Hale Barn** and then a junction off to **Bibury Farm**. Carry on towards Bibury whose buildings soon come into view ahead. Beyond a house, the way becomes partly metalled and eventually winds down to the main road at the edge of the village. Turn right and then left as if to walk down to Bibury Court, but instead, immediately leave via a gap in the low right-hand wall by a **telephone**

box. Follow the street ahead past cottages, turning right at the bottom in front of the church to return to the main road. Go left, but then cross the river at the first bridge to

Arlington Row. At the end of the terrace of cottages, swing right on a path that follows a stream back to Arlington Mill.

Bibury   GLOUCESTERSHIRE

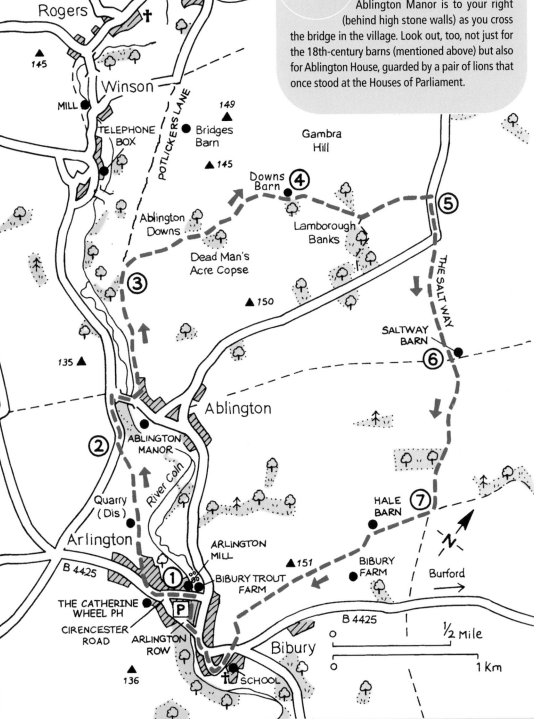

what to look for

Ablington Manor is to your right (behind high stone walls) as you cross the bridge in the village. Look out, too, not just for the 18th-century barns (mentioned above) but also for Ablington House, guarded by a pair of lions that once stood at the Houses of Parliament.

The Catherine Wheel

Fruit trees grow against the wall at each side of the entrance to this 500-year-old stone pub situated in this classic Cotswold village, a short stroll from Arlington Row (NT) – a group of ancient cottages – and the River Coln. Inside, the three small, low-beamed rooms have the mellow atmosphere of an unpretentious, unspoiled local. Most of the drinking is done in the first bar, which has a log fire in winter and ceiling beams taken from old wooden ships, when they were broken up in Gloucester dock – an example of 15th-century recycling. Most of the eating takes place in the other two rooms, both with wood-burning stoves, pictures of old Bibury, and traditional pub furnishings. Summer attractions include colourful hanging baskets and neatly tended terraced lawns full of picnic benches. There are four en suite bedrooms in well converted outhouses.

Food

Traditional home-made pub food ranges from lunchtime snacks such as filled jacket potatoes, hot and cold baguettes and plaice and chips to Thai fishcakes, lambs' liver and bacon, paella and Bibury trout.

Family facilities

Children are welcome away from the bar. You will find a children's menu, high chairs, baby-changing facilities, and activities to keep children amused. Lovely rear garden with rabbits constantly in residence.

Alternative refreshment stops

The Swan Hotel has a good restaurant and also serves teas. A variety of snacks are available at Bibury Trout Farm and at the mill.

about the pub

The Catherine Wheel

Bibury, Cirencester
Gloucestershire GL7 5ND
Tel: 01285 740250

DIRECTIONS: just up from the car park towards Cirencester

PARKING: 25

OPEN: daily; all day

FOOD: daily

BREWERY/COMPANY: Eldridge Pope

REAL ALE: Adnams Bitter, Wadworth 6X

DOGS: allowed in the garden only

ROOMS: 4 en suite

☛ Where to go from here

Bibury Trout Farm is a working farm where children can feed the fish and even catch their own – all tackle provided. There are also plenty of activities at the Cotswold Water Park and Keynes Country Park to keep children amused (www.waterpark.org).

The villages of Great Tew and Little Tew

Take a stroll through one of Oxfordshire's loveliest villages before exploring undulating countryside to the south.

The fall and rise of Great Tew

Arthur Mee, in his book *The King's England – Oxfordshire*, says that 'if our England is a garden, Great Tew is one of its rare plots.' Most would agree. The village is a gem of a place.

Designed as an estate village in the 19th century, with the intention of blending architectural beauty with utility and management, Great Tew went into decline in later years and virtually became derelict. However, the village has been given a new lease of life, with many of the thatched and ironstone cottages carefully restored, and it is now a designated Conservation Area.

The origin of its name is unclear, but Tew is thought to mean 'ridge', of which there are a great many in the area. The village has a long history and in later years became closely associated with Lucius Carey, 2nd Viscount Falkland, Secretary of State to Charles I. A later owner, G F Stratton, who inherited Great Tew in 1800, resided in a rather modest late 17th- or early 18th-century house which stood at the southern end of the village. During the early years of the 19th century, Stratton engaged in an ill-fated trial in estate management.

The estate changed hands several times before being acquired by Matthew Robinson Boulton. Outlying farms were rebuilt, cottages were re-thatched and other features such as mullioned windows and stone door

heads were added. The estate remained the home of the Boulton family for many years. Between 1914 and 1962 Great Tew was administered by trustees but by now the local workforce had decreased and the estate was all but abandoned.

It was Major Eustace Robb, an old Etonian and descendant of the Boulton family, who moved to the village with the aim of halting its steady decline. His efforts certainly paid off. A stroll through the village today is marked by a conspicuous air of affluence.

the walk

1 From the car park at the edge of Great Tew, walk left along the main lane and go past the turning into the village. Immediately beyond the junction, leave through a gate on the right, the path signposted to Little Tew. Climb diagonally across the field, heading for **Court Farm** on the brow of the hill. Enter the farmyard over a stile by a gate and bear right, skirting

Above: Little Tew is on the route of the walk

1h45 · 3.75 MILES · 6 KM · LEVEL 123

MAP: OS Explorer 191 Banbury, Bicester & Chipping Norton

START/FINISH: Free car park in Great Tew; grid ref: SP 395293

PATHS: field paths and tracks, stretches of quiet road, 3 stiles

LANDSCAPE: rolling parkland and farmland on edge of Cotswolds

PUBLIC TOILETS: none on route

TOURIST INFORMATION: Chipping Norton, tel 01608 644379

THE PUB: The Falkland Arms, Great Tew

❶ Paths at the edge of some crop fields may become overgrown in summer and may be difficult for young children

Getting to the start

Great Tew stands alongside the B4022, just south of its junction with the A361 and 7 miles (11.3km) south west of Banbury. There is a small car park on the edge of the village beside the lane as it enters from the north.

some silos to find another gate and stile behind them. Follow the right-hand field boundary to the top corner, emerging over a final stile at a junction.

2 Cross to a path at the left angle of the junction, again signposted to Little Tew. Head diagonally across the field, passing to the right of a **transmitter**. On reaching a lane, turn right and walk down the hill into **Little Tew**. At a junction by the church of St John the Evangelist turn left towards Enstone.

3 The lane climbs out of the village over a rise, dropping on the far side to a **bridge** bounded by white railings. Just beyond, go through an opening in the left-hand hedge into a field and follow the left boundary away. Through a gate in the corner, continue ahead in a meadow, shortly joining a track from a house, over to the left. Follow it out to the road.

4 Be careful, for traffic moves quickly, as you cross to a track opposite, signed to Sandford. It eventually swings left over a bridge in front of **Tracey Barn Farm**. Immediately turn right and walk away at the field edge. Entering trees at the far side, a track leads on through a gate, but leave it after 50yds (46m) through a small waymarked gate on the left. Climb away at the edge of successive fields. Approaching a **lodge** at the top, leave the field through a gate and walk along its drive out to the road by a junction.

5 Cross to the lane opposite, signposted for Great Tew, and follow it down past the entrance to **St Michael's Church**, which lies peacefully amid the trees of the parkland

what to look for

Little Tew is worth close inspection. The church, built by George Street, dates back to 1835 and the Methodist chapel to 1871. The Grange, also by Street, was built as a vicarage about the same time as the church. The school and almshouses were constructed in the 1860s. Walk along the splendid avenue of laurels and traveller's joy leading to Great Tew's fine medieval church, which lies peacefully amid the trees of the parkland. The church walk was originally the carriage drive to the mansion of Lucius Carey, 2nd Viscount Falkland.

on the right. Carry on, passing the school to return to the **village green**, at the back of which, you will find The Falkland Arms.

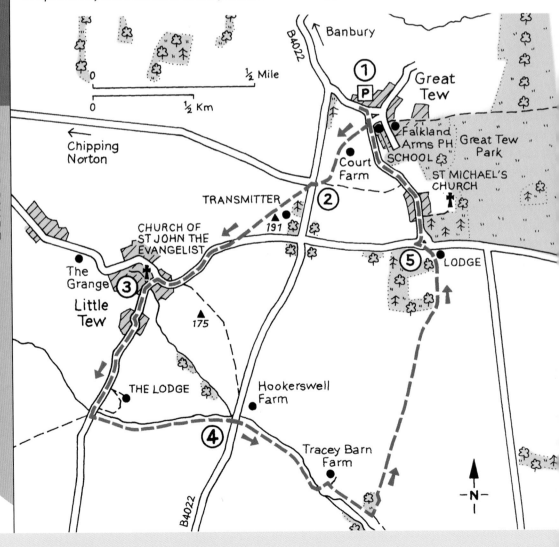

The Falkland Arms

An unspoiled and historic village is the tranquil setting for this 500-year-old, creeper-clad, Cotswold-stone inn which takes its name from Lucius Carey, 2nd Viscount Falkland, who inherited the manor of Great Tew in 1629. Nestling at the end of a charming row of Cotswold-stone cottages – the quintessential English village scene – The Falkland Arms is a classic gem. The intimate bar features flagstone floors, high-backed settles, a huge inglenook fireplace with winter log fire, and a collection of jugs and mugs hangs from the old beams. A pretty garden is shaded by a large hornbeam tree, complete with dovecote.

Food
Home-made specials such as beef and ale pie or salmon and broccoli fishcakes supplement the basic lunchtime menu (baguettes & ploughman's), served in the bar or the pub garden. In the evening, booking is essential for dinner in the small, non-smoking dining room. Expect parsnip soup or grilled goat's cheese salad, followed by chicken breast with mushrooms and bacon in shallot sauce, or salmon and prawns with lemon and dill sauce.

Family facilities
Children are welcome in the separate dining area at lunchtimes only.

Alternative refreshment stops
Nearby Chipping Norton has a range of restaurants, pubs and cafés.

☛ Where to go from here
At North Leigh, near Woodstock, is the remains of a large and well-built Roman courtyard villa. In Woodstock you can visit the award-winning Oxfordshire Museum and learn more about the archaeology, landscape and wildlife of the county.

about the pub

The Falkland Arms
Great Tew, Chipping Norton
Oxfordshire OX7 4DB
Tel: 01608 683653
www.falklandarms.org.uk

DIRECTIONS: see Getting to the start; pub along dead-end lane by the village stores, opposite the church

PARKING: use village hall car park

OPEN: daily; all day Saturday & Sunday mid-July–September

FOOD: daily; restaurant only in evening; no food Sunday evening

BREWERY/COMPANY: Wadworth Brewery

REAL ALE: Wadworth 6X & Henry's IPA, 4 guest beers

DOGS: allowed on a lead

ROOMS: 5 en suite

A circuit around Linwood

CYCLE

Linwood HAMPSHIRE

Venture off the beaten track and mix with wildlife in the heart of the New Forest.

New Forest deer

You'll often see deer along this trail, especially early in the morning or around dusk – go quietly for the best chance of seeing these timid woodland residents in their natural habitat. Keep an eye out for roe deer in the cultivated fields close to Dockens Water, between the start of the ride and the point where you join the tarred lane leading up to the Red Shoot Inn. These graceful creatures are 24–28 inches (61–71cm) high at the shoulder and the

males have short, forked antlers. Roe deer have rich reddish-brown coats from May to September, but turn greyer in winter and develop a white patch on the rump.

You'll occasionally spot red deer in the same area, especially on the open heath near Black Barrow. These are our largest native species, and a fully-grown male with his splendid russet coat and impressive antlers may stand nearly 4ft (1.2m) tall at the shoulder. The males are at their boldest when competing for females during the mating season in early autumn.

Fallow deer may pop up almost anywhere on the ride, but a favourite haunt is in Broomy Bottom, off to your right as you

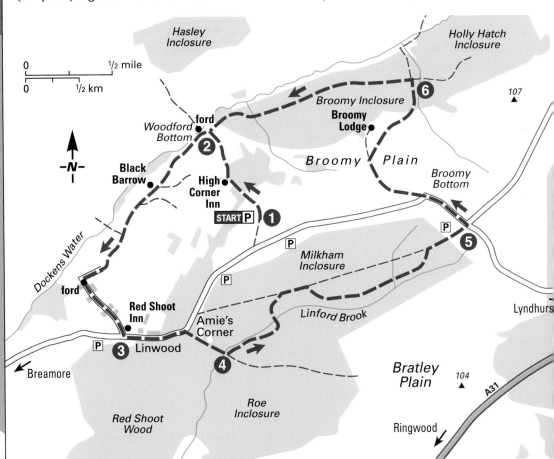

cross Broomy Plain. With their reddish-fawn coats dappled with white spots, these appealing animals have white rumps and a black line running up the tail. The males have broad antlers and stand up to 3ft (0.9m) tall at the shoulder.

the ride

1 Turn right out of the car park and pass the end of the gravel track which leads up to the **High Corner Inn**.

2 At Woodford Bottom bear left at the wooden barrier on your right and pass the ford across the Dockens Water stream, also on your right. Keep to the waymarked cycle route as it follows the gravelled track that winds across the open heath, past a few scattered houses and the tree-capped mound of **Black Barrow**. A few smaller tracks lead off to left and right, but the main gravelled trail is easy enough to follow. Keep straight on as a similar track leads in from your left near the thatched Bogmyrtle Cottage, until you join a tarred lane. Almost at once the lane turns sharp left through a tiny ford and climbs gently up to the road junction at the **Red Shoot Inn**.

3 Turn left opposite the post-box, still following the waymarked cycle route, and continue to climb until the road levels off and swings to the left at **Amie's Corner**. Fork right here, sticking with the waymarked cycle route as it joins a gravelled forest track. The trail dives into Milkham Inclosure through wooden gates beside an attractive whitewashed cottage, then drops to a bridge over the Linford Brook.

1h45 — **7 MILES** — **11.3 KM** — **LEVEL 123**

MAP: OS Explorer OL22 New Forest

START/FINISH: Spring Bushes car park, Linwood; grid ref: SU 196107

TRAILS/TRACKS: gravelled forest tracks, two short sections on rural lanes

LANDSCAPE: broadleaf and coniferous woodland interspersed with open heathland

PUBLIC TOILETS: none on route

TOURIST INFORMATION: Lyndhurst, tel: 023 8028 2269

CYCLE HIRE: Country Lanes, 9 Shaftesbury Street, Fordingbridge, tel: 01425 655022

THE PUB: The High Corner Inn, Linwood

❶ Moderate hills, some uneven and stony tracks. Suitable for older children, off-road riding experience useful.

Getting to the start

Linwood is a village on a minor road north east of Ringwood. Spring Bushes car park is on the road that runs west from Emery Down, near Lyndhurst, to Rockford, just north of Ringwood.

Why do this cycle ride?

This relatively remote ride offers peace and quiet, and the opportunity to see the New Forest at its best. You'll follow waymarked Forestry Commission off-road cycle tracks deep into the heart of the Forest, with two short sections on tarred roads where you will need to watch out for the occasional car. There are plenty of opportunities for birdwatching or studying the other wildlife.

A family cycles through the countryside at Linwood

4 A few yards further on turn left at the numbered waymark post 5, then follow the track as it winds through open mixed woodland and re-crosses the **Linford Brook**. Continue as the track bears right at the next **waymark post**, then right again in front of a pair of wooden gates where you enter an area of mainly coniferous woodland. A pair of wooden gates punctuates your progress to the top of the hill, where further gates lead you out into the Forestry Commission's **Milkham car park**. Go through here, cross the car park, and stop at the road junction.

5 Turn left towards **Linwood** and follow the narrow tarred lane for 500yds (457m) until it bears away to the left. Fork right here on to the waymarked cycle trail that follows the gravel track towards **Broomy Lodge** and **Holly Hatch**. Here your route crosses the

high heathland plateau of **Broomy Plain**. This is a good spot to see Dartford warblers, meadow pipits and stonechats, and you'll also enjoy long views towards Cranborne Chase and the Wiltshire Downs. Bear right at the next fork and follow the trail down into **Holly Hatch Inclosure**.

6 At the foot of the hill, numbered **waymark post 3** stands at the forest crossroads. Turn left here, on to a lovely tree-shaded track with soft green verges that leads you through the **oak woods**. Two pairs of wooden gates mark your progress through the inclosure, and at length the oaks give way to conifers. Follow the waymarked trail until you rejoin your outward route at a low wooden barrier. Turn left here, and climb the short hill back to the **High Corner Inn**.

The High Corner Inn

The High Corner is an early 18th-century inn, much extended and modernised. It is set in 7 acres (2.8ha) of the New Forest and hidden down an old drovers' track off a narrow Forest lane. A quiet hideaway in winter, mobbed in high summer due to its heart-of-the-Forest location, it is a popular retreat for families, offering numerous bar-free rooms, an outdoor adventure playground and miles of easy New Forest walks. Although extensively refurbished, this rambling old building retains a wealth of beams, wooden and flagstone floors, and a blazing winter log fire in the cosy main bar. There's a separate food servery, plus top-notch Wadworth ales on tap and overnight accommodation in eight well-equipped rooms.

Food
An extensive printed menu includes sandwiches, ploughman's lunches and salads, as well as freshly battered haddock and chips, beef and 6X pie and sizzling steak platters. Look to the blackboard for daily soups, daily roasts or the likes of baked trout with pine nuts and chargrilled pork loin with spiced apple cream.

Family facilities
This is a great family pub – there's a children's menu, family areas, some high chairs and a woodland garden with an adventure playground.

Alternative refreshment stops
Also owned by Wadworth Brewery, the Red Shoot Inn offers home-cooked meals and brews its own beer behind the pub.

about the pub

The High Corner Inn
Linwood, Ringwood
Hampshire BH24 3QY
Tel: 01425 473973

DIRECTIONS: a gravel track to the High Corner Inn branches off the road, 400yds (366m) west of the start point
PARKING: 200
OPEN: daily, all day in summer, and all day Sunday in winter
FOOD: daily, all day July and August
BREWERY/COMPANY: Wadworth Brewery
REAL ALE: Wadworth Henry's IPA, 6X and JCB
ROOMS: 7 en suite

☛ Where to go from here
Breamore House, north of here off the A338, is a handsome old manor house which dates back to 1583. It has a fine collection of paintings and china, and a countryside museum which includes steam engines (www.breamorehouse.com).

From Yarmouth to Freshwater

An exhilarating three-stage ramble in the footsteps of Alfred, Lord Tennyson.

Tennyson country

Away from the hustle and bustle of the traditional resort towns in the east of the island, West Wight is a quieter, less populated area of great natural beauty, offering areas of open countryside, rugged cliffs, wonderful views and fascinating wildlife. This three-part ramble encapsulates the contrasting landscapes of the area, from the wildlife-rich tidal estuary of the River Yar and the natural wetland habitat of freshwater marshes, to rolling farmland and the magnificent chalk headlands and hills with their breathtaking coastal views.

The poet Alfred, Lord Tennyson (1809–92) and his wife Emily first came to Farringford House (now a hotel) set in parkland beneath Tennyson Down, in 1853. The island inspired some of his greatest poems. 'The Charge of the Light Brigade' was written on the down that now bears his name, and 'Maud', 'Enoch Arden' and 'The Idylls of the King' were all composed at Farringford. The Tennysons later bought a house on the mainland and only returned to Farringford for the winter, where they would be undisturbed.

Memories of the great man and his family are dotted along this walk. On Tennyson Down, where he rambled, you will find the monument erected in his honour in 1897. You can take lunch or afternoon tea at Farringford Hotel. In Freshwater, view the memorials to the family in All Saints Church, while in the peaceful churchyard you will find Emily's grave.

the walk

1 From the car park in Yarmouth make for the town square. Head for the **church** and walk along St James' Street. Cross Tennyson Road into Mill Road and continue straight on towards and past the **old Tide Mill** (built in 1793 to harness the tidal flow of the estuary). Continue through the gate and turn right along the **old railway line**, following it for 1.5 miles (2.4 km) to **The Causeway**.

2 For the short walk back to Yarmouth, turn right, cross The Causeway to the Red Lion and Point 9. To continue the second stage of the walk, turn left at Point 2 and follow the lane to the **B3399**. Turn left

what to look for

On Tennyson Down you may see rare chalk-loving flowers and grasses, including bee orchids and nettle-leaved bellflowers, and hundred of small butterflies, such as common, chalkhill, small and Adonis blues, skippers and dark green fritillaries.

White cliffs, the bay and beach at Freshwater

| 4h30 | 9.5 MILES | 15.3 KM | LEVEL 2 |

SHORTER ALTERNATIVE ROUTE 1

| 3h00 | 6.5 MILES | 10.4 KM | LEVEL 1 |

SHORTER ALTERNATIVE ROUTE 2

| 1h30 | 3.5 MILES | 5.7 KM | LEVEL 1 |

MAP: OS Outdoor Leisure 29 Isle of Wight

START/FINISH: ferry terminal or pay-and-display car park opposite, Yarmouth; grid ref: SZ 354897

PATHS: disused railway, woodland and downland paths, some road walking, 4 stiles

LANDSCAPE: freshwater marsh and salt marsh, farmland, downland

PUBLIC TOILETS: at Yarmouth and Freshwater Bay

THE PUB: The Red Lion, Freshwater

❶ Care needed crossing main roads in Yarmouth and Freshwater. Nature reserve can be wet and muddy. Long ascent up Tennyson Down on longest walk. The full 9.5-mile (15.3km) route is recommended only for more experienced older children. Only children over 10 allowed in the pub

Getting to the start

Yarmouth is 10 miles (16.1km) west of Newport on the A3054, on the north west coast of the Isle of Wight. The car park is opposite the ferry terminal. Park at the ferry terminal in Lymington and cross to Yarmouth as a foot passenger on the Wightlink ferry (www.wightlink.co.uk).

and soon cross into the unsurfaced **Manor Road**. In 50yds (46m) bear off left, signposted '**Freshwater Way**', and ascend across grassland towards **Afton Down**.

3 Proceed ahead at a junction of paths beside the **golf course**, and follow the gravel track right to the **clubhouse**. Go through a gate by the building and walk down the access track, keeping left to reach the **A3055**. Turn right downhill into **Freshwater Bay**.

4 For the second loop option, walk past the **Albion Hotel** and continue, turning right at Blackbridge Road, at Point 8. For the third section of the long walk, turn left instead by the **bus shelter** and public toilets, along a metalled track signposted '**Coastal Footpath**'. As it bears left, keep ahead through kissing gates and soon begin a steep ascent up a concrete path on to **Tennyson Down**. Keep to the well trodden path to reach the **memorial cross** at its summit.

5 Continue down the wide grassy swathe, which narrows between gorse bushes, to

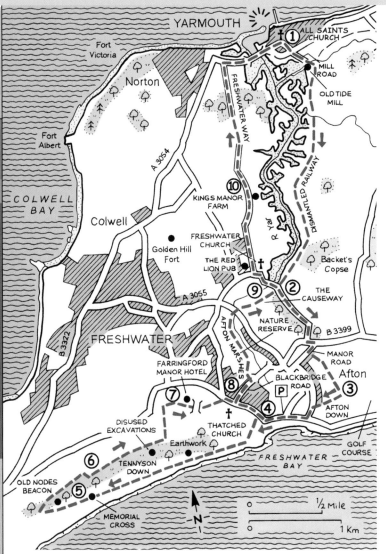

Pass beneath a **wooden footbridge** and continue downhill to a gate and the road. (Turn left to visit the hotel.) Turn right, pass the **thatched church**, and turn left down Blackbridge Road.

8 Just before Black Bridge, turn left into **Afton Marshes Nature Reserve**. Join the nature trail, go over the footbridge and turn left following the path beside the stream (this can be very wet) to the **A3055**. Turn left and almost immediately cross over to join **footpath F61** along the course of the old railway. After 0.5 mile (800m) reach **The Causeway**.

9 Turn left and follow the lane to All Saints Church and **The Red Lion** pub. Take the waymarked path (**Freshwater Way F1**) between a cottage and the churchyard wall. Cross two stiles and continue along the farm road. At the farmyard entrance cross the double stile on the left and bear right along the field edge to a stile.

reach the replica of **Old Nodes Beacon**. Here, turn very sharp right down a **chalk track**. Turn right into a car park and almost immediately ascend sharp left.

6 The path descends to a gate. Proceed along the **woodland fringe** and continue into more open countryside, then fork left at disused **excavations** on the right. Cross a stile, then keep left and after 50yds (46m) turn sharp left and descend to another stile. Cross the next field to a stile and turn right along the field edge to a stile.

7 After the next stile cross a **farm track**, go through a gate and walk along the track (F47) beside **Farringford Manor Hotel**.

10 At a track and the entrance to **Kings Manor Farm**, cross the stile ahead (by double gates) and follow the wide track to a gate and a junction of paths. Climb the stile on the right, pass through a copse, over another stile and bear left, uphill along the field edge. Cross a stile and maintain direction to another stile and descend into **woodland**, emerging onto a metalled track. Turn left to the **A3054** and turn right to the bridge over the River Yar, back into Yarmouth.

The Red Lion

A husband-and-wife team run this pub, in a picturesque setting beside All Saints Church. It's just a short stroll from the tidal River Yar, which makes it popular with the sailing set from nearby Yarmouth. The Red Lion's origins date from the 11th century, though the current red-brick building is much newer. The open-plan bar is comfortably furnished with country kitchen-style tables and chairs, plus relaxing sofas and antique pine. In addition to the pub's four real ales, including the island's Goddards Best, and a good wine selection (with 16 available by the glass), the pub is renowned for its daily blackboard menu of interesting food.

about the pub

The Red Lion
Church Place, Freshwater
Isle of Wight PO40 9BP
Tel: 01983 754925
www.redlion-wight.co.uk

DIRECTIONS: from the A3055 east of Freshwater by mini-roundabout and garage follow Yarmouth signs, then turn left for the church
PARKING: 15
OPEN: daily
FOOD: daily
BREWERY/COMPANY: Enterprise Inns
REAL ALE: Fuller's London Pride, Flowers Original, Wadworth 6X, Goddards
DOGS: welcome in the bar

Family facilities
Children under 10 are not permitted in the bar, but there is a fascinating dome structure in the pretty side garden where families can eat, also a gravelled area with tables and chairs beyond the herb garden.

Alternative refreshment stops
Choice of pubs and cafés in Yarmouth. Freshwater Bay has a family-friendly pub and café, and lunch or teas can be found at Farringford Manor Hotel.

☛ Where to go from here
Visit the Needles Pleasure Park. Take a boat trip to view the Needles and explore the Old Battery, with its viewing platform and exhibition (www.theneedles.co.uk).

Food
Everything is freshly made from tried and tested recipes. Typical dishes are whole crab salad, braised half-shoulder of lamb with minted gravy, fresh cod and chips, halibut with chilli and coriander sauce, steak and kidney pie, and apple pie with custard. Lunchtime snacks include baguettes and ploughman's lunch.

From Chichester to Hunston

WALK

Chichester WEST SUSSEX

A fascinating walk combining the ancient treasures of a cathedral city with the delights of the adjacent countryside.

Historic Chichester

A stroll through the quaint streets of Chichester is the best way to appreciate this beautiful city. Chichester's origins date back as far as the late Iron Age, and settled by the Romans in about AD 200. They built the walls and laid out the city plan, which can still be clearly identified.

From the car park you soon in the heart of Chichester. Make the cathedral your first port of call. This magnificent building includes the site of a shrine to St Richard, Bishop of Chichester in the 13th century, modern tapestries by John Piper and Romanesque stone carvings. Another memorable feature is Graham Sutherland's painting, which depicts Christ appearing to St Mary Magdalen on the first Easter morning.

From the cathedral the walk heads down West Street to the intricately decorated Market Cross, built at the beginning of the 16th century. Situated at the hub of the Roman street plan and distinguished by its flying buttresses, the cross provided shelter for traders. Head up North Street to the Council House, built in 1731 and famous for its huge stone lion and Roman stone. The Latin inscription records the dedication of a temple to Neptune and Minerva. From here it's an easy stroll south to the Pallants.

You then leave the city, by following the Chichester section of the Portsmouth and Arundel Canal out into the countryside and south to Hunston.

the walk

1 Leave the car park, cross the **footbridge** over the Avenue de Chartres and head towards the city centre. Turn right at the city map and then left into South Street. Bear left into **Canon Lane**, just beyond the tourist information centre. Turn right into St Richard's Walk up to **Chichester Cathedral**.

what to look for

In addition to the remains of the Roman city walls, there is St Mary's Hospital of the Blessed Virgin Mary in St Martin's Square, founded between 1158 and 1170. Originally a hospital, it later became almshouses. Visitors can make an appointment with the guide.

In the nearby Pallants is Pallant House, built by Henry Peckham, a Chichester wine merchant, in 1712. The house is Queen Anne style and each room reflects a particular period of its history.

2h00	4.5 MILES	7.2 KM	LEVEL 1 2 3

WALK

MAP: OS Explorer 120 Chichester, South Harting & Selsey

START/FINISH: fee-car park in Avenue de Chartres, Chichester; grid ref: SZ 857044

PATHS: urban walkways, towpath and field paths, 3 stiles

LANDSCAPE: mixture of city streets and open countryside

PUBLIC TOILETS: at car park and elsewhere in Chichester

TOURIST INFORMATION: Chichester tel: 01243 775888

THE PUB: The Spotted Cow, Hunston
🛈 Great care needed when crossing the A27. Suitable for children of all ages.

Getting to the start

Chichester is a city on the south coast between Portsmouth and Bognor Regis. Leave the A27 city bypass at the roundabout where the Witterings are signed to the south and the city centre and railway station to the north. Follow the city centre signs, cross over the railway, then in 200 yards (183m) take the first major turning left – Avenue de Chartres. Pass under the footbridge and exit off the next roundabout into the car park.

Chichester
WEST SUSSEX

2 Swing left at the **cloisters**, then left again to keep the stone wall on your left. Make for the West Door and pass the **Bell Tower** to reach West Street. Bear right here. Across the road is a converted church, now a bar. The north face of Chichester Cathedral is clearly seen as you head along West Street. On reaching the **Market Cross**, turn left into North Street and bear right immediately beyond the historic **Council House** into Lion Street.

3 Walk along to **St Martin's Square**, and opposite you at this point is **St Mary's Hospital**. Turn right and pass the Hole in the Wall pub to reach East Street. Glance to the left and you can pick out the **Corn Exchange**. Go straight over into North Pallant and walk along to **Pallant House**. Head straight on into South Pallant and follow the road round to the right, passing **Christ Church** on the left. Turn left at the next junction, make for the traffic lights and continue south into **Southgate**.

4 Cross the railway at **Chichester Station** and then swing left to reach the **canal basin**. Follow the tow path to Poyntz Bridge, dated 1820, and continue to the next bridge which carries the **A27 Chichester bypass**.

Left: Chichester Cathedral
Right: A tapestry and altar inside the cathedral

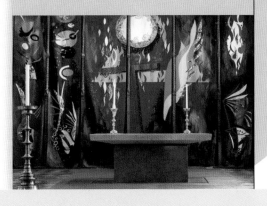

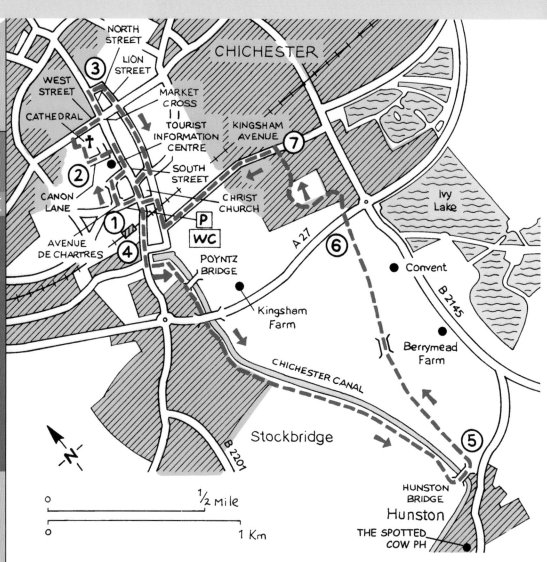

Keep going as far as the next footbridge and follow the path to the road. Confusingly this bridge is labelled Poyntz Bridge on OS maps. (Turn right here to **The Spotted Cow**, about 250 yards/229m on the right.)

5 Bear left for a few steps to a stile by the **car park** entrance. Cross into the field. The cathedral's spire can be seen above the city. Keep the **field boundary** on your right and make for a stile. Keep ahead, with a field on your left and follow the path to a small **footbridge** over a ditch and a stile. Follow the edge of the next field, keeping the same direction. Pass by a **broken stile** in the wooded corner and a few steps beyond you reach the **A27**.

6 Cross over with extreme care to join a footpath opposite. Turn left between **two terraces** of houses and follow the tarmac path to the **recreation ground**. Cross to the far side of the green, keeping the cathedral spire more or less straight ahead. Look for **Cherry Orchard Road**, with a post-box and a phone-box on the corner of the road.

7 Turn left at the crossroads into Kingsham Avenue and follow it into Kingsham Road. Turn right at the T-junction, cross the **railway line** and, on reaching the one-way system, bear left to cross over at the lights. Bear right into Southgate, then left into **Avenue de Chartres**. The car park is on the left.

The Spotted Cow

about the pub

The Spotted Cow
Selsey Road, Hunston
Chichester, West Sussex PO20 6PD
Tel: 01243 486718
www.thespottedcow.net

DIRECTIONS: village and pub are on the B2145 Selsey road south of Chichester
PARKING: 40
OPEN: daily, all day Friday, Saturday and Sunday
FOOD: daily
BREWERY/COMPANY: free house
REAL ALE: Gales BB and HSB, guest beer
DOGS: welcome on a lead
ROOMS: 2 bedrooms

The Spotted Cow was originally a dairy farm before being converted into a pub in 1955. It's close to the attractions of Chichester harbour and an easy stroll from the city centre via the towpath beside the old canal. Refurbishment in 2000 saw the pub carefully extended to incorporate an old barn, and today it successfully combines the charm and character of a classic country pub (flagstones, heavy beams, open fires) with a modern Mediterranean theme. Upgrading included developing the shaded patio and the sun-trap garden area to the front of the pub. Expect an informal atmosphere, good wines by the glass and local Gales ales on tap.

Food

From an extensive menu you can order snacks and starters such as roast beef and horseradish sandwiches, hearty ploughman's lunches with salad, pickles and crusty bread, fishcakes or scrambled egg and smoked salmon. Main courses include Lancashire hotpot, home-made venison meatballs, fish pie and steak and kidney pie, a range of hand-made sausages, and fresh fish dishes – perhaps sea bass with lemon and coriander.

Family facilities

Families are welcome and youngsters will find a play area in the garden, a children's menu and reduced price dishes from the blackboard menu. There are baby-changing facilities in the disabled person's toilet.

Alternative refreshment stops

As well as Chichester's many inns and hotels, there is Platters restaurant near the Avenue de Chartres car park, and Bishop Bell Rooms close to the cathedral.

☛ Where to go from here

There's plenty to see and do in Chichester, including harbour tours, or head just west of the city to the Roman palace at Fishbourne, with its stunning collection of mosaic floors (www.sussexpast.co.uk).

Around the Arun Valley from Arundel

WALK

Follow the River Arun to Arundel Park and then tour this handsome Sussex town.

Arundel

Arundel has rows of elegant Georgian and Victorian buildings, fine shops and a riverside setting, but the best attraction is the castle. Driving along the A27 to the south of Arundel, the great battlemented castle can be seen standing guard over the town, dwarfing all other buildings in sight.

There has been a castle here since the 11th century, though most of the present structure is Victorian. Arundel Castle has been the principal home of the Dukes of Norfolk since the 16th century. During the Civil War Parliamentary forces attacked the castle. However, it was extensively rebuilt and restored in the 18th and 19th centuries. Within its great walls lies a treasure trove of sumptuous riches.

The walk starts down by the River Arun and from here there are teasing glimpses of the castle, but it is not until you have

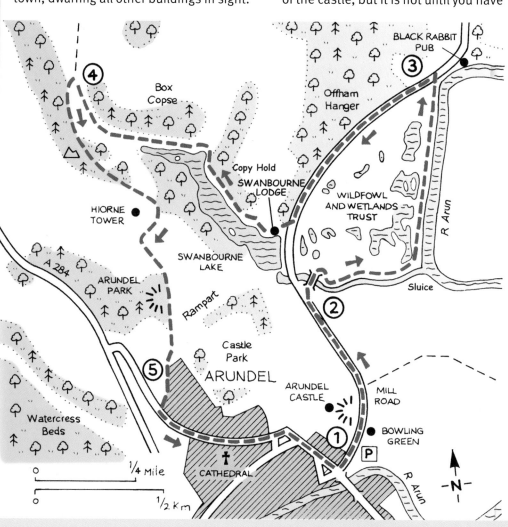

WALK

what to look for

Climbing up from Arundel Park brings you to Hiorne Tower, a remote but beautifully situated folly. Triangular in shape and newly restored, the folly was built by Francis Hiorne in an effort to ingratiate himself with the then Duke of Norfolk so that he might work on the restoration of Arundel Castle. The duke agreed to engage him but Hiorne died before he could begin any work.

The Wildfowl and Wetlands Trust Conservation Centre, which is directly on the route of the walk, has many attractions to divert your attention. Ducks, geese and swans from all over the world make their home here and the boardwalk enables you to explore one of the largest reed beds in Sussex, without getting your feet wet.

MAP: OS Explorer 121 Arundel & Pulborough

START/FINISH: fee-paying car park, Mill Road, Arundel; grid ref: TQ 020071

PATHS: riverside and parkland paths, some road walking, 2 stiles

LANDSCAPE: valley, rolling parkland and town

PUBLIC TOILETS: Arundel town centre and Swanbourne Lake

TOURIST INFORMATION: Arundel, tel: 01903 882268

THE PUB: Black Rabbit, Offham

❶ Section of road with no pavement (generally light traffic). Arundel Park is closed annually on 24 March. Dogs are not permitted in Arundel Park

Getting to the start

Arundel is located just off the A27 between Chichester and Worthing, 10 miles (16.1km) east of Chichester. If heading west on the A27, exit for the town centre at the first roundabout. Cross the River Arun and turn right into Mill Road. The car park is 100yds (91m) along on the right.

almost finished the walk that you reach its main entrance. Following the riverbank through the tranquil Arun valley, the walk reaches Arundel Park. Swanbourne Lake, a great attraction for young children, is by the entrance to the park, but beyond here the park assumes a different character. Rolling hills and tree-clad slopes crowd in and only occasional walkers will be seen in these more remote surroundings. You may feel isolated but you are soon back in Arundel's busy streets. Pass the huge cathedral, built in 1870, and head to the castle entrance. Walk down the High Street, said to be the steepest in England, and by the bridge you can see the remains of the Blackfriars monastery, dissolved in 1546 by Henry VIII.

Walking through an open stretch on the route

Swans in the Wildfowl and Wetlands Trust reserve at Arundel

the walk

1 From the car park in Mill Road, turn right and walk along the tree-lined pavement. Pass the **bowling green** and a glance to your left will reveal a dramatic view of Arundel Castle with its imposing battlements.

2 Follow the road to the elegant stone bridge, cross over via a **footbridge** and turn right. Ignore the path left, and follow the riverside path, partly shaded by overhanging trees. Emerging from the cover, the path cuts across lush, low-lying ground to reach the western bank of the **Arun**. Turn left and walk beside the reed-fringed river to the **Black Rabbit pub**, which can be seen standing out against a curtain of trees.

3 From the Black Rabbit, follow the minor road in a roughly westerly direction back towards Arundel, passing the entrance to the **Wildfowl and Wetlands Trust**. Make for the gate leading into Arundel Park and follow the path beside **Swanbourne Lake**.

Eventually the lake fades from view as the walk reaches deeper into the park. Ignore a turning branching off to the left, just before a **gate and stile,** and follow the path as it curves gently to the right.

4 Turn sharply to the left at the next **waymarked junction** and begin a fairly steep ascent, with the footpath through the park seen curving away down to the left, back towards the **lake**. This stretch of the walk offers fine views over Arundel Park. Pass through a gate with a stile on the left, then bear immediately right up the bank. Cross the grass, following the waymarks and keeping to the left of **Hiorne Tower**. On reaching a driveway, turn left and walk down to **Park Lodge**. Keep to the right by the private drive and make for the road.

5 Turn left, pass **Arundel Cathedral** and bear left at the road junction by the entrance to Arundel Castle. Go down the hill, back into the centre of Arundel. You'll find **Mill Road** at the bottom of the High Street.

Black Rabbit

This uniquely named pub is popular with walkers and tourists visiting Arundel and the nearby Wildfowl and Wetlands Trust reserve. It stands right beside the River Arun, and from its riverside terrace you can relax and enjoy excellent views down the river to Arundel's magnificent castle. Once a fashionable watering hole for the Edwardians, it retains the appearance of being an elegant riverside summer house, and what were once probably old boat sheds now form part of the pub's main dining area. Wood floors, traditional furnishings and a winter log fire are features of the long main bar. Seating is also provided under the attractive front verandah, which makes a real picture in summer with colourful hanging baskets and tubs.

Food

Sandwiches, filled baguettes and a choice of ploughman's lunches are listed on the blackboard in the bar. From the printed menu you can sample honey-roast ham, egg and chips, steak and Tanglefoot pie, warm chicken and bacon salad and garlic chicken, and round off with apple and blackberry crumble.

Family facilities

Children are most welcome, and although a 'junior menu' is available, children are encouraged to be adventurous and try a starter or smaller portions from the main menu. To keep youngsters away from the river there is a play area beside the car park.

Alternative refreshment stops

Arundel has a good choice of places to eat and drink. The Wildfowl and Wetlands Trust offers a café by the water's edge, and there is a picnic site by Swanbourne Lake.

☛ Where to go from here

Arundel Museum and Heritage Centre illustrates the town's colourful and lively past with a series of fascinating exhibits and photographs, providing a unique glimpse into the development of the town and the lives of its people.

about the pub

Black Rabbit

Offham, Arundel

West Sussex BN18 9PB

Tel: 01903 882828

DIRECTIONS: continue along Mill Road from Arundel town centre for Offham	
PARKING: 180	
OPEN: daily, all day	
FOOD: daily, all day	
BREWERY/COMPANY: Hall and Woodhouse Brewery	
REAL ALE: King & Barnes Bitter, Badger Best, Tanglefoot and Fursty Ferret	
DOGS: allowed in part of the bar and garden	

A circuit of Devil's Dyke by Poynings

A fine walk with glimpses over the most famous of all the dry chalk valleys.

Devil's Dyke

Sussex is rich in legend and folklore, and the Devil and his fiendish works crop up all over the county. The local landmark of Devil's Dyke blends the natural beauty of the South Downs with the mystery and originality of ancient mythology.

Devil's Dyke is a geological quirk – a spectacular, steep-sided downland combe or cleft 300ft (91m) deep and half a mile (800m) long. It was probably cut by glacial meltwaters in the Ice Age. Rising to over 600ft (180m), views from this beauty spot stretch for miles in all directions. Artist John Constable described this view as the grandest in the world.

Devil's Dyke has long been a tourist honey pot. During the Victorian era and in the early part of the 20th century, the place was akin to a bustling theme park, with a cable car crossing the valley and a steam railway coming up from Brighton. On Whit Monday 1893 a staggering 30,000 people visited the area. In 1928 HRH the Duke of York dedicated the Dyke Estate for the use of the public forever, and in fine weather it can seem just as crowded as it was in Queen Victoria's day. With the car park full and the surrounding slopes busy with people, Devil's Dyke assumes the feel of a seaside resort at the height of the season. Hang gliders swoop over the grassy downland like pterodactyls, and kite flyers spill from their cars. The views more than make up for all the visitors, and away from the chalk slopes and the car park the walk heads for more peaceful surroundings.

the walk

1 From the Summer Down car park go through the kissing gate and veer right. Join the **South Downs Way** and follow it alongside lines of trees. Soon the path curves left and drops down to the road. Part company with the South Downs Way at this point, as it crosses over to join the **private road** to Saddlescombe, and follow the verge for about 75yds (69m). Bear left at the footpath sign and drop down the bank to a stile.

1h30 — **3 MILES** — **4.8 KM** — **LEVEL 1 2 3**

2 Follow the line of the tarmac lane as it curves right to reach a **waymark**. Leave the lane and walk ahead alongside **power lines**, keeping the line of trees and bushes on the right. Look for a narrow path disappearing into the vegetation and make for a stile. Drop down some steps into the woods and turn right at a **junction** with a bridleway. Take the path running off half-left and follow it between fields and a wooded dell. Pass over a stile and continue to a stile in the left boundary. Cross a footbridge to a further stile and now turn right towards **Poynings**.

3 Head for a gate and footpath sign and turn left at the road. Follow the parallel path along to the **Royal Oak** and then continue to **Dyke Lane** on the left. There is a **memorial stone** here to George Stephen Cave Cuttress, a resident of Poynings for over 50 years, erected by his widow. Follow the tarmac bridleway and soon it narrows to a path. On reaching the fork, by a National Trust sign for **Devil's Dyke**, veer right and begin climbing the steps.

The South Downs seen from Devil's Dyke

MAP: OS Explorer 122 South Downs Way: Steyning to Newhaven

START/FINISH: free car park, Summer Down; grid ref: TQ 268112

PATHS: field and woodland paths, 6 stiles

LANDSCAPE: chalk grassland, steep escarpment and woodland

PUBLIC TOILETS: by Devil's Dyke pub

TOURIST INFORMATION: Brighton, tel: 0906 711 2255

THE PUB: Royal Oak, Poynings

❶ Steep steps up the South Downs. Suitable for fitter, older children.

Getting to the start

Poynings is north of Brighton, west of the A23. Take the A281 for Henfield, then turn left for Poynings. Turn left in front of the church, then at the next T-junction, turn right. Follow this road for about 1 mile (1.6km) and turn right, signposted 'Dyke'. The car park is on the right after about 500yds (457m).

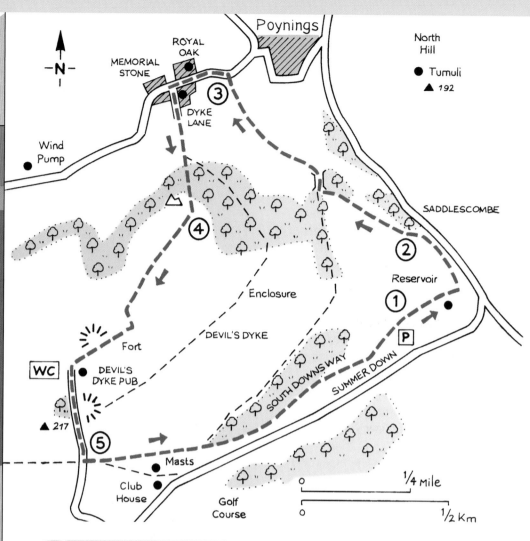

what to look for

Devil's Dyke consists of 183 acres (74ha) of open downland which is home to all manner of flora and fauna, including horseshoe vetch, the Pride of Sussex flower and the common spotted orchid. The adonis blue butterfly also inhabits the area. The Dyke lies within the South Downs Area of Outstanding Natural Beauty and is a designated Site of Special Scientific Interest (SSSI).

Take a stroll through the village of Poynings, pronounced 'Punnings' locally. The village takes its name from the Poynages family, which held the manor here during the Middle Ages. Michael de Poynages, a 14th-century lord of the manor, left two hundred marcs (£2,400) in his will towards the building of the Church of Holy Trinity.

4 Follow the path up to a gate and continue up the **stairs**. From the higher ground there are breathtaking views to the north and west. Make for a **kissing gate** and head up the slope towards the inn. Keep the **Devil's Dyke pub** on your left and take the road round to the left, passing a bridleway on the left. Follow the path parallel to the road and look to the left for a definitive view of **Devil's Dyke**.

5 Head for the **South Downs Way** and turn left by a National Trust sign for **Summer Down** to a stile and gate. Follow the trail, keeping Devil's Dyke down to your left, and eventually you reach a stile leading into **Summer Down car park**.

Royal Oak

Nestling at the foot of the South Downs, close to the famous Devil's Dyke, this white-painted pub is popular in summer for its excellent barbecues. So, if walking this way on a fine summer Sunday, time your walk to coincide with the sizzling barbecue and relax with the family in the large garden, which has a huge marquee for a play area. The Royal Oak is a great community pub and you might happen upon their jazz lunches, charity bungee jumps and dancing Morris Men in the garden – it's that sort of place. The unpretentious and comfortably furnished bars are equally welcoming on less clement days, and you'll find Sussex-brewed Harveys Bitter on tap.

about the pub

Royal Oak
The Street, Poynings
Brighton, East Sussex BN45 7AQ
Tel: 01273 857389
www.royaloakpoynings.biz

DIRECTIONS:	west of the village centre
PARKING:	50
OPEN:	daily, all day
FOOD:	daily, all day Saturday and Sunday
BREWERY/COMPANY:	free house
REAL ALE:	Harveys Best, Greene King Abbot Ale and Old Speckled Hen
DOGS:	very welcome inside (biscuits offered)

19

WALK

Devil's Dyke EAST SUSSEX

Food

Expect a varied menu that includes some good, hearty lunchtime snacks – thick-cut sandwiches, excellent cheese ploughman's (see the blackboard for the day's cheese selection), filled 'jackets', and 'best of British' meals – perhaps steak and kidney pie, beer-battered cod and local sausages and mash. Fresh dressed Selsey crab with crusty bread is a popular daily special.

Family facilities

Children are very welcome and the youngsters' menu is better than most, offering a child's portion of a roast on Sunday. There's a safe, large garden for summer days.

Alternative refreshment stops

The Devil's Dyke pub, three quarters of the way round the walk, has a family dining area and garden patio. Fish and chips, mixed grills and salads feature on the menu.

☛ Where to go from here

Explore the pair of windmills known as Jack and Jill at nearby Clayton. Jill Windmill is a restored post mill, originally constructed in Brighton in 1821 and moved to this location in 1852. She is still open for corn grinding demonstrations on summer Sundays, while her more solid, black-painted companion remains silent.

From Winchelsea to Rye and beyond

Two historic gems, and a castle in between, plus the biggest and best sandy beach in the south east.

Winchelsea and Rye

Today Winchelsea seems an idyllic sleepy village, yet in medieval times it was one of the prosperous 'Cinque Ports' – Channel port towns that supplied ships and men to the navy. It was built in the 13th century in a grid plan after the old town at the foot of the hill was washed away in a storm. Black Death and attacks from the French led to lean times over the next two centuries, and much of it was rebuilt later on; many houses still have vaulted cellars (some visible from the street) for storing wine, and there are three town gateways. The church stands partly incomplete, partly ruined, but inside it is grandly proportioned, with fine canopied tombs. Visit the Court Hall Museum for the full story.

Similarly lost in time, Rye was another Cinque Port, stranded inland as the sea has receded. Its knot of hilly streets, including cobbled Mermaid Street with its ancient Mermaid Inn, has a delightful array of tile-hung, timber-framed and brick buildings. The Landgate and Ypres Tower are medieval fortifications, and don't miss the glorious view from the top of the church tower. The Rye Castle Museum looks at the town's past.

The cobbled road and plant-festooned buildings in Rye's Mermaid Street

the ride

1 With the New Inn on your left and the churchyard behind you, take the road ahead to the **A259 sign**, turn right towards Rye and soon descend steeply. Take the first left, signposted **Winchelsea Station**, as the road hairpins sharp right. After the level crossing (stop and wait if the light is red), turn right at the T-junction on **Dumb Woman's Lane**. As the road starts to bend left uphill take the bridleway through the gate ahead (signposted **National Cycle Route 2**). This goes along the foot of what used to be sea cliffs in Roman times.

2 Turn right by a **pumping station** (with green turrets), avoiding the road ahead near houses, on a permissive cycle path to reach **Gibbet Marsh car park**. Keep right to skirt the car park (if you are starting from here, take the path at the back of the car park, near the **picnic benches**, and turn left). The path bends right, opposite a **windmill**, and crosses the railway line. You will later return to Winchelsea by following the road to the right, but first go left and round to the right into **Rye town centre**, wheeling your bike through town. Visit the tourist information centre/Rye Heritage Centre/Town Model, then turn left and go up cobbled **Mermaid Street**. Turn right at the top along West Street, then right and left to skirt the right side of the churchyard. In front of Ypres Tower, turn left, then right, soon passing **Rye Castle Museum**. Turn right at the next junction, and just before the **town gate** (Landgate), turn right at the end of the

3h30 | **9** MILES | **14.5** KM | LEVEL 1 **2** 3

SHORTER ALTERNATIVE ROUTE

2h30 | **5** MILES | **8** KM | LEVEL 1 **2** 3

MAP: OS Explorer 125 Romney Marsh

START/FINISH: New Inn, Winchelsea (free roadside parking near the pub and church); grid ref TQ 904174. Alternative start: Gibbet Marsh car park, Rye; grid ref: TQ 915203

TRAILS/TRACKS: roads, surfaced cycle paths, stony in places, grass track: mountain bikes recommended

LANDSCAPE: farmland, coast

PUBLIC TOILETS: Winchelsea, Rye, Camber Sands

TOURIST INFORMATION: Rye, tel: 01797 226696

CYCLE HIRE: Rye Hire, Rye, tel: 01797 223033; Sundays and bank holidays tel: 01797 227826

THE PUB: The New Inn, Winchelsea

🛈 Short sections on main road. Take care with road crossings in Winchelsea and Rye. Cross the railway with care at Winchelsea Station and at Rye. Wheel your bike through Rye when going in the Camber direction. One steep hill up into Winchelsea

Getting to the start

Winchelsea is signposted off the A259 between Rye and Hastings. You can also start at Rye: use Gibbet Marsh car park signposted from the B2089.

Why do this cycle ride?

Apart from the little hills on which the Rye and Winchelsea stand, this is a level route from Winchelsea to Camber Sands, and a more demanding close to Camber Castle.

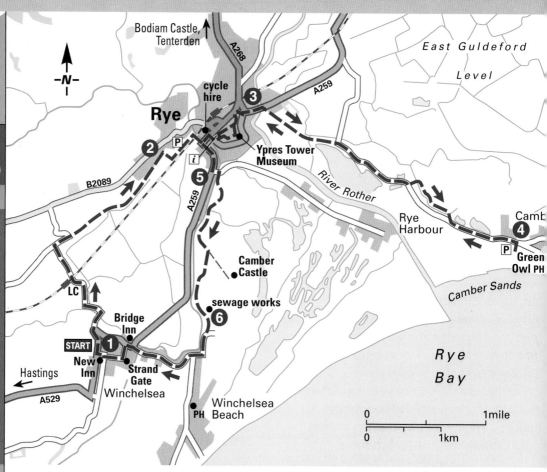

railings, go down a path and over a zebra crossing, then left through the car park and right through the park to join the pavement by the **A259**.

3 At a **bike symbol** you can now ride your bike again, along the pavement and over the A259 river bridge. Turn right on the other side on the **bike path**, signposted to Camber. This later crosses the road by a traffic island. After 2 miles (3.2km) the bike path ends by **houses**.

4 Cross the road, enter the car park and take the path over the dunes and on to **Camber Sands**. Return the same way to Rye: wheel your bike over the zebra crossing and up the path to the Landgate. Cycle left along Rye's main street, ignoring side turns, and drop downhill to reach a junction of roads. Take the road ahead (the continuation of Mermaid Street) to reach the **tourist**

information centre. Wheel over the zebra crossing away to your right and follow the A259 towards **Hastings** (cycling along the road or wheeling along the pavement).

5 Turn left, signposted **Rye Harbour**, over the canal, then turn right on a bridleway. At the next house, fork left through a gate. The route follows a raised **grassy dyke**. At a junction near **concrete sheds,** with Camber Castle ahead, keep right in the direction of the blue arrow (or leave your bike here and walk along the path to see the castle). The track is fainter and bumpier, following a slight ridge.

6 By a **sewage works** join a concrete road, then keep forward along a tarmacked road. Turn right on a larger road, left on the A259, and left up a steep road into **Winchelsea**. Go under Strand Gate and keep forward to reach **The New Inn**.

The New Inn

The comfortably old-fashioned, 18th-century New Inn is opposite the church in the centre of this ancient town. The cosy, rambling interior has three bustling beamed rooms, all sporting nice old furnishings and good warming winter log fires. There's a separate locals' bar, well-kept Greene King ales and simply furnished bedrooms with delightful views. An inviting walled garden to the rear of the pub is perfect for alfresco meals or simply to relax in following an energetic walk or cycle ride.

about the pub
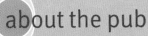

The New Inn

German Street, Winchelsea
East Sussex TN36 4EN
Tel: 01335 370396

DIRECTIONS: The New Inn is opposite the church in the middle of Winchelsea	
PARKING: 20	
OPEN: daily; all day	
FOOD: daily; all day Sunday	
BREWERY/COMPANY: Greene King	
REAL ALE: Greene King IPA and Old Speckled Hen, Morland Original	
ROOMS: 6 en suite	

Food

You can order home-made pies, roast chicken, a range of steaks with sauces, and hearty snacks such as sandwiches and ploughman's lunches from the printed menu. The special board includes local fish such as whole Dover sole and red mullet alongside lamb shank in red wine, and minced beef and onion pie.

Family facilities

Well-behaved children are allowed in the bar area and restaurant, where young children can choose from a standard kid's menu.

Alternative refreshment stops

There's the Tea Tree (tea room) and the Bridge Inn at Winchelsea, plus a full range of cafés, restaurants, pubs and shops in Rye, and cafés and the Green Owl pub in Camber.

☛ Where to go from here

Fifteen miles (24.1km) north west of Rye is Bodiam Castle (www.nationaltrust.org.uk), a fairytale, 14th-century ruin surrounded by a moat. The walls stand to their original height, and there are staircases and turrets to climb. You can reach it by riding a steam or diesel train on the Kent and East Sussex Railway (www.kesr.org.uk) from just outside Tenterden, a rewarding little Wealden town with many weatherboarded houses.

Around Hampton Court

Discover more about the game of kings on a walk through the regal landscape of Hampton Court.

Courting a historic ball game

The majority of visitors to Hampton Court come to see the State Apartments of William III and Henry VIII, the Tudor kitchens, the maze and the 60 acres (24ha) of riverside gardens. Most miss the subtle doorway in the wall that looks like the opening to a secret garden. In fact it is the entrance to one of the more unusual parts of the palace, and the most historic court in the world – the real tennis court.

The Royal Tennis Court at Hampton Court has serious royal connections. Henry VIII played real tennis here, as did Charles I. Cardinal Wolsey built the original real tennis court in the 1520s on the site of the present Stuart court, but it remained roofless until 1636. During World War Two it was once again roofless, when a bomb hit the adjacent apartments and completely shattered the court's windows. Apart from 'real tennis', any of the terms 'royal tennis', 'court tennis' and 'close tennis' may be used to distinguish this ancient game from the more familiar 'lawn tennis' (although that is rarely played on a lawn nowadays). The game, from which many other ball games – such as table tennis and squash – are derived, was probably being played as early as the 6th century BC. The word 'tennis' stems from the French *tenez* or the Anglo-French *tenetz* which translates as 'take it', referring to what the server might call to his or her opponent. The game was very popular in France with the aristocracy, but suffered considerably for this association during the Revolution. After World War One it declined in popularity in England, but it has seen a revival lately.

If you're a real tennis novice then the court will probably look like a cross between a badminton court and a medieval street roof. Yet it's a quirky game to watch, for the serve can be over or underarm as long as the ball bounces at least once on the roof (known as a penthouse) and then on the floor within the service court. The rackets are shaped more like a buckled bicycle tyre than a conventional tennis racket, but the game is fast, energetic and skilful. The world champion, Rob Fahey, admits to having been initially attracted more by the glitzy parties than the game itself, but the sport has grown in stature over the past few years and seems now to have the ball firmly back in its own court.

the walk

1 Cross **Hampton Court Bridge**, turn right through the main gates to **Hampton Court Palace** and walk along a wide drive. Just before the palace turn left through the gatehouse and then under an **arch**.

2 Turn right just before the tea room ahead of you, then immediately left through a gate and gardens. Take the next diagonal path on the right to **Lion Gate** (signposted Formal Gardens and East Front), passing the **Maze**.

3 Go through Lion Gate and turn right to walk along the main road. Follow the wall of the estate passing **Flowerpot Gate**. Re-enter the parkland at **Paddock Gate**. Go

Top: Hampton Court Palace façade
Left: Landscaped gardens at Hampton Court

Hampton Court

MIDDLESEX

1h45 **4.75 MILES** **7.7 KM** **LEVEL 1 2 3**

MAP: OS Explorer 161 London South

START/FINISH: Hampton Court Railway Station. Car park in Hampton Court Road; grid ref: TQ 174697

PATHS: gravel, tarmac and riverside tracks

LANDSCAPE: landscaped grounds of historic palace

PUBLIC TOILETS: Hampton Court Park

TOURIST INFORMATION: Kingston-upon-Thames, tel 020 8547 5592

THE PUB: The King's Arms, Hampton Court

❶ Take care near the water

Getting to the start

Hampton Court railway station is on the A309 between Esher and Sunbury, at the junction with the A3050 for Walton-on-Thames. It's easily accessed from Waterloo and Clapham Junction stations. The car park is on Hampton Court Road.

Hampton Court

MIDDLESEX

what to look for

The handsome façade of Hampton Court Palace is the nearest thing England has to Versailles, but it wasn't until Queen Victoria's reign that the gardens and maze were opened to the public. If you decide to explore the palace, allow yourself a few extra hours. Notice, too, the topiary on the gigantic yew trees leading down towards the river.

through a wooden gate and follow the path between the wall and fencing. At the end of the path go through another wooden gate and turn left through a door in the wall.

4 Turn right and bear left to walk along the railings at the bottom of the palace's **formal gardens** (by the horse carriage rides). At the **Long Wate**r, turn left and walk the length of it to the **fountains**. Turn right at the

end, then first left on to a tarmac track past a pond. Bear off to the right on a grass track to skirt the edge of **Rick Pond**. Go left through a metal gate, along an enclosed footpath and through a gate to reach the **River Thames**.

5 Turn left along this riverside path and follow it for 0.75 mile (1.2km) to **Kingston Bridge**. Here join the road leading to the roundabout.

6 Turn left along the main road past the roundabout. Bear left past a row of houses to enter a gate before the **Old King's Head** pub. Immediately after the cattle grid bear right along a grassy path running along the left side of the boomerang-shaped **Hampton Wick Pond**. Follow the straight path for about 0.75 mile (1.2 km) back to Hampton Court Palace and back through the door in the wall by the sign '**Hampton Court Palace and gardens**'.

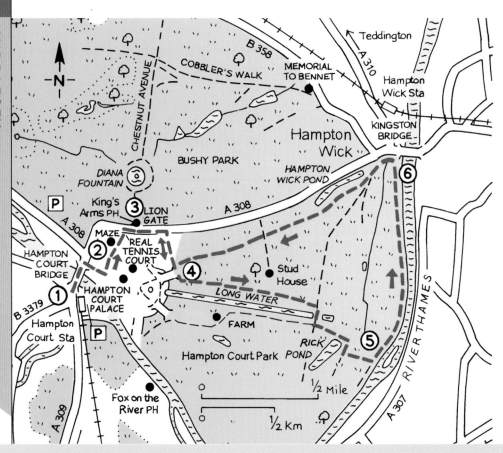

The King's Arms

Right on the edge of Hampton Court grounds, this character Georgian pub makes the ideal refreshment stop after the walk, or following a stroll around the Hampton Court Gardens. It's cosy and comfortable inside, with plenty of oak panelling, bare brick walls, heavy beams and wooden floors topped with deep sofas, large wooden tables and an eclectic mix of furnishings. Bric-a-brac, old pictures of Hampton Court and portraits of Henry VIII's wives decorate the bars, and there's a big open fireplace with a blazing log fire in winter and a super front terrace for summer drinking. Expect a relaxed, laid-back atmosphere, excellent Badger beers and a genuine love of dogs (biscuits on the bar).

Food
The blackboard lists a wide-ranging choice of pub food. For a snack tuck into thick-cut ham sandwiches, tomato and red onion bruschetta, or filled ciabatta rolls. For something more substantial try the steak and ale pie or lamb shank with mash, followed by strawberries and cream. There are also summer weekend barbecues and traditional Sunday roast lunches.

Family facilities
Children are very welcome in the pub.

about the pub

The King's Arms
Lion Gate, Hampton Court
Road, East Molesey, London KT8 9DD
Tel: 020 8977 1729

DIRECTIONS: on the A308 between Kingston Bridge and Hampton Court Bridge, next to Lion Gate
PARKING: 7
OPEN: daily; all day
FOOD: daily; all day Saturday and Sunday
BREWERY/COMPANY: free house
REAL ALE: Badger Best, Tanglefoot & Fursty Ferret, guest beer
DOGS: welcome in the pub

Alternative refreshment stops
There is a licensed café/restaurant at the Palace. South of Hampton Court Station (0.75 mile/1.2km) in Queens Road is the Fox on the River pub, which enjoys a prime spot overlooking the River Thames.

☞ Where to go from here
Visit the famous Hampton Court Maze, which was laid out in 1714. It's quite possible to wander round this for ages, but if you want to play safe, keep to the right-hand edge going in and the left-hand one coming out. The Privy Garden has been restored with plant species from William III's day. The Great Vine, planted by 'Capability' Brown, is thought to be the oldest in the world, and is still producing grapes. Allow time to visit Henry VIII's magnificent Tudor palace. Costumed guides and audio tours bring the palace to life and provide an insight into how living conditions in the palace would have been in the time of Henry VIII and William III (www.hrp.org.uk).

Around Richmond Park

Discover the capital's largest open space and enjoy amazing views of the city.

Richmond Park

At 2,500 acres (1,012ha) Richmond Park is Europe's largest urban walled park, which has an abundance of wildlife in its varied landscape of hills, woodland gardens and grasslands. Charles I brought his court to Richmond Palace in 1625 to escape the plague in London and turned it into a park for red and fallow deer. There are more than 750 deer in the park today. Pembroke Lodge was the home of Lord Russell, prime minister in the mid-1800s. His grandson Bertrand Russell grew up here. The restaurant that now occupies the building enjoys spectacular views of the Thames Valley. The Isabella Plantation is a stunning woodland garden that was created in the early 1950s from an existing woodland and is organically run, resulting in a rich flora and fauna. Over 1,000 species of beetle have been recorded in the park. The ancient oaks provide a rich habitat for many types of insect. The park enjoys the status of a Site of Special Scientific Interest and a National Nature Reserve.

the ride

1 On entering the park at Richmond Gate look for the path on the left-hand side. (From Pembroke Lodge car park return to Richmond gate and turn right.) The path skirts **Bishops Pond**. Keep straight on past Cambrian Gate. Adam's Pond is to your right just beyond **East Sheen Gate**. The bridge over Beverley Brook means you are nearly at **Roehampton Gate**.

2 At Roehampton Gate cross the road. The path continues past the café and car park, where cycle hire is available. The **golf course** is to your left. Soon the path crosses Beverley Brook once again, then it remains between the brook and the park road as far as **Robin Hood Gate**.

3 At **Broomfield Hill** the steepest ascent of the ride awaits; signs advise cyclists to dismount. There is a bench at the top where you can recover, and a r**efreshment kiosk** is just beyond. The Isabella Plantation is to your right. At **Kingston Gate** the route starts heading north.

4 At **Ham Gate** the path crosses the road and turns right, ascending

A busy stretch of the Tamsin Trail at Roehampton

1h30 · 7 MILES · 11.3 KM · LEVEL 123

MAP: OS Explorer 161 London South

START/FINISH: Richmond Gate at Richmond Park; grid ref: TQ 184737

TRAILS/TRACKS: largely compacted gravel

LANDSCAPE: parkland and woodland

PUBLIC TOILETS: around the park

TOURIST INFORMATION: Richmond, tel 020 8940 9125

CYCLE HIRE: Roehampton Gate, tel 07050 209249

THE PUB: Lass O'Richmond Hill, Richmond

🛈 Some short, steep climbs and a couple of longer ascents through woodland

Getting to the start

Richmond Gate is at the top of Richmond Hill (B321). You can approach from Richmond town centre or if you are coming from the south leave the A307 at Star and Garter Hill. There's parking at Pembroke Lodge in the park.

Why do this cycle ride?

This is an enjoyable circuit on an easy traffic-free trail shared with pedestrians. The stunning views of St Paul's Cathedral and other London landmarks are the only reminders that you are just 10 miles (16.1km) from the centre of the capital.

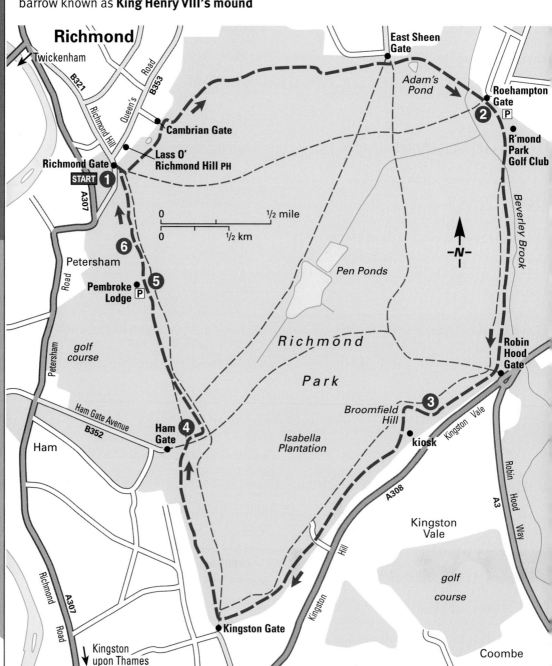

parallel to the road. At the T-junction turn left, remaining parallel to the road. Soon the path leaves the road and opens on to a wide tree-lined avenue. As you approach **Pembroke Lodge**, glorious views of the Thames Valley unfold to the left.

5 At Pembroke Lodge the path is sometimes congested with pedestrians. Just beyond Pembroke Lodge, with the barrow known as **King Henry VIII's mound**

on your left, the cycle path unexpectedly moves to the right. At this point a marker beside the path draws attention to the incredible view of **St Paul's Cathedral**, 10 miles (16.1km) away.

6 As you ride on, a panoramic view of other London landmarks opens out. Before long you will be back at **Richmond Gate**.

Lass O'Richmond Hill

Perched high on the steep Richmond Hill this pub is ideally placed for a cycle ride around the park. The sign outside promises 'home cooked food all day, every day, 8 days a week'. The fully air-conditioned interior means that this is a pleasant place to spend time in all weathers, and the main bar is spacious and airy. Abundant window boxes and hanging baskets add a colourful touch to the exterior. There are a few tables on the pavement, but the small garden terrace to the rear is a quieter and more pleasant place to eat and drink on sunny days.

Food

The printed menu has starters such as Wexford-style Stilton and pepper mushrooms and a duo of chicken satay and tiger prawn skewers. Main courses include roast duck with a ginger and scallion sauce and asparagus, pea and mint risotto. Banana toffee crumble and strawberry shortcake are among the puddings. There are also daily chalkboard specials.

about the pub

Lass O'Richmond Hill
8 Queens Road, Richmond
Surrey TW10 6JJ
Tel: 020 8940 1306

DIRECTIONS: on Queen's Road (B353), just to the northeast of Richmond Gate

PARKING: 25 spaces

OPEN: daily; all day

FOOD: daily; all day

BREWERY/COMPANY: Chef & Brewer

REAL ALE: Courage Best, Fuller's London Pride

Family facilities

Children are made welcome and there's a children's menu for younger family members.

Alternative refreshment stops

There are various cafés in the park and at Pembroke Lodge.

☛ Where to go from here

You're spoilt for choice for places to visit after your ride. Head off to Kew Gardens and explore some of the 3,000 acres (1,215ha) and the magnificent conservatories filled with exotic plants (www.kew.org). Take the children to Twickenham Stadium for a behind-the-scenes look at the home of England rugby and Britain's top sporting museum, the Museum of Rugby (www.rfu.com).

Around Hyde Park

Discover a green oasis in the heart of the capital.

Hyde Park

Henry VIII and his court once hunted deer in Hyde Park; the Tudor monarch acquired the land from the monks of Westminster Abbey in 1536. Public access was first permitted under James I, but it was Charles I who opened the park fully to the general public in 1637. During the Great Plague in 1665 many Londoners set up camp in the park, hoping to escape the disease. The Serpentine – the vast ornamental lake dominating the park – was created in the 1730s by Queen Caroline, wife of George II.

The latest in Hyde Park's long line of royal connections is the controversial £3.6 million Diana, Princess of Wales Memorial Fountain, unveiled by the Queen in 2004.

The fountain was designed by US architect Kathryn Gustafson, and is based on an oval stone ring. Water enters the fountain at its highest point, then bounces down steps. It picks up momentum and is invigorated by jets. As it flows westwards it resembles a babbling brook. Air bubbles are added as it approaches a waterfall before entering a water feature. Water from east and west meets at the reflecting pool, before being pumped out to restart the cycle.

the ride

1 From the West Carriage Drive car park, opposite the **Serpentine Gallery,** cross the road and join the cycle track on the pavement on the west side of West Carriage Drive. The Diana, Princess of Wales **Memorial Fountain** is on your right.

Safe, traffic-free cycling in Hyde Park in the heart of London

1h00 — **2.5 MILES** — **4 KM** — **LEVEL 123**

CYCLE

Hyde Park LONDON

MAP: OS Explorer 173 London North

START/FINISH: West Carriage Drive car park; grid ref: TQ 269800

TRAILS/TRACKS: well-surfaced paths

LANDSCAPE: urban parkland

PUBLIC TOILETS: in the park

TOURIST INFORMATION: London Line, tel 09068 663344

CYCLE HIRE: London Bicycle Tour Company, 1a Gabriels Wharf, 56 Upper Ground, SE1, tel 020 7928 6838

THE PUB: The Wilton Arms, Kinnerton Street

❶ Be sure to give priority to pedestrians on shared-use paths. Beware of unpredictable rollerbladers!

Getting to the start

The West Carriage Drive car park is south of the bridge over the Serpentine. It can be approached from the A402 Bayswater Road to the north or the A315 Kensington Gore/ Kensington Road to the south. The pay-and-display car park is open 8.30am-6.30pm.

Why do this cycle ride?

An ideal ride for families with very young children, this is a chance to make the most of a huge expanse of green space that Londoners often forget they have on their doorstep. Glance to your left as you cross the Serpentine Bridge and you'd never guess that you were in the heart of the capital. Yet elsewhere there are surprising views of familiar London landmarks.

2 The track drops down on to the road to cross the **Serpentine bridge**. Once across be sure to look out for the point where the path resumes on the pavement, as the cycle lane on the road surface stops abruptly.

3 At Victoria Gate cross the road and follow the cycle path along **The Ring**. The path here is on the road, but it is often traffic-free.

4 As you approach Cumberland Gate and Marble Arch, look for the **cycle route sign** for Chelsea Bridge and cross the road to pick up the cycle path on **Broad Walk**. You may need to reduce speed here as the cycle lane can be obstructed by crowds milling around at **Speakers' Corner**. It then heads south on Broad Walk, a pleasant, wide, tree-lined boulevard.

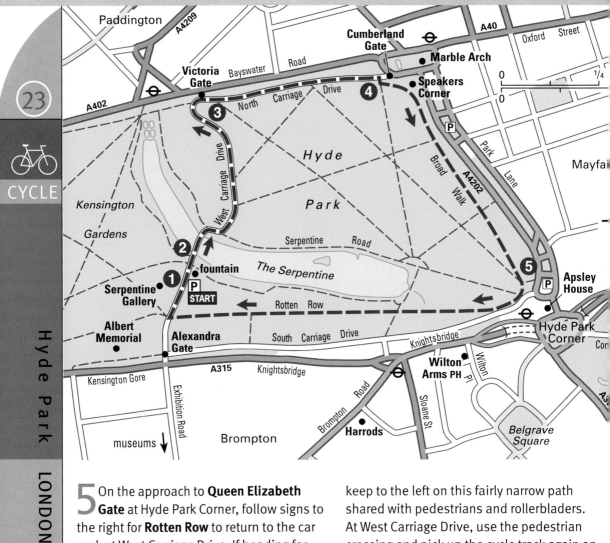

Paddington

A4209

Cumberland
Gate

Marble Arch

A40   Oxford   Street

Victoria
Gate   Bayswater   Road

Speakers
Corner

A402

North   Carriage   Drive   4

P

0   1/4
0

Hyde

West Carriage Drive

3

Park

Broad

Walk

A4202

Park   Lane

Mayfair

Kensington

Gardens

Serpentine   Road

2

The Serpentine

5

Apsley
House

Serpentine
Gallery   1   fountain

P
START   Rotten   Row

P

Hyde Park
Corner   Cor

Albert
Memorial   Alexandra
Gate   South   Carriage   Drive   Knightsbridge

A315   Knightsbridge

Wilton
Arms PH

Wilton
Pl

Kensington Gore

Exhibition Road

Brompton Road

Sloane St

A3

museums ↓   Brompton   Harrods

Belgrave
Square

5 On the approach to **Queen Elizabeth Gate** at Hyde Park Corner, follow signs to the right for **Rotten Row** to return to the car park at West Carriage Drive. If heading for **The Wilton Arms** pub, you will need to leave the park through this gate. On Rotten Row, keep to the left on this fairly narrow path shared with pedestrians and rollerbladers. At West Carriage Drive, use the pedestrian crossing and pick up the cycle track again on the west side in front of the **Serpentine Gallery**. (This simple circular ride can be easily extended eastwards with a foray along **Constitution Hill**'s excellent parallel cycle track to see Buckingham Palace, or to the west to explore Kensington Gardens. Notices at the park entrances show where cycling is currently permitted.)

The Wilton Arms

Exuberant hanging baskets and window boxes decorate this early 19th-century pub, and a tasteful conservatory occupies the garden, so arrive early to ensure a seat in summer. Inside, high settles and bookcases create cosy individual seating areas, all fully air-conditioned. Owned by Shepherd Neame, Britain's oldest brewer, it was named after the 1st Earl Wilton and is known locally as the 'Village Pub'.

Food

The chalkboard menu lists the house speciality – a doorstep sandwich of salt roast beef with horseradish and mustard dressing. There's also beef and Guinness pie, fish and chips, lamb hotpot and a choice of curries, alongside staples such as burgers and ploughman's meals.

Family facilities

Children are welcome inside the bar if they are eating, and smaller portions of main menu dishes can be ordered.

Alternative refreshment stops

You will find various cafés and kiosks in Hyde Park.

☛ Where to go from here

Along the ride, stop at Apsley House, The Wellington Museum at Hyde Park Corner, the 19th-century home of the first Duke of Wellington. From West Carriage Drive you are within walking distance of the South Kensington museums. Spend some time at the Science Museum (www.sciencemuseum.org.uk), the Victoria and Albert Museum (www.vam.ac.uk), the Natural History Museum (www.nhm.ac.uk) or the (www.sciencemuseum.org.uk). Explore Kensington Gardens and visit the restored Kings Apartments in Kensington Palace (www.hrp.org.uk). The Serpentine Gallery has fascinating exhibitions of contemporary art (www.serpentinegallery.org).

about the pub

The Wilton Arms

71 Kinnerton Street
London SW1X 8ER
Tel: 020 7235 4854

DIRECTIONS: tucked away behind Knightsbridge and best accessed from Wilton Place. From the Queen Elizabeth Gate of Hyde Park, leave the park and cross to the other side of Knightsbridge. Turn right, and then continue until you reach Wilton Place, Turn left here, and take the next right. You will soon spot the pub.

PARKING: none

OPEN: daily; all day

FOOD: all day; no food Sunday

BREWERY/COMPANY: Shepherd Neame

REAL ALE: Shepherd Neame Goldings, Spitfire and Master Brew

From St James's Park to Kensington Gardens

A healthy, linear walk from St James's Park to Kensington Gardens.

Nash to the rescue

St James's Park, the oldest of the Royal Parks, started life as a swamp, but Henry VIII started the changes. Charles II made it look as much like Versailles as possible and around 150 years later the architect John Nash replaced the French layout with the English one that you see today. The contrast of Green Park may be what's needed if you prefer a less manicured environment.

In Hyde Park there are lime trees, rose gardens and the Serpentine, a lake on which you can usually take a boat. Kensington Gardens is on the other side of the Serpentine Bridge and here you'll pass the gates in front of Kensington Palace.

the walk

1 From Charing Cross Station turn left into the **Strand** and left again into Northumberland Street. Bear left along Northumberland Avenue and, after a few paces, cross over into **Great Scotland Yard**, with the Nigerian Embassy on the corner.

| 2h30 | 4.25 MILES | 6.8 KM | LEVEL 1 23 |

2 As the road bears right turn left into Whitehall, cross to the other side and head for the arch of **Horse Guards Parade**, where the guards are on duty for an hour at a time. Go through the arch leading to a gravel square used for the Trooping the Colour ceremony in June.

3 At the far side of Horse Guards enter **St James's Park** to the left of the Guards Monument. Turn left following the path along the end of the lake. At the junction of paths turn right and take the right fork. Continue along this path by the lakeside, past weeping willow trees, to a **blue bridge**.

4 Cross the bridge, stopping half-way across to enjoy the views: westwards is Buckingham Palace and eastwards is Horse Guards Parade, where the skyline looks almost fairytale-like. Turn left, past the **Nash Shrubberies**, and leave the park on the right. Cross The Mall, walk around the monument of Queen Victoria and enter **Green Park** through the impressive gates by Constitution Hill.

5 With your back to the gates take the straight walkway, with benches, slightly to the left. Continue up the long path, past a **water sculpture** to the left, to the end at Piccadilly. Still inside the park, turn left at the end and continue up the slight incline that leads to **Hyde Park Corner**.

6 Use the underpass ahead to first reach the central island and Wellington Arch, and then Hyde Park itself. (For **The Grenadier** pub, exit the underpass on the south side of Knightsbridge, then turn left along Wilton

MAP: OS Explorer 173 London North

START: Charing Cross tube; grid ref: TQ 303803

FINISH: High Street Kensington tube; grid ref: TQ 255794

PATHS: mainly tarmac paths through the parks

LANDSCAPE: parkland with occasional busy road and hum of traffic

PUBLIC TOILETS: in each park

TOURIST INFORMATION: London, tel 020 7971 0027

THE PUB: The Grenadier, Belgravia, SW1

Getting to the start

Charing Cross railway station and tube can be reached via the Northern and Bakerloo lines and from mainline stations in south east London and beyond. There's a car park in St Martin's Lane.

St James's Park   LONDON

Crescent which leads into Wilton Row.) Go over the crossing on **Rotten Row**, and follow the left-hand path, bearing right through a rose garden with a dolphin fountain. Continue straight on, walking slightly downhill through a small metal gate, bearing right to reach the Dell Restaurant beside the **Serpentine**.

what to look for

Just across the Blue Bridge in St James's Park is an area called the Nash Shrubberies. It has been restored to Nash's original, 'floriferous' specifications, with an emphasis on foliage.

7 Continue over a junction of paths bearing left, along the northern edge of the Serpentine, past the **boat houses**

to reach the Serpentine Bridge. Pass underneath it and up some steps on the right. Turn right, crossing over the bridge to enter Kensington Gardens. Take the middle path and continue ahead, ignoring other paths. When you join the **cycling pat**h turn right and head towards Kensington Palace, with a **bandstand** on the left and a pond on the right.

8 Carry on over a junction and bear left on the path that runs to the left of the gates to **Kensington Palace** state apartments. At the end turn left to reach Kensington High Street. Turn right to pass the Royal Garden Hotel, Kensington Church Street and cross **Kensington High Street** to the tube station on the left.

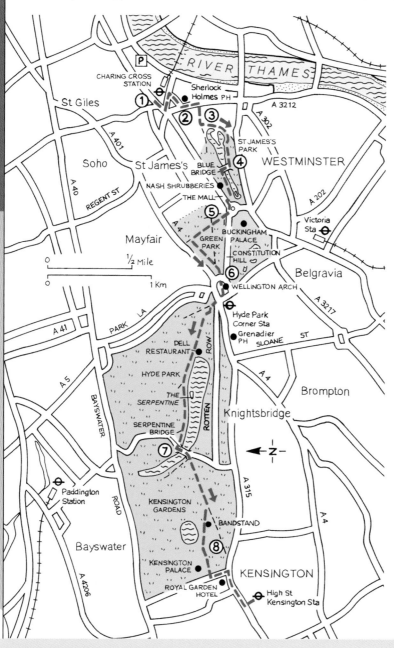

The Grenadier

The bright red, white and blue frontage of the patriotic Grenadier, regularly used for films and television series, can't be missed. Once the Duke of Wellington's officers' mess and much frequented by King George IV, it stands in a quiet cobbled mews behind Hyde Park Corner and remains largely undiscovered by tourists. The dark interior (candlelit even in summer) features dark wood panelling, wooden floors, heavy red curtains, cosy winter fires and the place is full of historical atmosphere with sabres, daggers, bugles and bearskins decorating the intimate bar. Outside is the remaining stone of the Duke's mounting block, and beside the little blue double doors there's even a sentry box.

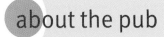

about the pub

The Grenadier

18 Wilton Row
Belgrave Square
London SW1 7NR
Tel: 020 7235 3074
www.thespiritgroup.com

DIRECTIONS: off Knightsbridge just west of Hyde Park Corner. Wilton Crescent leads to Wilton Row. Nearest tube: Hyde Park Corner	
PARKING: none	
OPEN: daily; all day	
FOOD: daily	
BREWERY/COMPANY: Spirit Group	
REAL ALE: Young's Bitter, Fuller's London Pride, Wells Bombardier, Courage Best	
DOGS: not allowed inside	

Food

Dishes range from black pudding stack, and spinach and Roquefort tart starters, to minted lamb shoulder, duck in red wine and chicken breast with thyme dumplings

Family facilities

Children are welcome in the restaurant area only, where smaller portions of adult dishes are available.

Alternative refreshment stops

The Sherlock Holmes in Northumberland Avenue serves its own label ale as well as Flowers and London Pride, and there are cafés in the parks.

☞ Where to go from here

The views from the fourth-floor balcony of Wellington Arch (www.english-heritage.org.uk) into the gardens of Buckingham Palace and along Constitution Hill are worth the small admission price alone. Arrive around 11.30am or 12.30pm and you'll see the Household Cavalry trotting past, on their way back to their barracks. Visit the State Apartments in Kensington Palace (www.hrp.org.uk), or spend some time at one or more of London's finest museums in South Kensington – the Victoria and Albert Museum (www.vam.ac.uk), the Natural History Museum (www.nhm.ac.uk) or the Science Museum (wwwsciencemuseum.org.uk).

St Non's Bay

Easy walking around the lovely coastline that gave birth to the patron saint.

St David's

This walk makes a great evening stroll. The paths from the city are pleasant and easy to follow but they're quickly forgotten as you step out into the glamorous surroundings of the coast. The all-too-short section of towering buttresses and jagged islets leads easily to the birthplace of St David.

Considering the immense influence he has had on Welsh culture, little is known about the patron saint. His mother is said to be St Non, who was married to a local chieftain. They settled near Trwyn Cynddeiriog, the rocky bluff that forms the western walls of the bay named after her.

Legend suggests that David was born in around AD 500, in the place where the ruined chapel stands today. Although a fierce storm raged throughout his birth, a calm light was said to have lit the scene. By the morning, a fresh spring had erupted near by, becoming the Holy Well of St Non.

Judging from his parentage, David would have been well educated and it is believed that he undertook a number of religious odysseys, including one to Jerusalem, before he finally returned around AD 550. He founded a church and monastery at Glyn Rhosyn, on the banks of the River Alun, on the site of the present cathedral, where he set about trying to spread the Christian word before his death in 589. St David's Day is celebrated on 1 March every year and St Non, who saw out her life in Brittany, is remembered on the following day.

St David's is little more than a pretty village, though it is a city due to its magnificent cathedral. It's a wonderful place and very popular. Known as Tyddewi –

Right: St David's Cathedral

1h30	3.5 MILES	5.7 KM	LEVEL 123

David's House – in Welsh, the city grew as a result of its coastal position at the western extreme of the British mainland. It would have been linked easily by sea with Ireland and Cornwall. As well as the cathedral and the ruins of the Bishop's Palace, it houses a plethora of gift shops and the National Park information centre, close to the car park, is one of the finest in the country.

the walk

1 Turn left out of the car park in **St David's** and walk down the road, as if you were heading for **Caerfai Bay**. As the houses thin out, you'll see a turning on the right that leads to more dwellings. Take this and then turn left on to a waymarked bridleway. Follow this bridleway between hedges, past the end of a road and on to a junction with another road.

2 Walk straight across and take the waymarked path down a pleasant track and pass through three gates. Keep to the left of the field to another gate, where you keep straight ahead again. Go through a gate, bear left then right through the farmyard into the **campsite**.

3 Keep the hedge on your right, where the drive swings off to the left. Continue across two fields and at the end drop down between gorse bushes to the road at **Porth Clais**. Before crossing the bridge, turn left on to the coast path.

MAP: OS Explorer OL35 North Pembrokeshire

START/FINISH: pay-and-display car park in St David's; grid ref: SM 757252

PATHS: coast path and clear footpaths over farmland

LANDSCAPE: leafy countryside and dramatic cliffs

PUBLIC TOILETS: next to tourist information centre

TOURIST INFORMATION: St David's, tel 01437 720392

The pub: The Glan-Y-Mor Inn, St David's

❶ One short climb; care to be taken on the cliff path

Getting to the start

St David's is located at the western tip of Pembrokeshire, 16 miles (25.8km) west of Haverfordwest on the A487. As you enter the town, turn left for the signed car park along Caerfai Road.

Left: Walkers on Pembrokeshire Coastal Path
Right: Lifeboat station and departure point for Ramsey Island

4 Climb up steeply on to the cliff tops and bear around to the left to walk towards **Porth y Ffynnon**. The next small headland is **Trwyn Cynddeiriog**, where there's a lovely grassy platform above the cliffs if you fancy a rest. Continue walking into **St Non's Bay** and look for a footpath on the left that leads to the ruined chapel.

5 From the chapel, head up to a gate that leads to **St Non's Well** and then follow the path beneath the new chapel and back out on to the coast path. Turn left to climb easily on to **Pen y Cyfrwy**, continue around this and drop down towards **Caerfai Bay**.

6 You'll eventually come to a gate beneath the Caerfai Bay car park. Go through the gate and climb the steps on the left into the car park. Join the access and follow this past **The Glan-Y-Mor Inn** to St David's and the start of the walk.

what to look for

Shortly after the stiff climb out of Porth Clais, you'll round Trwyn Cynddeiriog, the headland that divides Porth y Ffynnon from St Non's Bay. This is where St Non and Sant, St David's parents, were said to have lived. A short distance further along the coast path, at the head of the bay, you'll see a footpath on the left that leads to the ruined chapel. This is thought to have been built in the 13th century on the spot where St David was born. A path then leads to a gate, behind which you'll see St Non's Well and a grotto. Further up the hill is the newer chapel, dedicated to Our Lady and St Non. This was actually built in the 1930s using stone from other principal local evangelical sites, including the original chapel.

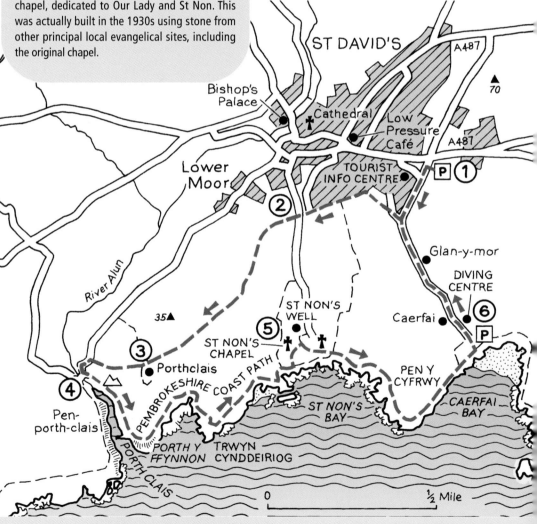

The Glan-Y-Mor Inn

Enjoying a rural setting close to town and just a short stroll from the Pembrokeshire Coast Path, the refurbished bar of this substantial old building looks out across St Bride's Bay towards the islands of Skomer and Skokholm. Modernised and open-plan, the bar is welcoming and informal, with leather settees, simple tables and chairs, and space for a pool table and television. There are separate raised dining areas and an adjoining restaurant with plants and access to a wooden platform for alfresco dining and savouring the sea views. There are also a campsite (tents only), rooms in the main building and a lodge in the garden.

Food

Menu choices range from sandwiches, paninis, lasagne, mixed bean chilli and steak, ale and mushroom pudding at lunchtime to Welsh leg of lamb with port, redcurrant and mint sauce, rump steak and fresh fish (sea bass, black bream) in the evenings. Puddings include sticky toffee pudding and apple and blackberry crumble. Curry menu on Sunday evening.

Family facilities

Children are welcome away from the bar until 9pm and kids' meals are available.

Alternative refreshment stops

Apart from the possibility of an ice cream van in the car park at Porth Clais, the best bet for refreshment is St David's where there's plenty of choice. A favourite pub is the Farmers Arms on Goat Street, which has a good garden and serves up all the usual pub fare. For non-alcoholic refreshment, try the excellent Low Pressure Café.

about the pub

The Glan-Y-Mor Inn
Caerfai Road, St David's
Pembrokeshire SA62 6QT
Tel: 01437 721788
www.glan-y-mor.co.uk

DIRECTIONS:	on entering St David's, turn left for Caerfai Bay, passing the main car park. Keep to the lane towards the sea; pub is on the left. At Point 6 of the walk
PARKING:	15
OPEN:	daily; all day
FOOD:	daily
BREWERY/COMPANY:	free house
REAL ALE:	Felinfoel Bitter
DOGS:	allowed in the bar area
ROOMS:	10 bedrooms; 5 en suite

☛ Where to go from here

St David's Cathedral is both architecturally stunning and spiritually moving. In 1120 Pope Calixtus II decreed that two pilgrimages to St David's were the equivalent of one to Rome – an honour indeed. The cathedral and the nearby Bishop's Palace play host to a series of classical concerts every summer (www.stdavidscathedral.org.uk).

St David's

PEMBROKESHIRE

Between the mountains and the Menai Straits

An old railway trail and country lanes lead you through gentle countryside south of Caernarfon.

Caernarfon and Dinas Dinlle

The centrepiece of this medieval walled town is the magnificent 13th-century castle built by King Edward I, splendidly sited by the lapping waters of the Menai Straits. The Slate Quay and Harbour Offices nearby are reminders of later centuries when the port bustled with commercial vessels loading Welsh slate for transportation to distant shores. There are several other attractions in the town, including the Seiont II Martime Museum at Victoria Dock, the Regimental Museum of the Royal Welsh Fusiliers, the Roman fort of Segontium and the Welsh Highland Railway, which runs parallel with Lon Eifion between Caernarfon and Dinas station.

Lon Eifion is a splendid cycle trail, forming part of the National Cycle Network and route number 8 that traverses Wales. It is a long stretch of dismantled railway, a green avenue of native trees and plants that stretches for 12 miles (18.2km) to Bryncir. This was the former Caernarfon to Afon Wen line, which was opened as standard gauge in 1867.

The large mound known as Dinas Dinlle is a natural deposit dating from the Ice Age, which has evidently been used several times as a fortification by different peoples. Roman coins, dating from the time of Emperor Alectus (AD293), have been found here. It is also a site rich in legend, a place woven into the tales of the Mabinogi.

Foryd Bay is a large shallow estuary rich in wildfowl which love the mud, reeds and saltmarsh. It is now a nature reserve where you can see shelduck, oystercatchers, dunlin and curlew with their distinctive beak and haunting call.

the ride

1 From Slate Quay car park, pass the Harbour Offices to join a road between the railway line and warehouses. In 300 yards (274m) join the old trackbed on the left and pass beneath the impressive Lon Eifion cycle route sign. With the Welsh Highland railway to your left, gradually climb above the harbour and leave the town. Cross a lane by a house, signposted 'Hendy', continue to cross another road and keep to the trail to reach Bontnewydd, where you cross the Afon Gwyrfai. Gently ascend through a cutting, pass Dinas station to reach a road at Llanwnda, with the village church to your left.

2 If you wish to continue south on the traffic-free trail (returning to Llanwnda), go round the gate opposite. Otherwise, go right along the narrow lane for two miles (3.2km), ignoring a turning on the right and soon drop down to the waters of the Afon Carrog. Climb to a junction, go right and then left at the next junction to reach Llandwrog. Turn right by the Harp Inn; the road descends to a junction in 0.5 mile (0.8km). Go right for Dinas Dinlle and soon reach the seafront.

CYCLE

2h30 · **14 MILES** · **22.8 KM** · **LEVEL 1 2 3**

MAP: OS Explorer 17 Snowdonia, Snowdon & Conwy Valley

START/FINISH: Slate Quay car park, Caernarfon; grid ref: SH 477627

TRAILS/TRACKS: gravel cycle trail, quiet country lanes

LANDSCAPE: gently undulating farmland, level coastline, views of mountains

PUBLIC TOILETS: Slate Quay, Dinas Dinlle

TOURIST INFORMATION: Caernarfon, tel 01286 672232

CYCLE HIRE: Beics Menai Cycles, Slate Quay, Caernarfon, tel: 01286 676804

THE PUB: The Harp Inn, Llandwrog

❗ Short stretch of busy road linking Slate Quay and the start of the cycle trail. A few short climbs and a couple of blind bends on the lanes. An easy ride for older children.

Getting to the start

Caernarfon lies southwest of Bangor on the A487. Follow signs to Caernarfon Castle and the car park beneath (pay on entry) on Slate Quay.

Why do this cycle ride?

For mountainous North Wales this ride is a delight for family cyclists looking for few hills and gentle pedalling. You can enjoy exceptional views across the mountain range of Snowdonia to the east and to the island of Anglesey in the west. You begin by riding the traffic-free Lon Eifion trail (former railway) out of Caernarfon, then follow narrow back lanes to Llandwrog and the Harp Inn, with an optional out-and-back ride to the nearby golden sands of Dinas Dinlle. The highlights are Foryd Bay and the lane that hugs the shores of the Menai Straits back to Caernarfon.

Caernarfon

GWYNEDD

3 Retrace your route to Llandwrog and turn left before the Harp Inn, still on your outward route. Keep to this lane for 0.75 mile (1.2km) to cross the Afon Carrog and pass a small cluster of buildings (telephone box). Continue to a sharp right bend and bear off left along a quiet narrow road leading to Foryd Bay. The lane bears right close to the water's edge, eventually reaching a crossroads. Go left here through the hamlet of Saron.

4 The road descends to a bridge at Pont Faen, crossing the Afon Gwyrfai, and rises to a junction, just before the Llanfaglan village sign. Turn left and continue for less than 0.5 mile (0.8km) to the water's edge at Foryd Bay, with excellent views across to the Isle of Anglesey. This delightful lane hugs the coast and passes the small windswept Llanfaglan church, isolated in a field to your right. The road bears right and runs along the front of the harbour at Caernarfon. Wheel your cycle across the Aber footbridge and return to the castle and the start point of the ride.

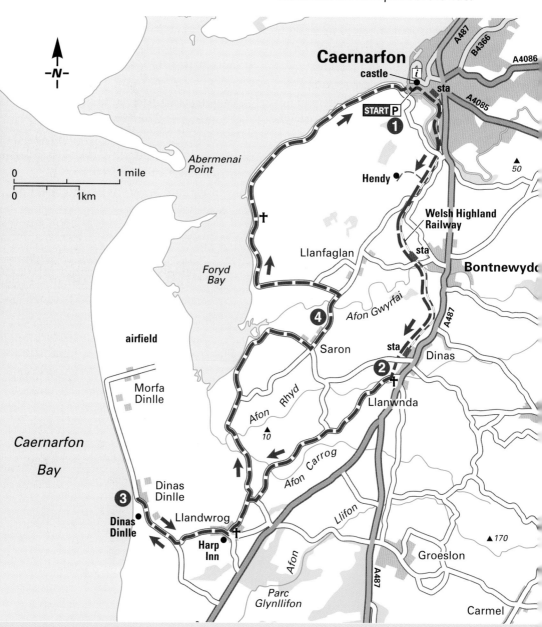

The Harp Inn

A long established haven for travellers, this stone Georgian building is located in the historic home village of the nearby Glynllifon Estate, close to the beautiful beaches of Dinas Dinlle. An inn has existed on the site since Roman times, as Llandwrog was on the pilgrim route from Holyhead to Bardsey Island. The traditional interior comprises a cheerful bar area, where you will find a good range of real ales and ciders, a comfortable restaurant and a popular games room. Note the tablet on the wall of the pub featuring a poem by the well-known Welsh poet Evan Fardd.

Food

A proudly Welsh menu offers lob scouse with roll and red cabbage, Welsh mackerel rarebit on toast, trio of local bangers and mash, Welsh lamb steaks with a laverbread and citrus sauce, and local sea bass with ginger and sesame seeds. There's also lasagne, cod and chips and filled baked potatoes and homemade hoggies filled with hot beef. Sunday roast lunches.

Family facilities

Children are welcome in the eating areas and the games room. There are healthy eating options for "little people" on the menu, a safe garden and overnight accommodation in one large family room.

Alternative refreshment stops

There are pubs and cafés in Caernarfon and at Dinas Dinlle, and a pleasant picnic site by Foryd Bay.

☞ Where to go from here

Just a short ride away from the Harp Inn is Parc Glynllifon, a 70-acre country park with exotic gardens, 18th-century follies, contemporary sculptures, a restored steam engine, a craft centre and signed walks. It is also home to a rich and diverse wildlife, including the largest roost in Europe for the Lesser Horse Shoe Bat.

about the pub

The Harp Inn
Tyn'llan, Llandwrog
Gwynedd LL54 5SY
Tel: 01286 831071

DIRECTIONS: village and pub signposted off the A499 south of Caernarfon

PARKING: 20

OPEN: all day in summer and Saturday in winter. Closed Monday except Bank Holidays

FOOD: daily; all day Sunday in summer

BREWERY/COMPANY: free house

REAL ALE: Bass, Black Sheep Best, Plassey Bitter, guest beers

ROOMS: 4 bedrooms (1 en suite)

The Mortimer Trail around Aymestrey

What have 'Capability' Brown, Richard Payne Knight and Hanson Aggregates got in common? Find out on this brief walk through time.

Natural and man-made landscapes

Shobdon Airfield was one of the many airfields built in 1940, as part of wartime preparations. The government compulsorily purchased the modest, privately owned quarry at Aymestrey, ensuring a local supply of stone for the airfield. In its latter years the quarry was run by Hanson Aggregates. The company may not expect to be remembered for its landscape architecture in the same way as Lancelot 'Capability' Brown, or Richard Payne Knight, but it should be commended for trying.

Towards the end of the walk, as you descend to the former quarry area, there is little to indicate that the landscape has been recently manufactured, although your curiosity may be alerted by the absence of any really substantial trees. Unlike many quarries, the plan here was to return the land to a mixture of agricultural use and woodland. People tend to dislike quarries in their backyards, so unsurprisingly they often get a bad press. The quarry companies will argue that 'restoration' and 'environmental sensitivity' were among their objectives a decade or two before their current fashionability.

West of Aymestrey the River Lugg runs in a small but spectacular gorge. This is a glacial overflow channel that exploited a fault in the rock, associated with the glacial Wigmore Lake. The paucity of contours on the map a few grid squares to the north shows the position of the former lake. At Mortimer's Cross, Richard of York's son, Edward, defeated the Lancastrian army in 1461 in one of the battles that changed the course of the Wars of the Roses (Edward was crowned king later that year). The battle site is 0.5 mile (800m) south of the road junction named Mortimer's Cross. The cross itself dates from 1799.

the walk

NOTE: You may experience some access problems with the path to the west of the A4110 (**Point 2**). A major overhaul will be carried out at some stage but in the meantime the landowner has given permission to use the 'unofficial' parallel path a short distance to the south of the described route.

1 Walk up the access road for almost 0.5 mile (800m), until beyond the garden of a newish house and just before a **junction of tracks**. Note a stile on the right – your route returns over this.

2 Go 30yds (27m) further and turn left. Go left at a fork and walk along to a **T- junction**. Turn left to the A4110. Cross directly to a stile, walking along the left-hand field edge. Through a gate go forward then skirt round the right edge of an oak and ash embankment, to find a corner stile. Walk up the left edge of this field but, at the brow, where it bends for some 70yds (64m) to a corner, slip left through a gap in the hedge to walk along its other side. Within 60yds (55m) you will be on a clear path, steeply down through woodland, a ravine on your left. Join the driveway of **River Bow,** to a minor road. (The glacial overflow channel is directly ahead.)

3 Turn left here, joining the **Mortimer Trail**. Enjoy this wooded, riverside lane for nearly 0.75 mile (1.2km), to reach the A4110 again. Cross, then walk for just 25yds (23m) to the right. (**The Riverside Inn** is about 175yds/160m further.) Take a **raised green track**, heading for the hills. Then go diagonally across two fields, to a stile and wooden steps.

4 Ascend steeply through the trees. Leave by a stile, to cross two meadows diagonally. Take the stile on the right to walk along the left-hand edge of a field, still heading downhill. At the trees turn left. Soon reach a tarmac road. Turn left along

Open farmland by the Mortimer Trail

MAP: OS Explorer 203 Ludlow

START/FINISH: at old quarry entrance, on east side of A4110, 0.25 mile (400m) north of Aymestrey Bridge; grid ref: SO 426658

PATHS: excellent tracks, field paths, minor roads, steep woodland sections, 11 stiles

LANDSCAPE: wooded hills and undulating pastures

PUBLIC TOILETS: none on route

TOURIST INFORMATION: Ludlow, tel 01584 875053

THE PUB: The Riverside Inn, Aymestrey

! Several steep climbs, busy road crossing, lengthy section of quiet country lane. Not suitable for young children.

Getting to the start

Aymestrey is on the A4110 road between Ludlow and Hereford. The layby/parking area where the walk starts is just to the north of the village, on the right coming from the south.

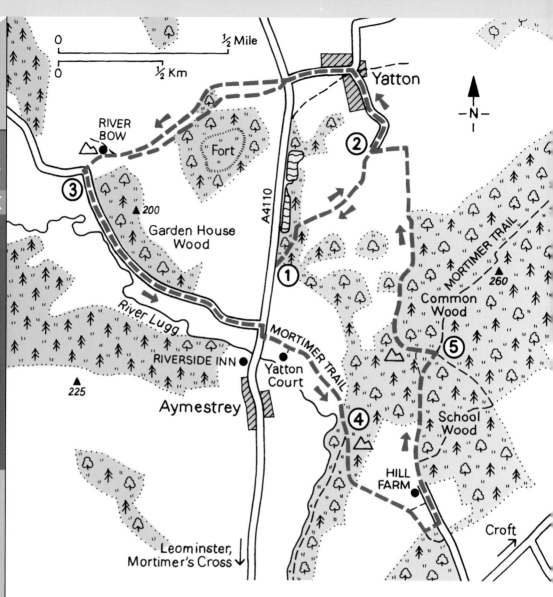

the road, now going back uphill. Beyond **Hill Farm**, enter the **Croft Estate**. Walk along this hard gravel track. After 110yds (100m) ignore a right fork but, 550yds (503m) further on, you must leave it. This spot is identified by an end to the deciduous trees on the left and a **Mortimer Trail marker post** on the wide ride between larches and evergreens on the right.

5 Turn left (there is no signpost). Within 110yds (100m) go half right and more steeply down. This aged access track gives expansive views over **felled forest**. Within 250yds (229m) look out for a **modern wooden gate**, waymarked, leading out of the

woods. Walk along its right-hand edge (and beside a recently appended small **plantation**). At the far corner, within the field, turn left to Point 2. Retrace your steps to the start of the walk.

what to look for

As you walk through Yatton there are stunning brick-arched barns on the right. These tall stone structures have brick apertures; one is filled in with attractive gridded brickwork. Later, look back from the other side of the A4110 to see more arches.

The Riverside Inn

An attractive half-timbered Welsh longhouse, dating from 1580, set on the banks of the River Lugg. An inn since 1700 it is perfectly placed midway along the Mortimer Trail and makes the ideal stop-off point for walkers. The interior, with its low beams and open fires, provides a relaxing atmosphere in which to sample local Wye Valley beers and some excellent food from an imaginative menu that utilises locally grown produce, notably fruit and vegetables from the pub garden. Lovely terraced and riverside gardens for summer sipping.

about the pub

The Riverside Inn
Aymestrey, Leominster
Herefordshire HR6 9ST
Tel: 01568 708440
www.theriversideinn.org

DIRECTIONS: see Getting to the start; pub just south of parking area by the River Lugg

PARKING: 40

OPEN: daily; closed Sunday & Monday evenings October to March

FOOD: daily

BREWERY/COMPANY: free house

REAL ALE: Woods & Wye Valley Brewery beers

DOGS: allowed inside

Food

Here you can eat anything from simple baguettes to proper country fare, including local black pudding and apple compôte, lamb's kidneys, saddle of rabbit with mustard and red wine jus, and roast venison on sweet and sour cabbage.

Family facilities

Children are welcome in the dining areas of the pub. There are high chairs and two family bedrooms, and smaller portions of adult dishes can be provided.

Alternative refreshment stops

The Mortimer's Cross Inn, at the junction of that name, has a beer garden and a children's play area.

☞ Where to go from here

You'll have to do this walk on a Thursday if you want to visit Lucton Mill (also called Mortimer's Cross Water Mill), managed by English Heritage. Remarkably, this 18th-century mill was still grinding corn commercially in the 1940s. The wheel still turns today from time to time. You could spend the best part of a day on the Croft Estate. As well as viewing the castle, there are waymarked walks (www.nationaltrust.org.uk).

A circuit taking in Great Witley

A mostly woodland walk up and down some of Worcestershire's hills.

Pollen research

What sort of walker are you – 'any weather' or 'fair weather'? Or are you a 'low pollen count walker', suffering from hay fever? Grasses are the most common cause, but allergy is by no means confined to these – just about any pollen can produce allergenic reactions. Between 10 per cent and 35 per cent of us suffer from 'pollinosis' (allergy to pollen), but these reactions may be species-specific. In addition, some species of tree seem to have more potent pollen, birch in particular.

Pollen is typically released from grasses from May to August, oilseed rape from April to June, and stinging nettles from May to mid-September. These are all good reasons for walking in the winter, but if you are afflicted in January it could be pollen from alder or hazel, and in March it could be birch. Studies show that the season for birch pollen has shifted to five days earlier every decade over the past 30 years, a clear indication of global warming.

The National Pollen Research Unit (NPRU), at University College, Worcester, is at the forefront of the science of 'aerobiology'. Supplying pollen forecasts is just one of the NPRU's activities; others include studying changes in pollen seasons in relation to climate change, and studying asthma in relation to fungi and house-dust mites. The unit is undertaking a local 3-year study (2003–6) into chronic bronchitis (chronic obstructive pulmonary disease – COPD). It is caused primarily by smoking, but there are other, secondary factors at work – this must be so, because in some southern European countries people smoke more but there is less COPD. Suspicion is aimed at Britain's higher humidity. The research is focused on whether this can increase the occurrence of this illness.

From early spring until mid-December the lane around Walsgrove Farm is awash with geese – about 3,500 of them. They are prepared for sale using an on-site 'low throughput processing unit'. Until then, these free-range birds wander very freely. Nearly all are destined for the Christmas table, mainly through retail outlets, but you can buy at the farm gate too.

the walk

1 From the pub cross the road and take the path waymarked **Wynniatts Way & Worcestershire Way**. Turn left at the entrance to a house, then swing right and climb steeply through fields, crossing four stiles. Go up through the woods to and up steps to the road. Turn right and then left to join the **Worcestershire Way North**.

2 In about 400yds (366m) reach a bright **trig point**. Walk along the ridge path a further 650yds (594m) to a Worcestershire Way sign at a path junction, just beyond which are four trees growing in a line across the path.

3 Take the path down to the right, initially quite steeply. Take a path on the left on a right-hand bend, emerge from the woods over a **stile** to walk down two large fields, meeting the road beside the **Hundred House Hotel**.

2h45 — **4.75 MILES** — **7.7 KM** — **LEVEL 2**

4 Cross the A451 with great care. Through an opening, strike half right, aiming for the **hedge end** beside the **last house**. Step over the fence then turn left on this lane. Walk for 0.5 mile (800m) along here, soon passing firstly **Walsgrove Farm** and secondly (most of the year) thousands of strutting, wailing geese. Do not turn right up a lane but go half right, taking the path that becomes a beautiful avenue of conifers, to the top of **Woodbury Hill**. At a **marker post** go straight over on a narrower track. In 130yds (119m) reach a farm track above **Lippetts Farm**. Shortly rejoin outward route, descending flight of steps on the left and return to Abberley.

5 Turn right, descending. At a hairpin bend, aim away from the farm to walk along the inside edge of a **wood**. Skirt to the left of the buildings at **Birch Berrow**, resuming on a service road. As this goes up,

The Perseus Fountain in front of the 17th-century Witley Court

MAP: OS Explorer 204 Worcester & Droitwich Spa

START/FINISH: Adequate roadside parking by the church in Abberley; grid ref: SO 754679

PATHS: woodland paths, field paths, tracks, 9 stiles

LANDSCAPE: wooded hills and farmed valleys

PUBLIC TOILETS: none on route

TOURIST INFORMATION: Worcester, tel 01905 762311

THE PUB: The Manor Arms at Abberley, Abberley

❶ The route crosses several busy roads and involves some steep walking in places

Getting to the start
Follow the A443 between Droitwich and Tenbury. Go through Great Witley heading west, then turn off to follow signs for the pub which is near the church in Abberley.

right, to an **exercise ring** for horses, take the right-hand of two gates ahead. Go steeply down, taking a stile into thick **pines**. Very soon, over another stile, turn right along the tarmac road for 100yds (91m), so that you are past **1 Hillside Cottages**, not before it.

6 Turn right again, back uphill. Continue north for nearly 1 mile (1.6km), over several **stiles**, walking mostly in trees but later enjoying fine views westwards. Then, on top of **Walsgrove Hill**, you'll see the elaborate

and magnificent **clock tower** (1883) of Abberley Hall. Now go steeply down this meadow, to take a stile into a lane. Turn right for 80yds (73m) to the **B4203**.

7 Cross carefully. Turn left, along the verge. Take the driveway to **Abberley Hall School**. Keep ahead to some signs with a tarmac drive on the right. Maintain the same direction as before, following the track beside the clock tower to reach the A443. Take the road opposite, **'Wynniatts Way'**, up to the brow of the hill.

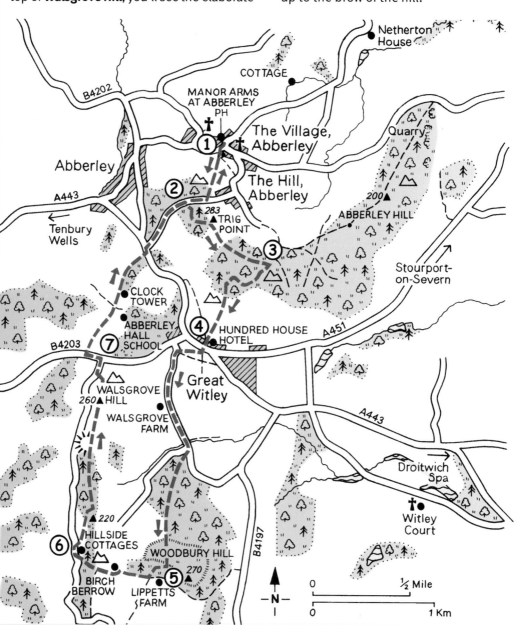

The Manor Arms at Abberley

Set just across the lane from the Norman church of St Michael in this delightful village high in the Abberley Hills, the exterior of this 300-year-old inn is emblazoned with fascinating coats of arms. Inside, original oak beams, log-burning fires and a fine collection of toby jugs in the two comfortable bars enhance the relaxing and welcoming atmosphere you can expect before or after your walk. There's a peaceful summer garden and a pretty patio for summer alfresco eating.

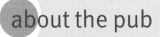

about the pub

The Manor Arms at Abberley
Abberley, Worcester
Worcestershire WR6 6BN
Tel: 01299 896507
www.themanorarms.co.uk

DIRECTIONS: see Getting to the start

PARKING: 25

OPEN: daily; all day Saturday & Sunday; closed Monday lunchtime October to April

FOOD: daily

BREWERY/COMPANY: Enterprise Inns

REAL ALE: Hook Norton Bitter, Flowers IPA, Timothy Taylor Landlord, guest beer

DOGS: allowed in the back bar

ROOMS: 12 en suite

Food

In addition to home-made soups, beef and ale pie, battered cod, fish pie and Cajun chicken, you can expect a choice of grills and roasts and a blackboard listing daily specials and fresh fish dishes, perhaps poached haddock with a simple chive and butter sauce.

Family facilities

Children under 5 are not allowed in the bars. There's a children's menu for younger appetites.

Alternative refreshment stops

The Hundred House Hotel in Great Witley has an enclosed beer garden to the side and an extensive menu.

☛ Where to go from here

Despite its size, Witley Court, 1.25 miles (2km) south east of Great Witley, is unseen on the walk itself. No public footpaths go near Witley Court, and the road that serves it (and the church) is unadopted. But do make an effort to visit this spectacular building. The Court's spectacular architecture, mostly Victorian, is just stunning. Only the skeleton remains, since its flesh was burned by a fire in 1937. English Heritage describe it as their number one ruin (www.english-heritage.org.uk). Adjacent to Witley Court, St Michael's Church is also worth a visit.

Revolution at Coalbrookdale

An absorbing walk in the wooded hills and valleys where the Industrial Revolution began.

Coalbrookdale

At Coalbrookdale in 1709 Abraham Darby perfected a method of smelting iron with coke instead of charcoal and sparked a revolution that changed the world. By 1785 the Coalbrookdale district had become the foremost industrial area in the world. It was particularly celebrated for its innovations: the first iron bridge, the first iron boat, the first iron rails and the first steam locomotive. Decline eventually set in due to competition from the Black Country and South Wales and the area fell into decay.

Since the 1960s, the surviving industrial relics have been transformed into museums and the gorge has been designated a UNESCO World Heritage Site. Perhaps even more remarkable than the industrial heritage is the way nature has reclaimed sites of industrial despoilation and made them beautiful again.

The ironmasters built decent houses for their workers and took an interest in their well-being. When you walk through Dale Coppice and Lincoln Hill Woods you will be using the Sabbath Walks, designed by Richard Reynolds to provide healthy Sunday recreation for his workers.

the walk

1 Follow the River Severn upstream, using the **Severn Way,** and pass under two bridges. After the second one, bear away from the river towards **Buildwas Road,** following a sometimes overgrown path. At the road, turn left for a few paces, then cross to a footpath that ascends through **woodland**. Keep close to the edge until a waymarker directs you obliquely right.

2 Cross a stile and continue in the same direction over pastureland. Pass under a **pylon,** then join a farm track and turn left through a gate. Follow the hawthorn hedge on your right to a junction, turn left on a **bridleway** and follow it along field edges, then across the middle of a meadow, avoiding a path on the right, to reach a lane at the top of the rise. Turn left.

3 Leave the lane when it bridges a road, turning right on a farm access track (**Shropshire Way**). Go through a white gate on the right, just before **Leasows Farm,** then downfield to enter **Lydebrook Dingle**. A path descends through the wood, beyond which you continue along a path called **Rope Walk**.

4 Descend some steps on the left into Loamhole Dingle. Cross **Loamhole Brook** at a footbridge and

2h00 — 5 MILES — 8 KM — LEVEL 1 2

MAP: OS Explorer 242 Telford, Ironbridge & The Wrekin

START/FINISH: Dale End Riverside Park, just west of Museum of the Gorge; grid ref: SJ 664037

PATHS: woodland paths, lots of steps (mostly descending), may be fallen trees at Strethill, 2 stiles

LANDSCAPE: wooded hills of Severn Gorge

PUBLIC TOILETS: in Museum of the Gorge car park

TOURIST INFORMATION: Ironbridge, tel 01952 884391

THE PUB: The Malthouse, Ironbridge
● Crosses a busy road, lots of up-and-down steps and several sections of boardwalk. Not suitable for very young children or inexperienced walkers

Getting to the start
Follow the A4169 south of Telford and then signs for Ironbridge and Coalbrookdale. The car park is signposted – by the river just west of the Museum of the Gorge.

climb steps on the other side to a T-junction. Turn right on what is mostly boardwalk and, when you reach **Upper Furnace Pool**, cross it on a footbridge to meet the road.

5 Your onward route is to the left, but a short detour right leads to the **Darby Houses**, Tea Kettle Row and the Quaker Burial Ground. Resuming the walk, go down to Darby Road and turn right beside the viaduct and the **Museum of Iron**. Turn left under the viaduct at a junction with Coach Road. Follow the road past the museum and **Coalbrookdale Works** to a junction.

6 Cross to Church Road, turn left after the Wesleyan chapel on the corner and take the stepped path (signposted **Woodside**) to enter **Dale Coppice**. Follow signs for **Church Road** at the first two junctions, but at the third ignore the Church Road sign and keep straight on. Leave the wood to enter grassland and go forward a few paces to meet a track. Turn left, then follow it as it bends right, passing a grassy path on the left. Keep left at the

The former warehouse building of 1843 in Coalbrookdale now houses the Museum of Iron

next junction and then fork right, staying on the track . **Dale Coppice** is on your right, a cemetery on your left.

what to look for

Upper Furnace Pool in Loamhole Dingle is the pool that powered the bellows that blew the furnace where Abraham Darby first smelted iron with coke. The area of open water has been reduced by a profuse growth of marsh horsetail. This primeval-looking species is the evolutionary successor to the giant tree-like horsetails that were a major element in the swamp vegetation that 300 million years ago formed the coal measures.

7 A gateway accesses Dale Coppice. Turn right, avoid a left path after a few paces, and then further on swing sharp left, going downhill to a junction marked by a bench. Turn right, then left when a sign indicates **Church Road**, and left again beside the road.

8 Turn right into **Lincoln Hill Wood** and follow signs for the **Rotunda**, soon arriving at a viewpoint where the Rotunda formerly stood. Descend a very steep flight of steps to a junction. Turn right, then left down more steps and left again, signposted to **Lincoln Hill Road**. Cross the road to a footpath opposite, which descends through rather overgrown ground to the **Wharfage**. Turn right past **Lincoln Hill lime kilns** and the Swan to **Dale End Riverside Park**.

The Malthouse

Smartly converted and extensively
refurbished this former malthouse has
been an inn since the turn of the 20th
century. It's set on the banks of the River
Severn in the heart of this spectacular
World Heritage Site, just 250yds (229m)
from Ironbridge's main visitor centre.
A successful gastropub with-rooms,
it is set around a cobbled courtyard and
the bright and spacious Jazz Bar is the place
for post-walk refreshment. Pine beams,
scrubbed wooden tables, candles and an
informal atmosphere set the scene for some
contemporary bar food and, if you're here
on Wednesday to Saturday evening, some
live music. The rest of the pub is given over
to dining and a more elaborate menu.

Food
Refuel on French bread pizzas, the Jazz Bar
cheeseburger with salad and chips, various
sandwiches and salad platters (steamed
salmon), chicken and red wine casserole,
and ribeye steak and chips.

Family facilities
Children are welcome in the eating area
of the bar and in the restaurant. You'll find
high chairs, baby-changing facilities, half-
portions of main menu items, and two
family bedrooms.

Alternative refreshment stops
There is lots of choice, such as the Swan, a
very attractive place, which is open all day.

☞ Where to go from here
The Museum of Iron brings the Darby
family's achievements to life. It includes the
Darby Furnace where it all began and it has
much to say about the lives of those who
lived and worked in the area during this
period of momentous change. Equally
fascinating are the ironmasters' homes near
by (known as the Darby Houses) and the
charming terrace of workers' houses at
Tea Kettle Row. For information on all the
museums and attractions at Ironbridge visit
www.ironbridge.org.uk.

about the pub
The Malthouse
The Wharfage, Ironbridge
Telford, Shropshire TF8 7NH
Tel: 01952 433712
www.malthousepubs.co.uk

DIRECTIONS: see Getting to the start; pub
is beside the river to east of the museum
and car park
PARKING: 15
OPEN: daily; all day
FOOD: daily; all day Sunday
BREWERY/COMPANY: free house
REAL ALE: Flowers Original, Boddingtons
DOGS: not allowed inside
ROOMS: 9 en suite

Kingsbury Water Park

WALK

Kingsbury

WARWICKSHIRE

A lovely stroll through old Kingsbury and around the pools of its magnificent water park.

Kingsbury village and Water Park

The water park around Kingsbury was once 620 acres (251ha) of old sand and gravel pits, but today it has become a major leisure facility with more than 30 beautiful lakes and pools attracting around 200,000 visitors each year.

Raised planks lead into the water park where you can stroll around a number of the larger pools to enjoy watching a wide variety of contemporary activities taking place such as sailing, windsurfing, fishing and horse-riding. There are also several hides where you can do a spot of bird-watching.

The old village of Kingsbury sits on a small hill overlooking this wonderland of water. On this high ground is the Church of St Peter and St Paul from where you get a delightful view over the lakes. The church contains a 12th-century nave, a 14th-century tower and a 16th-century belfry. One of its old arches is incised by deep grooves in which it is believed the local bowmen used to sharpen their arrows.

Kingsbury village has been associated with many famous families over the years. In the Middle Ages the Bracebridge and Arden families were involved in a Romeo and Juliet-type feud when Alice Bracebridge married John Arden against the wishes of both families. John's brother's granddaughter was Mary Arden, the mother of William Shakespeare.

By the middle of the 19th century most of the land in the village was owned by Sir Robert Peel. The long-serving MP for Tamworth, one-time Prime Minister and founder of the modern police, lived at nearby Drayton Manor and was buried at Drayton Basset, a few miles up the Tame Valley. The main business of the area had been agriculture, but coal mining took over. Later sand and gravel was extracted from the land on the other side of the River Tame. Today the river divides a thriving village from the Kingsbury Water Park.

You leave the water park over Hemlingford Bridge which crosses the River Tame. This bridge was first built by public subscription in 1783 and takes its name from the Hundred of Hemlingford in which Kingsbury stands (a hundred was an old Saxon local administrative area). There used to be a toll house at one end of the original bridge, but this was demolished in 1937. On New Year's Day in 1982 the original bridge was destroyed by catastrophic floods. Flooding has been a regular feature of the area, with the water frequently rising and spreading over the flood plain between Kingsbury village and the nearby hamlet of Bodymoor Heath. Most people now live on the east side of the River Tame.

the walk

1 From the car park, go left along **Pear Tree Avenue** to reach the A51 road. The Royal Oak can be seen over to the left. Go straight over the road, pass the White Swan and at the corner of the road, take the path on the left. Pass the **churchyard**, keep to the right of the church and descend the steps to reach a footbridge over the **River Tame**. Cross the bridge and walk along the raised footway planks to enter **Kingsbury Water**

Park. Follow the signs for the visitor centre, pass **Hemlingford Water** and **Bodymoor Heath Water** and keep right at the fork.

2 From the visitor centre make for the roundabout and go straight over following the signs for the **sailing club** and North Warwickshire Cycle Way. Pass by the entrance gate to **Tamworth Sailing Club** and continue on the right-hand side of **Bodymoor Heath Water,** along a mixture of tarmac lane and grass footpaths.

3 At the end of the stretch of water swing left, then right and follow the waymarks for the **Centenary Way.** Go diagonally across an access road, still following the waymarks, and take the path alongside lakes. Beyond **Swann Pool,** follow the path round to the left

Trees and lawns surround a lake in Kingsbury Water Park

MAP: OS Explorer 232 Nuneaton & Tamworth

START/FINISH: Pear Tree Avenue car park (free, off the A51 near the White Swan in the centre of Kinsgbury); grid ref: SP 217962

PATHS: reservoir paths and footpaths, 2 stiles

LANDSCAPE: reservoir and parkland

PUBLIC TOILETS: Visitor centre in Kingsbury Water Park

TOURIST INFORMATION: Tamworth, tel 01827 709581

THE PUB: The Royal Oak, Kingsbury

🔴 Two busy road crossings

Getting to the start
Kingsbury is on the A51 between junctions 9 & 10 of the M42, south of Tamworth.

Kingsbury   WARWICKSHIRE

Kingsbury WARWICKSHIRE

what to look for

Many wild birds visit the water park and you will certainly see plenty of ducks, swans, coots and moorhens, especially Canada geese. Look out for herons, kingfishers, common terns, great crested grebes, cormorants, little ringed plovers and lapwings. Some 200 species of bird have been recorded here and the park has one of the UK's largest inland breeding colonies of common terns.

and then you can see **Mill Pool** on the right through the trees.

4 Cross **Hemlingford Bridge** towards the busy A51, go left over a stile and cross the field to the next stile by the road, near the middle of the village of **Kingsbury**. Turn left for 100yds (91m), following the pavement to a path on the right, beside a detached house. There is a **Heart of England Way sign** here. Take the path, avoid the footbridge and carry on, keeping houses visible. Keep right at the fork just beyond the **bridge**, take the next left, then turn right. Turn left after a few paces into **Meadow Close**, then left again into Pear Tree Avenue to return to the car park.

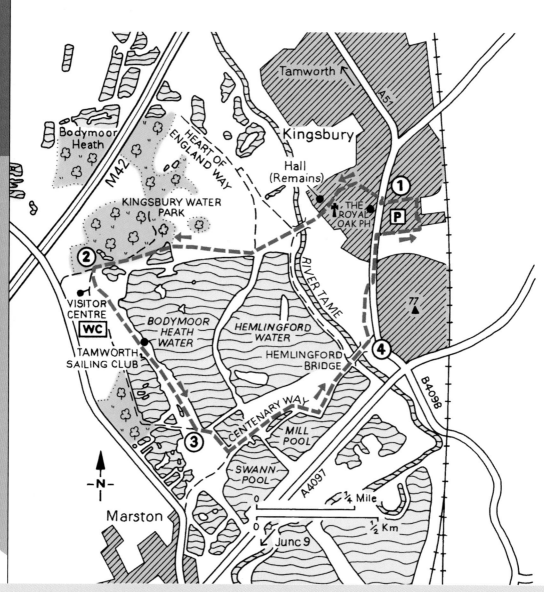

The Royal Oak

Kingsbury

WARWICKSHIRE

about the pub

The Royal Oak
Coventry Road, Kingsbury
Tamworth, Staffordshire B78 2LP
Tel: 01827 872339

DIRECTIONS: beside the A51 opposite the car park	
PARKING: 40	
OPEN: daily; all day	
FOOD: no food Sunday evening and Monday lunchtime	
BREWERY/COMPANY: Marston's	
REAL ALE: Marston's Pedigree, Banks's Bitter & Original	
DOGS: not allowed inside	

The 'Oak' is handily placed for refreshment before or after this stroll around the Water Park as it's right opposite the car park. Expect a bustling and traditional town pub, with loyal local trade filling the split-level bar and dining area. It's a friendly place and is justifiably popular with walkers, birdwatchers and passing cyclists.

Food

A wide-ranging menu takes in sandwiches and traditional pub favourites such as steak and ale pie and cottage pie. There are roast lunches on Sundays.

Family facilities

The welcome towards children extends to smaller portions of adult meals, a menu for younger family members and a play area in the garden.

Alternative refreshment stops

The White Swan is a regular haunt of local rambling groups. You might like to try the Old Barn Coffee Shop at the visitor centre in the park.

☞ Where to go from here

Off the M42 (junction 11) is Twycross Zoo, set in 50 acres of parkland and home to around 1000 animals, most of which are endangered species. It specialises in primates, with a big range of apes, gibbons, orangutans and chimpanzees. There are other animals such as lions, elephants and giraffes, a pets' corner for younger children, a Penguin Pool with underwater viewing, and a children's adventure playground (www.twycrosszoo.com).

CYCLE

Foxton Locks

LEICESTERSHIRE

Foxton Locks and the Grand Union Canal

Enjoy varied and challenging traffic-free riding along one of England's most famous canal systems.

Foxton Locks and the Grand Union Canal

The Grand Union Canal actually started its life as lots of separate canals, which were joined to provide a navigable waterway from Birmingham to London (the name 'Grand Union' comes from the amalgamation of a number of different companies in 1926). In 1793, long before this name was coined, a canal was begun in Leicester to link up with the Grand Junction Canal, which had started north from the Thames a year earlier. In 1814,

the two were finally joined by the ten locks at Foxton, which raised the level of the Leicester canal by some 75ft (22.8m). It takes about 50 minutes for a boat to negotiate all ten locks, and each boat requires about 25,000 gallons of water. The history of the locks is explained in more detail at the Foxton Locks Museum, near the start of the ride.

Also worth exploring is Millfield Wood, one of 200 woods created around the country as part of the Woods on Your Doorstep Project to celebrate the Millennium. The 18.8-acre (7.6ha) site was acquired by the Woodland Trust after a successful fund-raising appeal by Fleckney Village. Oak, ash, silver birch and small numbers of field maple are the dominant species.

the ride

1 From the car park exit, turn left along a gravel track to get to the **bridge** over the canal. Cross the bridge and turn right to reach the **canal** and, after about 300m (330 yards), the **locks** themselves. Cycling isn't permitted on this section, so you'll have to walk your bikes down the side of the locks (the Foxton Locks Museum is situated on the far side of the passing pond about half-way down this long, steep slope, and can be reached on foot). Stay to the left at the bottom to reach the shop and **café**.

2 Continue past the shop to cross a **cobbled bridge**. On the far side, keep going in the same direction. The shingle track along this part of the canal is wide and smooth, although there are one or two places where the left hand edge has collapsed a little, so it's a good idea to stay right. After 1.5 miles (2km), you come to **Debdale Wharf**. Beyond Debdale Wharf, the path becomes narrow and grassy, and on dry days it may be quite bumpy. In the summer, this section may also be quite overgrown with reeds and bull-rushes, but it should still be passable. At **Gumley Road**, the track becomes smoother and wider again, before continuing on to **Saddington Road**.

The towpath of the Grand Union Canal

2h00 — **9.6 MILES** — **15.5 KM** — **LEVEL 1 2 3**

MAP: OS Explorer 223 Northampton & Market Harborough

START/FINISH: Foxton Locks car park; grid ref: SP 692892

TRAILS/TRACKS: smooth gravel, narrow grassy track, road and rutted farm track

LANDSCAPE: towpath, village and farmland

PUBLIC TOILETS: at the start

TOURIST INFORMATION: Market Harborough, tel 01858 821270

CYCLE HIRE: none locally

THE PUB: The Bell Inn, Gumley

❶ A fairly challenging ride along an often bumpy tow path and some rough tracks – mountain bikes recommended. One short, steep descent to a railing over the canal (can easily be walked). Care is required crossing Kibworth Road. Suitable for older, more experienced children.

Getting to the start

Foxton is well signed off the A6 between Leicester and Market Harborough, off the A4304 to the west of Market Harborough, and off the B6047 to the north of Market Harborough. From Foxton, follow signs for the Foxton Locks car park, which is at the top end of the locks.

Why do this cycle ride?

This ride provides the perfect challenge to budding young mountain bikers, combining easy gravel towpath, flat grassy single tracks, a few gentle climbs, and some rough farm roads at the end of an alternative return route. The wonderfully preserved locks at the start are merely an added bonus.

---

3 Just beyond Saddington Road, a short sharp climb takes you up to the right of **Saddington Tunnel**. A longer but gentle rise, still on a wide gravel track, takes you along the top of the tunnel, before a gentle descent carries you back down to **Kibworth Road**. From here it's possible to return the way you came, but if you're feeling energetic, here follows an alternative.

4 If the gate is locked here, you'll have to carry your bikes over a **narrow stile**, before crossing the road with care to another, wider stile. Another gradual downhill then takes you to a short, steep slope down to a **fence** above the canal. This can be ridden, but you may prefer to walk it. At the fence turn left to continue along the canal. The path is quite narrow, and can be slippery in wet weather, so take great care. At the next **bridge**, continue past it for about 30 yards to reach a gate – go through this gate to reach the bridge.

5 Cross the bridge and continue to the top of the field ahead, where you'll find an enormous slab of granite welcoming you to **Millfield Wood**. Go through a gate and continue along a wide bridleway across a field. Follow the track as it bears left to reach **Kibworth Road** and then cross the road to continue in the same direction along another **gravel track**.

6 After 1.5 miles (2km) of gentle downhill riding on a wide, occasionally pot-holed **track**, turn right at the road in **Smeeton**, and then first left along Debdale Lane. This rough **farm track** rises gently and then more steeply to reach the canal. At the top of the track, bear left towards **Debdale Wharf Farm** and then turn right at the farm to regain the **towpath**. From here, turn left to retrace your tracks back to the start.

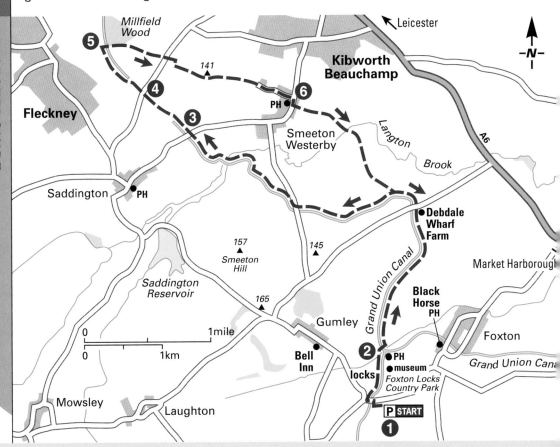

The Bell Inn

about the pub

The Bell Inn
2 Main Street, Gumley
Market Harborough, Leicestershire
LE16 7RU
Tel: 0116 279 2476

DIRECTIONS: signposted off the A6 north west of Market Harborough

PARKING: 20

OPEN: closed Sunday evening

FOOD: no food Monday evening

BREWERY/COMPANY: free house

REAL ALE: Bass, Batemans XB, Greene King IPA, guest beer

Note the collection of miniature cricket bats in a case in the lobby as you enter this early 19th-century village pub. Beyond lies an L-shaped bar furnished with dark wood tables and chairs and decorated by more cricket bats and cricketing prints and cartoons, china jugs and mugs, hunting prints, and gleaming horse brasses on black beams. You'll also find a good range of beers, a warming log fire and a small no-smoking dining room. Pretty summer garden for alfresco eating and drinking.

Food

Good value bar meals take in sandwiches, ploughman's lunches, home-made soups, salmon mornay, steaks and home-made puddings like sherry trifle. Popular three-course Sunday roast lunches.

Family facilities

Children over 5 are welcome in the restaurant but not in the terraced garden to the rear of the pub.

Alternative refreshment stops

Cold drinks, ice-creams and hot and cold snacks are available from the shop at Foxton Locks.

☛ Where to go from here

Market Harborough is a very picturesque medieval town with an interesting local museum and is well worth a visit if you have an hour or two to spare. Further afield, up the

A6 to Leicester and a must if you have kids in tow, is the National Space Museum (www.nssc.co.uk), which offers five themed galleries, cutting-edge audio-visual technology and glimpses into genuine space research. More great cycling and walking can also be found on the Brampton Valley Way, which starts behind the Bell pub, on the A508 near the southern edge of Market Harborough.

Around Pitsford Water

CYCLE

Pitsford Water

NORTHAMPTONSHIRE

Look out for the abundant birdlife along this purpose-built, waterfront cycle track.

with each numbering many hundreds of thousands on a good day. Butterflies add to the colour with 23 different species recorded. Other attractions at the park include a brand new playground, a sensory

The Reservoir

Established in 1997 with the help of a substantial grant from the Millennium Fund, Brixworth is the newest country park in Northamptonshire, while Pitsford Water was designated as a Site of Special Scientific Interest (or SSSI) in 1971. The latter is home to numerous species of wading birds, is the site of the county's largest winter gull roost, and is regularly visited by ospreys on their spring migrations. In the winter, wildfowl numbers have been known to reach 10,000, with ducks, grebes, geese and swans being the most common residents. The wide variety of habitats around the reservoir also provides food and shelter for migrant birds in spring – surveys show a breeding population of 55 species.

In the summer, meanwhile, the reserve comes alive with dragonflies and damselflies. Common blue and emerald damselflies are probably the most abundant species,

garden, a boules area (balls are available for hire), three wheel-chair accessible nature trails and a human sundial. Sailing, windsurfing and canoeing lessons are available from the Marina (April to October) and fly fishing can be arranged at the Lodge on Holcot Causeway (the reservoir is stocked with 35,000 trout each year).

the ride

1 From the main exit of the car park, turn left on a **gravel track**, following the obvious cycle path signs. Take this track down towards the water's edge, heading to the right of the **playground**, until you reach the **main cycle track** around the reservoir, with the marina off to your right.

2 Turn left here, along the wide and smooth gravel track, following the water's edge. You shortly pass through a sequence of gates

1h30 — **7.5 MILES** — **12 KM** — **LEVEL 123**

and continue to follow the shore around a series of **shallow bays**. As the reservoir starts to narrow, you come to the first gradual rise of the ride, followed by the option of a quick up-and-down single track for the more

MAP: OS Explorer 223 Northampton & Market Harborough

START/FINISH: Brixworth Country Park car park; grid ref: SP 752695

TRAILS/TRACKS: smooth gravel or tarmac all the way round

LANDSCAPE: woodland, waterside and causeway

PUBLIC TOILETS: at the start

TOURIST INFORMATION: Northampton, tel 01604 622677

CYCLE HIRE: Pitsford Water Cycle Hire, tel 01604 881777

THE PUB: The White Horse, Old Northampton

❶ Care needs to be taken when exiting the car park at the west end of the causeway.

adventurous. This whole stretch is dotted with little coves, benches and **picnic tables**, while signs along the water's edge warn of back-casting by anglers.

3 Within sight of the causeway, proceed through another **swing gate**, and then just before you reach the causeway, go through another gate and over a **cattle grid** to reach a car park and picnic area (during the summer, there may be an ice-cream van here, providing the perfect excuse for a rest). This is also a good place for a spot of bird watching.

4 Take care when exiting the car park to reach the cycle path across the **causeway** (this path, which is marked with a bike symbol, is on the car park side of the causeway, so you don't need to cross the main road). Continue to the end of the causeway and up a short rise.

Getting to the start

Brixworth Country park is signed from the A508 between Market Harborough and Northampton. The route starts at the visitor centre on the reservoir's western shore just to the south of Brixworth.

Why do this cycle ride?

This is a gentle and enjoyable ride on smooth gravel tracks. With great views of the reservoir and little in the way of hills or other challenges to contend with, it's ideal for families with younger children.

An orientation sign at Pitsford Water

some **trees**. Go through a gate and follow the track along the left-hand edge of a wood until you reach a pair of gates and a tarmac road (to the left is **Moulton Grange**). Turn right on the road, over a miniature causeway. Immediately after the causeway, turn right again, back onto the **cycle track** (this is not well signed) and follow it around to the **dam**. Continue across the dam, taking a moment to soak in the expansive views of the reservoir. At the end of the dam, go through a gate and then turn right onto the wooded cycle track just past the **sailing club entrance**. At the end of the woods, you reach the point where you first joined the **main trail**. Turn left here to get back to the car park and the start.

5 Just before the top of this gradual rise, turn right, through a gate and into some **woods**. Enjoy the ride's first little stretch of downhill through the trees, before negotiating a sweeping left-hand turn. Proceed through a gate and follow the water's edge into a long, narrow **inlet**. Go through a gate just before the end of the inlet. A tight turn at the end of the inlet will take you back along the other side.

6 Continue to skirt around the reservoir until you come to a corridor through

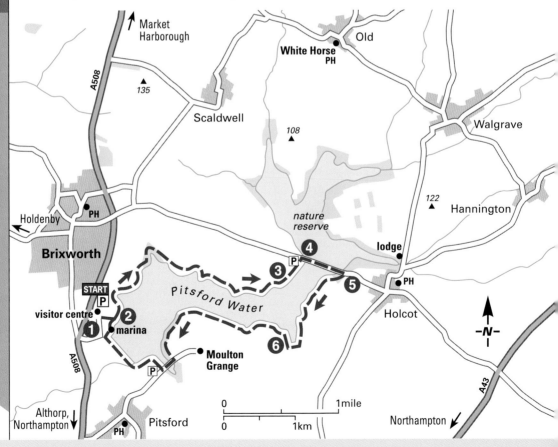

The White Horse

Small, friendly village local in a superb village setting overlooking the 13th-century St Andrew's church, a view best appreciated from the lovely enclosed garden which also features a fine restored red-brick chimney. Inside, the character bar and comfortable lounge areas, are spotlessly maintained, with hunting prints and collections of china decorating the walls, and splendid log fires to cosy-up to on cold winter days.

Food

Traditional home-cooked meals range from good-value sandwiches and filled baguettes to lamb and mint suet pudding, spinach and ricotta cannelloni, grilled tuna steak, and beef Wellington. Regular theme nights.

Family facilities

Children are welcome in the bars.

Alternative refreshment stops

A wide selection of hot and cold snacks and meals are available from the Willow Tree Café at the start. Ice creams may be available at the causeway car park during the summer, and snacks and hot and cold refreshments are available from the nature reserve lodge, near the eastern end of the causeway.

☛ Where to go from here

Holdenby House, about 4 miles (6.4km) to the west of the reservoir, boasts a splendid Elizabethan garden and a falconry centre (www.holdenby.com). Also nearby, about the same distance to the south, is the Northampton and Lampton Railway, on the Brampton Valley Way, just to the east of Chapel Brampton (www.nlr.org.uk). About five miles (8km) to the southwest is Althorp, the final resting place of Diana Princess of Wales (www.althorp.com).

about the pub

The White Horse
Walgrave Road, Old
Northampton, Northamptonshire
NN6 9QX
Tel: 01604 781297

DIRECTIONS: Old is located north of Northampton between the A508 and A43; pub is in the village centre next to the church

PARKING: 10

OPEN: closed Monday & Tuesday lunchtime

FOOD: daily

BREWERY/COMPANY: Banks Brewery

REAL ALE: Banks's Bitter, two guest beers

A loop from Exton

Exton

RUTLAND

Explore the open countryside and parkland around Exton, a thatched village north of Rutland Water.

Exton

A couple of miles north of Rutland Water, Exton is a picturesque village of ironstone and thatched cottages laid out around a green, ringed by mature sycamore trees and overlooked by the tall, creeper-covered village pub.

There has been a community here since Norman times, and the manor once belonged to King David of Scotland. Since then it has changed hands a number of times, finally passing to the Noels, Viscounts Campden, Earls of Gainsborough, in the 1620s. The family still owns neighbouring Exton Hall, which was built to replace the Old Hall after it was largely destroyed by a fire in 1810.

The ruins of the Old Hall are inside the grounds (accessible to the public from the road to the south) close to the Church of St Peter and St Paul, which itself was struck by lightning in 1843, causing the spire to collapse. Although some of the original work was lost, most of the fine monuments survived, including some medieval sculptures and various tombs. Also look out for the giant statue by the master carver Grinling Gibbons of the 3rd Viscount Campden, his wife and 19 children, which is considered something of a rarity since Gibbons is far better known for working in wood rather than stone. The film *Little Lord Fauntleroy* (1980) was shot on location in Exton and featured, among other places, the village church.

The grounds and parkland were mainly developed in the late 17th century by the 6th Earl of Gainsborough, when water features such as cascades, artificial ponds and streams were created. Among the ornamental follies on the estate is an elaborate Gothic summer house known as Fort Henry, overlooking Fort Henry Lake, which you will see half-way round the walk. Behind it stood the even more bizarre Bark Temple, an elaborate wooden structure that not surprisingly has rotted away over time.

Measuring less than 20 miles (32.4km) across, Rutland has a resident population of around 37,000, and apart from Oakham and Uppingham most of its inhabitants live in tiny villages and hamlets. The county's name may derive from the 11th-century word 'Roteland', denoting the red colour of the soil in the east of the region; or it could have been part of the estate belonging to an early landowner called Rota. For many years this tiny place was in the hands of either the Crown or the Church, but in 1974 local government reorganisation ended its independence and relegated it to a mere district of Leicestershire.

That decision was reversed in 1997, and Rutland is once more England's smallest county, whose Latin motto 'Multum in Parvo' means 'so much in so little'.

the walk

1 With your back to the pub leave the Green on the far right-hand side on **Stamford Road** and, at the end, turn right. This becomes Empingham Road and, when the houses finish, continue over the stream and turn left to follow a **public footpath**.

A row of 18th-century thatched cottages

3h00	6.5 MILES	10.4 KM	LEVEL 123

2 Just before the fence ahead veer off half right onto a lower **grassy path** and follow the wide track along the shallow valley for just under 1 mile (1.6km), at one point climbing into a field on the left to avoid Cuckoo Farm. Look for a stile and **footbridge** and clamber up through the fields on the right to reach a lane.

3 Turn left and walk the verge until just beyond the bend, then go left on a footpath indicated **'Fort Henry and Greetham'**. Follow this route above the trout hatchery, then head diagonally right via a small concrete bridge to reach the fence at the top. Turn left and walk along to **Lower Lake**, then go ahead/right on the surfaced drive for a few paces, keeping to the left of the bar gate, and out across open pasture above the water.

Pretty gardens in a Rutland village

MAP: OS Explorer 234 Rutland Water

START/FINISH: roadside parking in centre of Exton; grid ref: SK 924112

PATHS: mainly field paths and firm farm tracks, 12 stiles

LANDSCAPE: open and undulating fields and parkland, mixed woodland

PUBLIC TOILETS: none on route

TOURIST INFORMATION: Oakham, tel 01572 724329

THE PUB: The Fox & Hounds, Exton

Getting to the start

Follow the A606 between Oakham and Stamford. Turn off at Rutland Water at the sign for Exton and drive to the village. There are spaces in the vicinity of the Fox & Hounds.

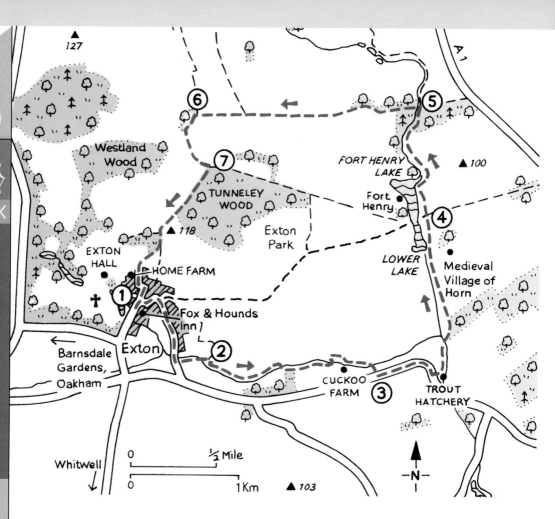

At the far side turn right on to another
lane then, in a few paces, left for the
footpath indicated **'Greetham'**. Follow this
beside **Fort Henry Lake**, then on along a
corridor between lovely mixed woodland. At
the far end climb the **stairs** to reach the lane.

Turn left and walk up through more
woods and, when the semi-surfaced
drive bears left, go straight on through an
area of newly planted **trees**. The wide,
unmade track now heads directly out across
the **open fields** for a mile (1.6km).

When you reach the **trees** on the far side
turn left on to a track that drops down
and bears left. Here go straight on via a stile
and **wooden plank footbridge** and head up
diagonally left towards the top of the field.
Go over the stile and turn left on to the **farm
track** once more.

At the junction turn right on to the
straight, metalled **lane**. Bear left at a
fork before woods and follow this back to
Exton. Follow signs around **Home Farm**, then
turn left at the end of West End and right by
the stone shelter into High Street and return
to the Green.

what to look for

Although the gentle farmland of
Rutland and South Lincolnshire is by
and large a peaceful place, every now and then
you may be aware of a distant roar and a fast-
moving object zooming through the sky. A few
miles to the north lies the busy airfield at
Cottesmore, which opened in 1938 and was a
base for American bombers throughout World War
Two. Today Tornado pilots train there.

The Fox & Hounds

about the pub

The Fox & Hounds
Exton, Oakham
Rutland LE15 8AP
Tel: 01572 812403
www.foxandhoundsrutland.com

DIRECTIONS: see Getting to the start
PARKING: 20
OPEN: daily
FOOD: no food Sunday evening in winter
BREWERY/COMPANY: free house
REAL ALE: Greene King IPA, Grainstore Ales, guest beer
DOGS: allowed in the bar
ROOMS: 4 bedrooms

Exton   *RUTLAND*

Rutland Water is only 2 miles (3.2km) away from this rather proud-looking and ivy-covered 17th-century coaching inn overlooking the picturesque village green. It is also a handy refreshment stop for ramblers on the Viking Way. The attraction in summer is the fine walled garden for alfresco dining, as well as pints of local Grainstore ales and imaginative pub food with an Italian twist, served in the civilised high-ceilinged lounge. Here you'll find sturdy pine tables, hunting prints on the walls, fresh flowers, and a crackling winter log fire in the large stone fireplace.

Food

From the 'casual lunch' menu order soup and sandwiches or filled jacket potatoes, or look to the main menu for interesting pasta meals, starters of asparagus and gruyère cheese tart or seared scallops with salad and dill dressing, and main dishes such as halibut with Mediterranean vegetables, or marinated lamb shank. Separate pizza menu.

Family facilities

Children of all ages are welcome. High chairs and half-portions of main meals are available and there's a children's menu and a play area in the garden.

Alternative refreshment stops

Nearby Greetham also has three thriving pubs. Alternatively visit the coffee shop at Barnsdale Gardens, which is open daily all year round (weekends from November to February).

☞ Where to go from here

Rutland County Museum in Oakham has displays of farming equipment, machinery and wagons, rural tradesmen's tools, domestic collections and local archaeology, all housed in a splendid 18th-century cavalry riding school. Don't miss Oakham Castle, a fine Norman Great Hall of a 12th-century fortified manor house (www.rutland.gov.uk). At the Rutland Railway Museum in Cottesmore there are over 40 industrial steam and diesel locomotives and other wagons and vehicles used in the ironstone quarries and industry.

A walk around Southwold

WALK

Southwold

SUFFOLK

Walk around this old-fashioned holiday resort on an island surrounded by river, creek and sea.

Southwold Pier

The arrival of the first steamboats for more than 70 years marked a return to the glory days for Southwold Pier in the summer of 2002. The pier was originally built in 1899, when Southwold was a flourishing holiday resort. Mixed bathing had just been introduced on the beach, on condition that men and women were kept at least 20yds (18m) apart and changed in separate 'bathing machines' into costumes that covered their bodies from neck to knees. The *Belle* steamer brought holidaymakers on its daily voyage from London and the pier was a hive of activity as porters carried cases to their lodgings.

The T-end, where the boats docked, was swept away in a storm in 1934. During World War Two, the pier was split in two as a precaution against a German invasion. By the time Chris and Helen Iredale bought the pier in 1987, storms and neglect had reduced it to a rotting hulk. Years later, the couple have realised their dream of rebuilding and reopening the pier, so that visitors can once again stroll along the boardwalk with the sea spray in their faces and watch the boats unloading their passengers at a new landing stage.

An exhibition on the pier tells the history of the seaside holiday, complete with saucy postcards, kitsch teapots, palm readers, end-of-the-pier shows, high-diving 'professors' and old-style arcade machines, such as the 'kiss-meter' where you can find out whether you are flirtatious, amorous, frigid or sexy. A separate pavilion contains modern machines by local inventor Tim Hunkin, who also designed the ingenious water clock, with chimes and special effects every half-hour. You can eat ice cream or fish and chips, drink a pint of the local beer, play pool in the amusement arcade or watch the fishermen while taking in the sea air. Especially in summer, the pier provides a focus for good old-fashioned fun.

Southwold, situated on an island between the River Blyth and the sea, is one of those genteel, low-key seaside resorts where, in spite of the pier, everything is done in good taste. Make no mistake, this is a popular spot but it has none of the brashness of kiss-me-quick Felixstowe or Lowestoft. The character of Southwold seems to be summed up by the rows of brightly coloured beach huts on the seafront promenade – some of which have been sold

what to look for

It's worth a visit to the cathedral-like St Edmund's Church, whose 100ft (30m) flint tower stands guard over the town. The greatest treasure here is the 15th-century rood screen which spans the width of the church, a riot of colour as vivid as when it was painted, with angels in glory and a set of panels depicting the twelve apostles.

for the price of a three-bedroom cottage elsewhere – and the peaceful greens with their Georgian and Edwardian houses. Adnams brewery dominates the town and it is no surprise to discover that the beer is still delivered to pubs on horse-drawn drays. Southwold is that sort of place.

The Walk

1 Leave the **pier** and turn left along the seafront, either following the promenade past the beach huts and climbing some steps or walking along the clifftop path with views over the beach. After passing **St James' Green**, where a pair of cannon stand either side of a mast, continue along the clifftop path to **Gun Hill**, where six more cannon, captured at the Battle of Culloden near Inverness in 1746, can be seen facing out to sea.

2 From Gun Hill, head inland alongside the large South Green, then turn left along Queen's Road to the junction with Gardner Road and Ferry Road. Cross the road and take the footpath ahead, that passes a hut and follows a stream beside the marshes as

MAP: OS Explorer 231 Southwold & Bungay

START/FINISH: beach car park (pay-and-display) or free in nearby streets; grid ref: TM 512767

PATHS: riverside paths, seaside promenade, town streets, 2 stiles

LANDSCAPE: Southwold and its surroundings – river, marshes, coast

PUBLIC TOILETS: beside pier, near beach and car park at Southwold Harbour

TOURIST INFORMATION: Southwold, tel 01502 724729

THE PUB: The Harbour Inn, Southwold

Getting to the start

Southwold is signposted off the A12 between Woodbridge and Lowestoft. Take the A1095 north of Blythburgh and head east for 4 miles (6.4km). Pass through Reydon and turn left just before Southwold town centre, signed to the beach and pier. A car park is at the pier.

WALK

Southwold SUFFOLK

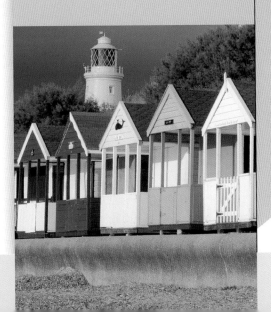

it heads towards the river. Alternatively, stay on the clifftop path and walk over the dunes until you reach the mouth of the **River Blyth**.

3 Turn right and walk beside the river, passing the **Walberswick ferry**, a group of fishing huts where fresh fish is sold, and **The Harbour Inn**. After about 0.75 mile (1.2km) you reach an iron bridge on the site of the old Southwold-to-Halesworth railway line.

4 Keep straight ahead at the bridge, crossing a stile and following the path round to the right alongside **Buss Creek** to make a complete circuit of the island. There

are good views across the common to Southwold, dominated by the lighthouse and the tower of **St Edmund's Church**. Horses and cattle can often be seen grazing on the marshes. Keep straight ahead at a four-finger signpost and stay on the raised path to reach a white-painted bridge.

5 Climb up to the road and cross the bridge, then continue on the path beside Buss Creek with views of beach huts in the distance. The path skirts a **boating lake** on its way down to the sea. Turn right and walk across the car park to return to the pier.

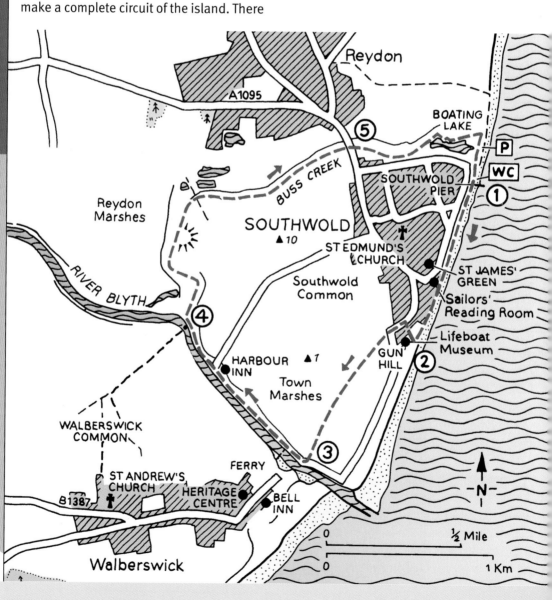

The Harbour Inn

Nautical memorabilia adorn the rambling bars of this appealing old Adnams pub situated away from the town on the bustling quay close to the working boatyard and fishing sheds beside the tidal River Blyth. There is a classic wood-panelled front bar with tiled floor, low beams and old settles. Local ship and boat photographs, model ships and flags fill the charactered back bar. It's the place to sup pints of superb Adnams ale, brewed just up the lane. Good summer alfresco tables on the front gravel overlooking the river and boats, or in the rear garden. Note the 1953 flood level mark on the pub wall.

Food

Expect a good range of freshly prepared food ranging from soups, baguettes, pint of prawns, ploughman's, lasagne and steaks. Draws a good crowd for first-rate fish – beer-battered haddock and daily specials.

Family facilities

Children are welcome in the bottom bar and restaurant until 9pm. There's a children's menu and high chairs are available.

Alternative refreshment stops

There are numerous cafés and restaurants in Southwold, many of them specialising in fresh local fish. Among the pubs serving Adnams beer are the Sole Bay Inn, a Victorian pub opposite the brewery on East Green, and the Red Lion on South Green.

☛ Where to go from here

The Southwold Sailors' Reading Room on East Cliff was opened in 1864 in memory of Captain Rayley, a naval officer at the time of the Battle of Trafalgar. Although it still retains its original purpose as a library and meeting place, it is now a small museum containing model boats, figureheads and portraits of local sailors and fishermen. Near by, on Gun Hill, a former coastguard look-out houses the tiny Lifeboat Museum, open on summer afternoons, with exhibits on the history of the Southwold lifeboats. Among the items to look for is a hand-operated foghorn, similar in appearance to a set of bellows.

about the pub

The Harbour Inn
Blackshore, Southwold
Suffolk IP18 6TA
Tel: 01502 722381

DIRECTIONS: in Southwold turn right at the Kings Head and follow the road to Blackshore Quay. At **Point 3** of walk

PARKING: 50

OPEN: daily; all day

FOOD: daily

BREWERY/COMPANY: Adnams Brewery

REAL ALE: Adnams Best, Broadside, Fisherman & seasonal ale

DOGS: allowed in the bar

Willaston to Parkgate

Start from an old railway station and follow the Wirral Way to a seafront resort with no sea.

Parkgate

Unique in the North West, Parkgate looks very much like a traditional Victorian seaside resort with terraced houses, shops and hotels. Once the seafront gave onto golden sands, but the sea abandoned Parkgate more than 50 years ago, leaving the sands to revegetate into the grassy marshes you see today. The encroaching marsh finally reached the sea wall along The Parade at the end of World War Two.
To the south of Parkgate, you can still find what remains of the Old Quay, evidence of the flourishing 16th century, now wholly landlocked. It is hard now to believe that once the water here was deep, and provided a safe anchorage.

Where the trackbed runs through the rock cutting, note the grooves made by the railway engineers as they cut through the sandstone bedrock. On one side, a lower wall and small sandstone cliffs are covered with mosses and ferns that love this kind of sheltered, moist environment.

the ride

1 Set off by riding to the far end of the car park and turning right through a narrow gap to gain the **Wirral Way cycle**

Shaded view across fields at Willaston

1h30 **7.5 MILES** **12 KM** **LEVEL 1**23

MAP: OS Explorer 266 Wirral and Chester

START/FINISH: Hadlow Road railway station, Willaston; grid ref: SJ 332774

TRAILS/TRACKS: former railway trackbed, rough-surfaced and muddy in a few places, but generally in good condition. Short section of road, in Parkgate, which can be avoided by stopping before reaching it and returning from there

LANDSCAPE: mainly farmland, with light woodland along the old trackbed

PUBLIC TOILETS: at the start (in Ticket Office) and at Parkgate

TOURIST INFORMATION: Birkenhead, tel 0151 647 6780; www.visitwirral.com

CYCLE HIRE: none locally

THE PUB: The Nag's Head, Willaston

Getting to the start

The village of Willaston lies between Neston and Ellesmere Port, and is best reached from the A540, along the B5151, or from the M53 (Junction 6) along the B5133. The car park is at the former Hadlow railway station, just at the southern edge of the village.

Why do this cycle ride?

Tree-lined tracks, picturesque villages, an authentic railway station complete with ticket office, views of the Dee Estuary and the Welsh hills, rock cuttings and a wealth of wildlife – and delicious home-made ice cream available in Parkgate.

track, which immediately passes the station platform, before reaching a gate. Cross the road with care, and continue on the other side, riding through lush arable farmland, along a fine corridor of trees and shrubs.

2 For a while after a **stone bridge**, the track is a little more rough, and runs on to a gate immediately before a road underpass. Go through the **underpass** and on the other side, pass through another gate to resume the Wirral Way. Eventually the track continues to run through a **railway cutting**, with steep sides and overhanging vegetation.

Railway station museum at Willaston, recalling early 20th-century rail travel

3 When the track emerges at a road (Mellock Lane) keep forward into **Station Road**, and cycle down to pass beneath a railway line and reach a small car park. Ride past this and resume the **Wirral Way**. Continue until the cycle route emerges near a car park, beyond which a broad track leads down to a main road on the edge of **Parkgate**.

4 Return from this point, back the same way you came.

Optional Extension

Extend the ride a little by emerging with care onto the road, and riding to the right for just over 100 yards (90m), and, as the road bends to the right, leave it by branching left onto a continuation into **light woodland** of the Wirral Way.

Keep going as far as a bridge where the cycle route circles right and passes beneath the bridge, to go forward along an estate road leading down into Parkgate. At **The Parade** (the seafront), turn left. This is always busy, and it may be safer if parties with young children dismount and walk to the far end of **Parkgate**. Either way, press on to the southern end of Parkgate and turn left as the road now climbs steadily to return to Point 4 above. Turn right, back onto the original route and retrace the outward ride.

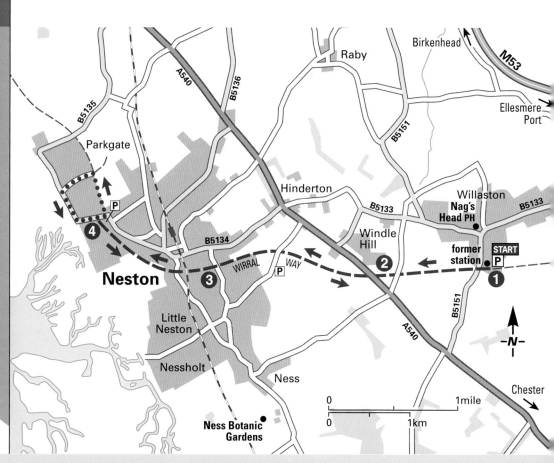

The Nag's Head

Built in 1733 and tucked away in the old part of Willaston, The Nag's Head is a welcoming pub to retreat to after the ride, with cushioned settles, comfy chairs and open log fires in the relaxing bars. In summer, the alfresco decking terrace with big benches and umbrellas provides a convivial setting for outdoor eating and drinking.

Food

Expect a straightforward pub menu offering snacks – ploughman's lunches and sandwiches – and main meals such as broccoli and cream-cheese bake, home-made steak and kidney pie, gammon steak and pineapple, and home-made curries.

Family facilities

There's a genuine welcome towards families and young children have their own menu.

Alternative refreshment stops

Pollards in Willaston and the Ship and the Red Lion on the Parade in Parkgate.

☛ Where to go from here

Discover how canals shaped Britain's heritage and see the world's largest collection of canal craft in a 200-year-old dock complex at the Boat Museum in Ellesmere Port (www.boatmuseum.org.uk). Ness Botanic Gardens overlooking the Dee estuary offer all round interest (www.nessgardens.org.uk), while the Blue Planet Aquarium near Ellesmere Port features two floors of interactive displays and an underwater moving walkway that takes you on a journey through the waters of the world. View huge sharks, deadly poisonous frogs and over 2,500 fish (www.blueplanetaquarium.com).

about the pub

The Nag's Head
Hooton Road, Willaston
Cheshire CH64 1SJ
Tel: 0151 327 2439

DIRECTIONS: in Willaston village centre on the B5133. Within walking distance of Hadlow Road Station

PARKING: 40

OPEN: daily; all day

FOOD: daily; all day until early evening

BREWERY/COMPANY: Enterprise Inns

REAL ALE: changing guest ales

A circuit outside Frodsham

WALK

A short and simple walk along the flanks of a red sandstone escarpment.

Sandstone Trail

Frodsham is at the northern end of the Sandstone Trail. The sandstone ridge that bounds the western edge of the Cheshire Plain is not continuous but does dominate the lowlands along much of its length. In a few places it breaks out into real crags, notably at Beeston, Frodsham and Helsby.

On Woodhouse Hill, near the southern end of the circuit, there was once a hill fort, probably dating back to the Iron Age. It can be hard to discern the remains now, though it's easier if you go in the winter when they're less obscured by vegetation. After a steep descent the walk returns along the base of the scarp then climbs up through Dunsdale Hollow to the base of the crags. Here you can return to the crest by a flight of steps, though there's an alternative for the adventurous in the steep scramble known to generations of Frodsham people as Jacob's Ladder. Above this the path passes more small crags, before emerging into the open at Mersey View, crowned by the village war memorial. As the name suggests, the grand curve of the Mersey is unmistakable. Hugging the nearer shore is the Manchester Ship Canal, joined almost directly below by the Weaver Navigation. Beyond it you can pick out Liverpool's airport and the city's two cathedrals.

the walk

1 Go right along the lane for 100yds (91m), then left down a sunken footpath and over a stile on to a **golf course**. The path is much older than the golf course and officially walkers have priority, but don't take it for granted! Head straight across and you'll arrive at the **17th tee**, where there's an arrow on a post. Drop down slightly to the right, to a footpath into the trees right of a

Frodsham's war memorial

1h10 — **3 MILES** — **4.8 KM** — **LEVEL 1 2 3**

MAP: OS Explorer 267 Northwich & Delamere Forest

START/FINISH: small car park on Beacon Hill, near Mersey View; grid ref: SJ 518766

PATHS: clear woodland paths, golf course, 4 stiles

LANDSCAPE: largely wooded steep slopes and gentler crest with a few open sections

PUBLIC TOILETS: in Frodsham village and at Castle Park

TOURIST INFORMATION: Runcorn, tel 01928 576776

THE PUB: The Ring O'Bells, Frodsham

❗ Generally suitable for all ages; a steep descent at Jacob's Ladder means that children will need to be closely controlled on this section.

Getting to the start

Frodsham, 2.5 miles (4km) south of Runcorn, and overlooking the Mersey Estuary, is easily reached from the M56 motorway and by rail (though it's quite a climb from the station to the start of the walk). The car park lies up a convoluted series of minor lanes, but it's easily figured out with the aid of a map.

green. Bear left at a sign for Woodhouse Hill, down a few steps. Keep to the left, passing above crags, then go down steps into **Dunsdale Hollow**.

2 Go left, rising gently, below more **crags**. Pass a stile on the right then go up scratched steps on the corner of the rocks ahead. Follow a level path through trees, near the edge of the golf course. Soon after this ends, the path rises slightly and passes a **bench** and after another 20yds (18m), the path forks. Keep straight on along the level path, soon passing a **Woodland Trust sign**, to a wider clearing with a signpost on the left near the corner of a field beyond.

3 Just before the corner of the field there's a break in a very overgrown **low wall** on the right, from which a narrow path slants steeply down the slope. There's some bare rock and it can be slippery

The view across Frodsham golf course towards Helsby

when wet, so it needs a little care. Near the bottom it turns directly downhill to the bottom of the wood. From a **gate**, go right along the base of the hill. After 800yds (732m) the path twists and descends a little into the bottom of **Dunsdale Hollow**. Cross this and go up the other side alongside a stone wall and up a flight of steps. Go right on a **sandy track**, climbing steadily then passing below a **steep rock face**.

4 Go left up steps, briefly rejoining the outward route. **Jacob's Ladder** is just to the left here, up the right-hand edge of the crags. When you reach the top, follow a sandy track, and then bear left at a signpost for **Mersey View**, with occasional Sandstone Trail markers, along the brink of the steeper slope. This passes below some small steep crags before emerging near the **war memorial**.

5 Turn right just at the memorial on a grassy footpath, aiming for **telecommunications towers** ahead. Go through the ornate **iron gates** on to the lane and turn right, back to the car park at the start of the walk.

what to look for

New red sandstone is about 200 million years old, which is fairly new in geological terms. It's a relatively soft rock, as you can see from the worn footholds of Jacob's Ladder. Curious knobbly shapes in some of the crags often result from wind erosion. Despite strenuous efforts at clearance, rhododendrons remain abundant in parts of the woods. Originating in the Himalayas, they are very hardy plants which frequently crowd out native species.

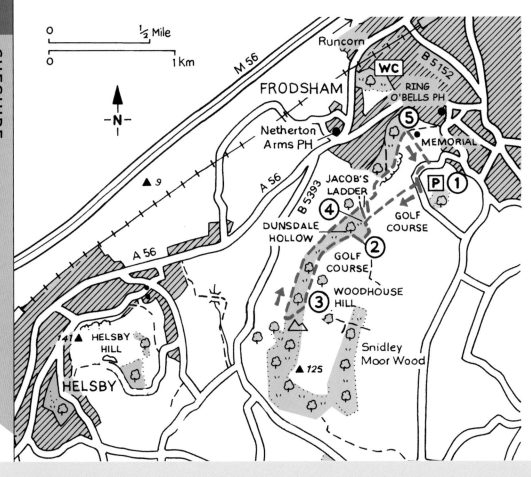

The Ring O'Bells

Rustic, white-painted 17th-century pub, festooned in summer with colourful hanging baskets, and pleasantly situated opposite the parish church. Three small, rambling rooms have antique settles, beams, dark oak panelling and stained glass, logs fires and lovely views over the church and the Mersey Plain. From a hatchway bar you can order pints of Black Sheep or the guest brew, and blackboard menus list some good-value lunchtime food. The secluded rear garden has a pond and plenty of shady trees for summer eating and drinking.

Food

Blackboards list sandwiches and filled baked potatoes and hearty walking fare such as steak and mushroom pie, Cumberland sausage and mash, and apple and blackberry crumble.

Family facilities

Children are welcome in the eating area of the bar only, where young children can choose from a standard children's menu.

Alternative refreshment stops

Also near the church in Frodsham is the Helter Skelter pub or you could try the Netherton Arms on the A56 between Frodsham and Helsby.

☛ Where to go from here

You can hardly ignore the chemical industry, especially from Mersey View, and you can find out a lot more about it at the Catalyst Science Discovery Centre near Widnes. Science and technology come alive through 100 interactive exhibits and hands-on displays (www.catalyst.org.uk). Just across the unmistakable Runcorn Bridge is Norton Priory Museum and Gardens (www.nortonpriory.org), where 38 acres (15.4ha) of peaceful woodland gardens provide the setting for the medieval priory remains, museum galleries and walled garden.

about the pub

The Ring O'Bells

Bellemont Road, Overton
Frodsham, Cheshire WA6 6BS
Tel: 01928 732068

DIRECTIONS: off B5152 at parish church sign; pub opposite Overton church	
PARKING: 20	
OPEN: daily	
FOOD: daily; lunchtime only	
BREWERY/COMPANY: Punch Taverns	
REAL ALE: two changing guest beers	
DOGS: allowed in the bar	

Tatton Park to Dunham Park

CYCLE

Link two great estates –
Tatton and Dunham – and
get the best of both worlds.

A pub and two parks

It is always fascinating to research pub names. They invariably tell a great deal about the surrounding communities and countryside. This route passes the Swan with Two Nicks (corrupted in some parts of England as the Swan with Two Necks, an improbable likelihood). The name comes from an association with the Vintners Company, founded in 1357 by importers of wine from Bordeaux. The company was incorporated by Henry VI (1422–1461) into one of the oldest of the Trade Guilds of London. Its symbol is a swan with two nicks on its beak. Then, as now, swans were the exclusive property of the Crown, but a Royal Gift was made to the Vintners, and each year the Vintners would put a nick on each side of the beak of cygnets to identify them as Vintner's swans.

The ride also links two of Britain's old estates, which offer a wealth of exploration and learning for all ages.

Tatton Park: the Mansion and Tudor Old Hall are set in 1,000 acres (405ha) of beautiful rolling parkland with lakes, tree-lined avenues and herds of deer. There are award-winning gardens, a working farm, play area, speciality shops and a superb programme of special events. There is plenty here to entertain the family, but there are extra charges for admission to the mansion, garden, farm or Tudor Old Hall.

Dunham Park: An early Georgian house built around a Tudor core, Dunham Massey was reworked in the early 20th century, to produce one of Britain's most sumptuous Edwardian interiors. It houses collections of 18th-century walnut furniture, paintings and Huguenot silver, as well as extensive servants' quarters. Here is one of the North West's great plantsman's gardens with richly planted borders and ancient trees, as well as an orangery, Victorian bark-house and well-house. The deer park contains beautiful avenues and ponds and a Tudor mill, originally used for grinding corn but refitted as a sawmill c.1860 and now restored to working order.

the ride

1 Leave the car park and ride out along the driveway to the **Rostherne Entrance** – keep an eye open for deer roaming in the park. Cross the road onto the **Cheshire Cycle Way West**, and ride on towards the village of Rostherne. Just on entering the village, turn left into **New Road**, climbing steeply for a short while, and then descending as it

The award-winning gardens in the grounds of Tatton Park

2h30 | **12.5 MILES** | **20 KM** | **LEVEL 1 2 3**

MAP: OS Explorer 267 Northwich and Delamere Forest and 276 Bolton, Wigan and Warrington

START/FINISH: Tatton Park (charge for admission); grid ref: SJ 741815

TRAILS/TRACKS: Outside Tatton Park, the route is entirely on minor roads, with a major A-road crossing (at lights)

LANDSCAPE: Cheshire farmland and two major estate parks

PUBLIC TOILETS: at Tatton Hall

TOURIST INFORMATION: Knutsford, tel 01565 632611

CYCLE HIRE: none locally

THE PUB: Swan with Two Nicks, Little Bollington

🛈 Two major A-road crossings, one using traffic lights

Getting to the start
The main entrance is at Rostherne. You can take the A50 from Knutsford, then branch onto the A5034 and then on to a minor road (signed for Tatton Park).

Why do this cycle ride?
The opportunity to link two of Cheshire's important estates should not be missed. The ride follows quiet lanes across farmland landscape and reaches a mill and weir on the edge of Dunham Park. Both parks have family attractions. The nearby village of Rostherne is a lovely community of brick houses with a few thatched cottages.

becomes **Cicely Mill Lane**, and leads out to a junction of two A-roads, near the **Swan Hotel** at Bucklow Hill. The easiest thing to do here is dismount and cross the two roads (at traffic lights) as a pedestrian.

2 Cross into **Chapel Lane**, initially a long, straight road, leading to Hulseheath. Keep on, riding round bends, and then turn right into **Back Lane**. At a junction go left into Thowler Lane, and at the next junction, bear right for Bollington, along **Boothbank Lane**.

3 On reaching **Booth Bank**, keep forward into **Reddy Lane** (signed for Bollington and Dunham Massey). Descend a little to pass beneath the M56 motorway, and then climbing around bends. The road eventually straightens and leads out to meet the A56, opposite a pub.

4 Cross the road with care, going left and then immediately right into **Park Lane**. Continue past the **Swan with Two Nicks** pub, to the end of the surfaced lane, where a narrow bridge crosses the **River Bollin**.

5 At **Bollington Mill**, go forward, but as the road bends left leave it by branching right onto a fenced and tree-lined path into **Dunham Park**.

6 Retrace the outward route. Avoid tempting alternative routes, as **Bucklow Hill** is the safest place to cross the Chester Road (A556).

The 18th-century Dunham Massey Hall

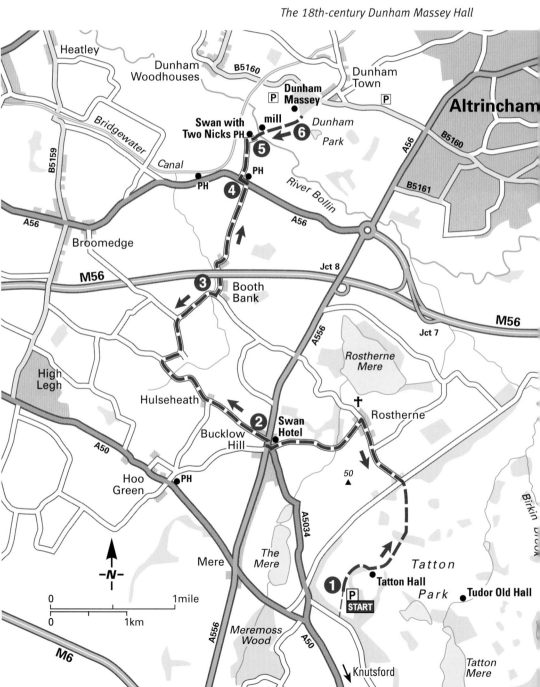

Swan with Two Nicks

Tucked away in a tiny hamlet close to Dunham Hall deer park, this distinctive, smartly refurbished pub is a real find and a super place for refreshments on this ride. Welcoming features include heavy ceiling beams, lovely antique settles, roaring winter log fires, while gleaming brass and copper artefacts and a wealth of bric-a-brac decorate the bars. There's also good seating in the patio garden, freshly prepared pub food, decent wines and three real ales on handpump.

Food

Typically, tuck into filled baguettes, various omelettes, sandwiches and salads at lunchtime, with main menu dishes including a hearty steak and ale pie, sausages and mash, grilled gammon and egg, and a range of pasta dishes.

Family facilities

A good welcome awaits families as children are allowed throughout the pub. Half portions of main meals are provided and there's a children's menu for younger family members.

Alternative refreshment stops

Stables Restaurant at Tatton Park serves hot meals, snacks and hot or cold drinks.

☛ Where to go from here

Take a closer look at Tatton Park, one of England's most complete historic estates (www.nationaltrust.org.uk), or visit nearby Tabley House, west of Knutsford, (www.tableyhouse.co.uk), the finest Palladian house in the North West, which holds the first great collection of English

about the pub

Swan with Two Nicks
Little Bollington, Altrincham
Cheshire WA14 4TJ
Tel: 0161 928 2914

DIRECTIONS: Little Bollington is signposted off the A56 between Lymm and the M56. The pub is in the village centre at the halfway point of the ride

PARKING: 80

OPEN: daily; all day

FOOD: daily; all day Sunday

BREWERY/COMPANY: free house

REAL ALE: Timothy Taylor Landlord, Greene King Old Speckled Hen, Swan with Two Nicks Bitter

pictures ever made, and furniture by Chippendale, Gillow and Bullock. Further afield is Jodrell Bank Visitor Centre (www.jb.man.ac.uk), where a pathway leads you 180 degrees around the massive Lovell radio telescope as it surveys the Universe. There's also an arboretum, and a 3-D theatre explores the solar system.

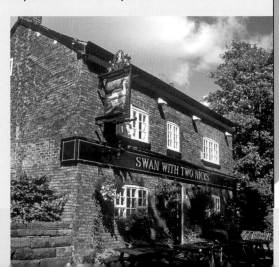

Flash Village

Rogues, vagabonds and counterfeiters meet the righteous in England's highest village.

Flash

At an altitude of 1,518ft (463m), the village of Flash proclaims itself as the 'Highest Village in Britain', and at this elevation winter comes early and lingers past the point where spring has visited its lower neighbours. Winters here can be cold. Once, during wartime, it got so cold that the vicar had icicles on his ears when he ventured from his house to the church. On another occasion a visiting minister arrived by motorcycle. The congregation were surprised to see him because heavy snow was imminent. They told him to watch for it falling at the window opposite his pulpit and that, should he see any, he should stop the service and depart immediately. Just after he left, it started to snow and within 20 minutes the village was cut off.

Despite being a devout community, Flash also has the dubious honour of giving its name to sharp practice. The terms 'flash money' and 'flash company' entered the English language as a consequence of events in Flash. A group of peddlers living near the village, travelled the country hawking ribbons, buttons and goods made in nearby Leek. Known as 'Flash men' they initially paid for their goods with hard cash but after establishing credit, vanished with the goods and moved on to another supplier. Their name became associated with ne'er-do-wells in taverns, who helped people drink their money and were never seen again.

Flash money on the other hand was counterfeit, manufactured in the 18th century by a local gang using button presses. They were captured when a servant girl exposed them. Some of the gang members were hanged at Chester.

the walk

1 Walk through the village, pass the **pub** and an old **chapel**. Turn right at a footpath sign and head towards the last house. Go over a stile, turn right and follow the path over two walls. Veer left towards a gate in the corner of the field to a lane

what to look for

Look for evidence of the network of packhorse trails on the moors covered by this walk. These ancient routes were used from medieval times to transport goods between communities. Packhorse trains could have anything up to 50 horses and were led by a man called a 'jagger' (their ponies were Galloway cross breeds called Jaegers). Today you will find their paved routes across the moors, descending into the valleys in distinctive 'hollow ways' or sunken lanes. Jaggers drove their hard-working beasts across the moors until the early 19th century, when canal transport.

4h00	6 MILES	9.7 KM	LEVEL 1 2 3

MAP: OS Explorer OL24 White Peak

START/FINISH: Flash village; parking on roadside near school, grid ref SK 026672

PATHS: some on road but mostly footpaths which can be boggy in wet weather. Around 35 stiles and gates

LANDSCAPE: hills, moorland and meadows

PUBLIC TOILETS: none on route

TOURIST INFORMATION: Buxton, tel 01298 25106

THE PUB: Travellers' Rest, Flash, see Directions to the pub

❶ The route explores a relatively remote area of the National Park and should not be attempted in bad weather, especially in low cloud or mist. Suitable for adventurous older children/family groups

Getting to the start

The village of Flash is off the A53 between Buxton and Leek. Drive south from Buxton for just over 4 miles (6.4km) passing the Travellers' Rest pub on your left. In a further 0.25 mile (400m), fork right on to a minor road to Flash. Park with care on the roadside before the school.

between walls. Follow this for 200yds (183m) then turn left at a waymarker along another walled track.

2 Continue through a gate then follow the waymarker right and uphill to **Wolf Edge**. Pass the rocks, veer left downhill over a stile and across heather moorland. Cross a stile on the right and continue downhill to a marker post. Cross the wall, then a bridge and turn left on to the road. Where the road forks keep right and continue through **Knotbury** then, after the last house on the left (Knotbury Lea), take the path on the left. Walk beside a wall. Where this bends left, go ahead and bear right to two nearby stiles. Turn left beside the fence past the second stile to find another stile, then go ahead on a path through heather to a further stile.

3 Follow the path down across moorland to join a ledged path through gnarled oakwoods before dropping on to a sandy bridleway. Turn left, veer right off the track at the next waymarker along a narrow path that leads to a stony farm lane. Turn left along this. At a bend beyond an open

Rushton Spencer at the western edge of the Peak District National Park

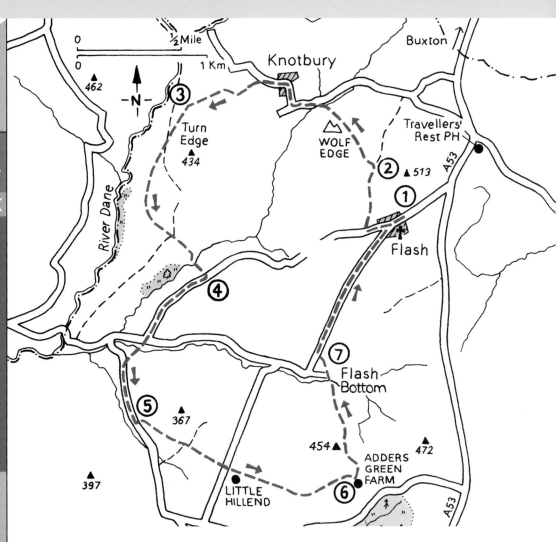

gateway leave this lane at a fingerpost along a faint green field road. Cross a stile then keep straight ahead at the next signpost. Follow this track until it crosses a hidden bridge over a stream (look carefully left for this), then climb steeply uphill to a barn and a lane.

4 Turn right. At the junction, turn right then left through a gap stile. Go downhill, over a bridge then uphill, following the path gradually left across the field to a gap stile. Here, turn left up the road and pass a house.

5 Go left at the next fingerpost, following the waymarked path to a farm track. At farm buildings go through a gate then fork

right. Continue on to reach the road, cross it then continue on the path through **Little Hillend**. Follow this waymarked path to **Adders Green Farm**.

6 Turn left through a gate signed to **Flash Bottom** and alongside a wall. At the end of the wall turn left, follow the wall, cross a gate then follow the path round the foot of the hill. Aim to pass left of the small plantation, cross a flat bridge to a small gate, turn left and go over a stile into a farm drive.

7 Cross a stile opposite, follow the path over a field and up steps left of the house to the road. Turn right and walk this quiet road back up to **Flash**.

Travellers' Rest

The Travellers' Rest, one of the highest pubs in England, is set back from the main road and enjoys grand views to the nearby moorland gritstone edges and across rolling pastures to the White Peak. Built of local stone some 250 years ago, it's a rambling place with a warren of small rooms leading off a central wooden bar. Expect heavy beams, grand old fireplaces with blazing log fires, and old tables and chairs. The walls are covered with clocks, and shelves and windowsills display old scales and stone jars, while ceilings are hung with farming implements and horse tack. Walkers and families can be assured of a warm welcome.

Food

All meals are home cooked using fresh local produce whenever possible. Pub favourites include fish and chips and steak and Guinness pie, with daily blackboard dishes like beef in port and Stilton, liver and bacon in red wine, and mango and ginger chicken. Lighter lunchtime snacks are available.

Family facilities

Children are welcome and they will love the museum-like interior. There's a standard children's menu and on fine days you can make use of the patio which offers extensive valley views.

Alternative refreshment stops

The New Inn in Flash village centre or drive north to Buxton where there are plenty of options.

about the pub

Travellers' Rest
Flash, Quarnford, Buxton
Derbyshire SK17 0SN
Tel 01298 23695

DIRECTIONS: the pub is beside the A53, a mile (1.6km) from Flash village and the start of the walk

PARKING: 40

OPEN: all day Saturday and Sunday, closed Monday

FOOD: daily (except Monday)

BREWERY/COMPANY: free house

REAL ALE: Tetley, Marston's Pedigree and Hartington IPA

DOGS: welcome on a lead

☞ Where to go from here

After the walk take a short pony trek (over 8s only) from Northfield Farm in Flash village. You must book in advance for this (www.northfieldfarm.co.uk), or visit the former spa town of Buxton (www.visitbuxton.co.uk).

Mam Tor and Rushup Edge

Approaching from the Edale side, discover the ancient secrets of the great 'Shivering Mountain'.

The 'Shivering Mountain'

With its spectacular views and close proximity to the road it's hardly surprising that Mam Tor is the most popular of the Peak District hill forts. Unfortunately this popularity has resulted in the National Trust having to pave the footpath and a large area around the summit to prevent serious erosion.

Called the Shivering Mountain because of the instability of its shale layers, Mam Tor is the largest of the Peak's hill forts and has the distinction of being the only one to be excavated. In the mid-1960s Manchester University selected Mam Tor as a training site for its archaeology students and this produced a wealth of fresh information about the fort. What can be seen today are the ramparts of a heavily fortified Iron-Age settlement. The single rampart with an outer ditch and another bank can still be traced round the hillside. There were two entrances, one leading to the path from Hollins Cross and the other to the path

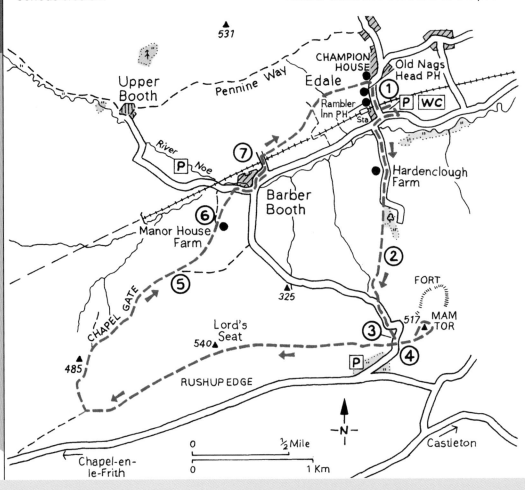

to Mam Nick. Mam Tor was probably a partially defended site with a timber palisade that was later replaced with stone.

The excavations revealed that there had been a settlement here long before the Iron Age. Two Early Bronze-Age barrows were discovered on the summit, one of which the National Trust has capped in stone to make sure it is preserved. An earlier settlement on the ground enclosed by the ramparts was excavated. Here several circular houses or huts had been built on terraced platforms on the upper slopes of the hill. The pottery and other artefacts uncovered are of a style often found in house platforms of this type and date from the Late Bronze Age. Radiocarbon dating of charcoal found in the huts put them somewhere between 1700 and 1000 BC.

Archaeologists, GDB Jones and FH Thomson, writing about the discoveries at Mam Tor, suggested that the fort might have been built as a shelter for pastoralists using the hills for summer grazing, but decided in the end that it was more likely to have had a strategic military purpose. Depending on when it was actually built, it could have seen action during inter-tribal struggles of the native Brigantes. It may well at a later period have been used as a strategic defence against the advancing Romans. Like most settlements from this far back in time Mam Tor will probably never reveal all its secrets, but standing on the summit and looking away down the valleys on either side, back along the path to Hollins Cross or forward to Rushup Edge it's enough just to try and imagine the effort that went into building such an enormous fortification with nothing but the most primitive of tools.

MAP: OS Explorer OL1 Dark Peak

START/FINISH: good public car park at Edale, grid ref SK 124853

PATHS: mainly good but can be boggy in wet weather, 15 stiles and gates

LANDSCAPE: woodland, hills and meadows

PUBLIC TOILETS: at car park

TOURIST INFORMATION: Edale, tel 01433 670207

THE PUB: The Rambler Inn, Hope Valley, near the start of the walk

❶ To be tackled by older, fitter children. There is a long and fairly arduous stretch near the start of this route.

Getting to the start

From Sheffield take the A625 and follow the brown tourist signs for the caverns at Castleton. At Hope, turn right for Edale opposite the church; in 5 miles (8km) turn right into the main car park at Edale. The adjoining Edale Station is served by regular trains on the Sheffield to Manchester line.

Mam Tor

DERBYSHIRE

the walk

1 Exit the car park entrance at **Edale** and turn right on to the road past a phone box. In 200yds (183m) turn left along a farm road for Hardenclough Farm. Just before this road turns sharply left take the public footpath that forks off to the right and goes uphill through a wood.

2 At the end of the wooded area cross a stile and continue uphill. Cross another stile, follow the path across open hillside, then cross yet another stile and turn left on to the road. Just before the road bends sharply left, cross the road, go over a stile and follow this path towards a hill.

3 Near the foot of the hill cross the stile to the left and turn right on to the road. Continue to find the steps on the left leading through the ramparts of an Iron-Age fort to the summit of **Mam Tor**. From here retrace your steps back to the road.

what to look for

Look out over Edale from Rushup Edge to Kinder Scout, scene of a mass trespass by ramblers in 1932. They were exercising what they saw to be their right to roam the hills and moors. Several were jailed and the severity of their sentences made them martyrs and heroes. Many people today believe that this act is what led ultimately to the creation of national parks.

4 Cross the road, go over a stile and continue on the footpath uphill and on to **Rushup Edge**. Follow this well-defined path along the ridge crossing five stiles. When the path is intersected by another, go right. This is **Chapel Gate** track, badly eroded by off-road motorbikes. Go through a kissing gate then head downhill.

5 Near the bottom of the hill go through a gap stile on the left. Go through another stile, join a raised path and go through a handgate, then cross another stile on the left. This leads to some tumbledown buildings. Cross over a stile by the corner of one building then veer right and cross another stile on to a rough farm road.

6 Cross this diagonally and follow the path beside a brook. Cross this and walk through to a lane. Turn right, then left at the junction. Cross the bridge and fork ahead on to the lane through the hamlet of **Barber Booth**. Near the far end fork left up a gated, rough lane signposted for Edale Station.

7 Follow the path across a series of meadows, going through several gates and stiles to join the road to Edale Station next to **Champion House**. Turn right on to the road then, near the junction, turn left into the car park.

Above: A view over the Peak District from Mam Tor

The Rambler Inn

The Rambler is a thriving pub which welcomes walkers, cyclists and the countless day visitors that descend on this beautiful area. Built of honey-coloured gritstone, with gables and large windows, it stands in its own grounds at the bottom of Edale's one village road. From the lawned gardens, with mature trees, there are stunning views down the valley of the River Noe. Inside, three airy rooms have high ceilings, reflecting the Rambler's Victorian origins, and a mix of flagstone, quarry tiled and carpeted floors. The comfortable furnishings consist of a mix of lived-in old wing armchairs, wooden seats and chairs and a mish-mash of tables. Blazing winter log fires in each room draw weary walkers in for Grays ales and traditional pub food.

about the pub

The Rambler Inn
Hope Valley, Edale
Derbyshire S33 7ZA
Tel 01433 670268.
www.theramblerinn.co.uk

DIRECTIONS: next to Edale Station and near the main village car park– see Getting to the start

PARKING: 20

OPEN: daily, all day

FOOD: all day

BREWERY/COMPANY: free house

REAL ALE: Grays Best, Premium and L S Lowry Bitter, guest beer

DOGS: on a lead in the bar only

ROOMS: 9 bedrooms

Family facilities
Children are welcome in the pub away from the bar area and can choose from a standard children's menu. On sunny summer days they can enjoy the spacious gardens and let off steam in the large activity playground.

Alternative refreshment stops
Café near Edale Station, also Old Nags Head pub in Edale.

☛ Where to go from here
Treak Cliff Cavern in Castleton is the main source of the famous Blue John stone, unique to this Derbyshire village (www.bluejohnstone.com).

Food
The menus offer traditional pub food ranging from large ploughman's lunches, sandwiches and basic pub snacks, to lamb chops, chips and peas, haddock and chips, and a mammoth Ramblers' Grill.

Pilsbury Castle and the Upper Dove Valley

Hartington

DERBYSHIRE/STAFFORDSHIRE

The upper valley of the Dove is one of quiet villages and historic remains.

Hartington and Pilsbury Castle

Hartington, lying in the mid-regions of the Dove Valley, is a prosperous village with fine 18th-century houses and hotels built in local limestone and lined around spacious greens. The settlement's history can be traced back to the Normans, when it was recorded as Hartedun, the centre for the De Ferrier's estate. Hartington Hall, now the youth hostel, was first built in 1350 but was substantially rebuilt in 1611.

As you leave the village, the lane climbs past the church of St Giles, which has a splendid battlemented Perpendicular tower. It continues up the high valley sides of the Dove and on through an emerald landscape of high fields and valley.

Pilsbury Castle hides until the last moment, but then a grassy ramp swoops down to it from the hillsides. Only the earthworks are now visible, but you can imagine its impregnable position on a limestone knoll that juts out into the valley. You can see the motte, a man-made mound built to accommodate the wooden keep, and the bailey, a raised embankment that would have had a wooden stockade round it. The castle's exact history is disputed. It was probably built around 1100 by the Normans, on the site of an Iron-Age fort. It may have been a stronghold used earlier by William I to suppress a local rebellion in his 'Wasting of the North' campaign. Being in the middle of the De Ferrier estate it was probably their administrative centre. In the 1200s this function moved to Hartington.

what to look for

The Dairy Crest Creamery is one of only a few places which are licensed to make Stilton Cheese. There's a visitor centre in Hartington, where you can sample and buy. Look too for Hartington Hall, an impressive three-gabled manor house, now the youth hostel (see photo).

Views up-valley are fascinating with the conical limestone peaks of Parkhouse and Chrome Hills in the distance. Now the route descends into Dovedale for the first time, crossing the river into Staffordshire. The lane climbs to a high lane running the length of the dale's east rim. Note the change in the rock – it's now the darker gritstone. The crags of Sheen Hill initially block the view east, but once past them you will be able to see for miles, across the Manifold Valley to the Roaches and Hen Cloud beyond. A field path takes the route on its finale, descending along a line of crags with lofty views of Hartington and the end of the walk.

the walk

1 Turn left out of the car park and follow the lane to the right beside the village green. Turn left up **Hide Lane** by the **church** and take the second path on the left in 600yds (549m), just past a large modern barn. This heads northwards across fields. Below a farm complex, the path swings left to follow a dry-stone wall on the left.

2 The path cuts down the concrete drive coming up the hill from **Bank Top Farm**. Waymarking posts highlight the continuing route along the high valley sides, about 50yds (45m) up from the break of slope.

Hartington Hall dates from 1611 and is now a youth hostel

3h30 — **7.5 MILES** — **12.1 KM** — **LEVEL 1 2 3**

3 West of **Carder Low** (grid ref 126627) the path goes through a gateway by an intersection of walls and becomes indistinct. Here, climb half right to another gateway, then head for a group of trees. Below these another footpath signpost shows the way uphill and half right to a step stile in a ridge wall, where you look down into a small valley.

4 Descend into the valley and turn left at a fingerpost for **Pilsbury** and Crowdecote to reach a lane by a stone barn. A stile across the road allows you on to the continuing path, rounding the high slopes above Pilsbury. The footpath rakes left down the hill slopes to a farm track and wall alongside the ancient earthworks of **Pilsbury Castle**. Go through the stile here.

5 Turn right along the path, which takes a well-used course heading up the valley, gradually losing height to join the valley floor. Cross straight over a rough, walled field track. The path develops into a farm track; remain with this past **Bridge End Farm** to reach **Crowdecote** and the **Packhorse Inn**.

6 Retrace your steps to Bridge End Farm. Beside the barn look right for a footbridge across the **Dove** (there's a hidden fingerpost, left). Walk ahead up the field.

7 The path steepens up the valley side. After a walker's gate veer right, away from the wall, climbing up through scrub to reach the Longnor road. Turn left along the lane to reach **Harris Close Farm** in 2 miles (3.2km).

Right: The hamlet of Pilsbury

MAP: OS Explorer OL24 White Peak
START/FINISH: Hartington pay car park, grid ref SK 127603
PATHS: field paths and lanes, some steep climbs, about 32 stiles and gates
LANDSCAPE: pastures, limestone valley
PUBLIC TOILETS: at car park
TOURIST INFORMATION: Ashbourne, tel 01335 343666
THE PUB: The Packhorse Inn, Crowdecote, see Point 5 on route
❶ This is a long walk with several ascents and is best suited to older children

Getting to the start
From Buxton take the A515 south towards Ashbourne. Pass the Jug and Glass Inn and then look for the right turn on the B5054 for Hartington.

8 Turn into the drive and look immediately on the right for a narrow passage right of the low barn. This leads to a fieldside path. In all but one field there's a wall on the right for guidance. After going through a wood, in 50yds (45m) the path descends through scrub into the valley. It joins a farm track southwards towards **Bridge End Farm**.

9 At the fingerpost for **Hartington**, turn left through a gate and cross a field. Cross the **Dove** by a footbridge hidden by trees. The path gradually swings right (south east) across fields, aims for the woods to the left of the dairy and enters them via a stile. At the other side go into the forecourt of the dairy and turn left along the lane to return to **Hartington**.

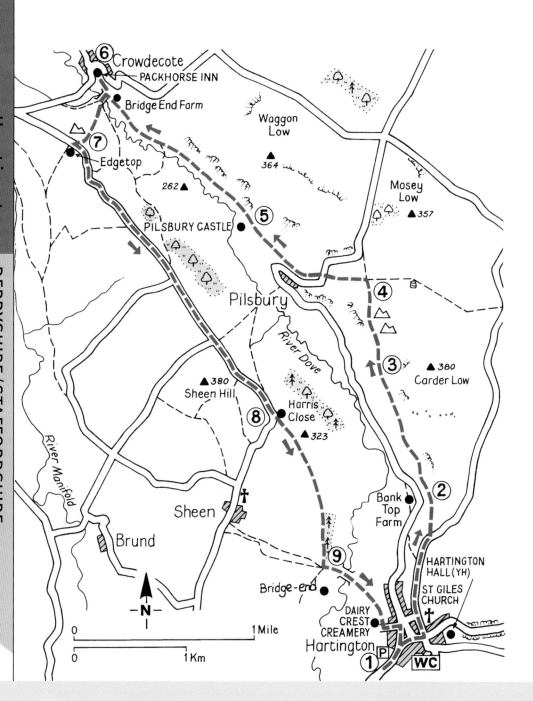

The Packhorse Inn

Crowdecote consists of a huddle of cottages and farms clinging to a steep hillside above the juvenile River Dove. Tucked away in this hamlet is the 300-year-old Packhorse Inn, once frequented by trains of packhorses and their overseers, the jaggers. Although the little interconnecting rooms have been updated over the years they retain some of their original character, with solid beams, stone walls and open fires. With Timothy Taylor Landlord on tap, decent pies and sandwiches on the menu, and a terraced lawn rising up behind with views to the steep slopes of the Dove Valley, this homely, unassuming little pub makes a great halfway stop.

Food
From a weekly changing menu choose starters such as red mullet and cod fishcakes or a bowl of *moules* with crusty bread, or tuck into something more substantial like home-made steak and Guinness pie. There is a good sandwich menu.

Family facilities
On fine sunny days the terraced garden, with the added attractions of ducks and chickens, is the place to be. Inside, children can choose from their own menu, or order a small portion of many of the dishes featured on the main menu.

about the pub

The Packhorse Inn
Crowdecote, Buxton
Derbyshire SK17 0DB
Tel 01298 83618

DIRECTIONS: on Point 5 of the route, see Getting to the start, in the centre of Crowdecote off the A515 north west of Hartington
PARKING: 20
OPEN: all day Saturday and Sunday, Easter to September. Closed Monday, except Bank Holidays when it closes on Tuesday instead
FOOD: daily
BREWERY/COMPANY: free house
REAL ALE: Worthington Cask, Timothy Taylor Landlord, guest beer
DOGS: welcome throughout pub
ROOMS: 2 bedrooms

Alternative refreshment stops
The Charles Cotton Hotel in Hartington (free house).

☞ Where to go from here
Poole's Cavern in Buxton Country Park offers guided tours of the illuminated chambers and their amazing crystal formations (www.poolescavern.co.uk).

CYCLE

Long Dale

DERBYSHIRE

Long Dale and the White Peak

From the Tissington Trail on to peaceful backroads near Hartington, returning via Long Dale and the new Pennine Bridleway.

Fossils

The main reason for building the railway on what is now the High Peak Trail was to move limestone from quarries to canals and lowland railways. The line itself burrows through cuttings and across embankments of limestone, and embedded in the limestone you'll find fossils of the creatures that lived in the shallow tropical seas that covered this area 300 million years ago. The most recognisable are the remains of crinoids. These were a kind of primitive starfish that attached themselves to rocks by a cord made up of small segments. It is these that you'll find in blocks and slabs of limestone, often in great numbers and looking like the mixed up contents of a necklace box. Belemnites are another fossil that are also found in numbers here. The fossil is that of the shell and looks very like a bullet casing!

On warm and sunny summer days stop for a break in Long Dale and take a close look at the limestone walls, where you may be lucky enough to catch a glimpse of a common lizard basking in the heat. Only about 4in (10cm) long, they're very agile and the slightest movement will see them disappear into the wall crevices and cracks they call home.

the ride

1 From **Parsley Hay** head south along the **High Peak Trail**. The firm, level surface means you can concentrate on the views as much as the way ahead – but look out for walkers and horse riders, as this is a multi-user trail.

2 In a short distance the route forks; keep right here, joining the **Tissington Trail**, the former trackbed of the line down to Ashbourne. Passing through a deep cutting, the trail emerges to reveal good views across towards the Staffordshire Moors. Shortly, to your left, the distinct hill is **Lean Low**, the burial site of our distant forefathers – a tumulus, or burial mound, was found on this windswept summit. The trail sweeps close to **Hartington-moor Farm** before crossing a bridge and reaching the former **Hartington Station**.

3 Take time to explore the site here before continuing south – and start counting the bridges. At the **seventh bridge** – three over you, four that you cross – you need to dismount and wheel your bike down the footpath on the right. There's a **barn** and trees off to the right and an old **quarry** to the left as additional locator points (if you reach the main road on your left you've gone too far). This drops to a quiet lane bound for **Biggin-by-Hartington** and is now your route to the left, a long and very gentle climb between the characteristic walled pastures and hay meadows of this fertile plateau. Cresting a low ridge, splendid views open out across the western Peak District and ahead to **Biggin**.

4 To visit **Biggin** itself you can divert right along **Drury Lane** to find the village shop and the **Waterloo Inn** (to return to the main route just pass by the pub on your right, the main route then comes in from the left at a junction). The main route avoids the village and descends to a couple of sharp bends at **Cotterill Farm** before reaching a junction. Keep ahead here (the village option rejoins here) to and straight through the next junction (pond on the right). An easy, all-but-level stretch ends with a narrow descent down **Harding's Lane** to a junction with the B5054.

5 Take great care crossing here; it's easiest to cycle down the main road a few yards to allow a clear view of traffic before crossing into the lane directly opposite. This is the start of a delightful, easy ascent along the valley floor of **Long Dale**. The lane meanders lazily beneath limestone crags and screes, imperceptibly rising for about 2 miles (3.2km) where a lane joins from the left. Ignore this and keep ahead, passing **Vincent House Farm** to a junction. You can turn right here to return to Parsley Hay, but continuing along the main lane allows you to visit a fine country pub.

6 The lane continues to rise gently, soon leaving the dale behind, unveiling views across the Staffordshire moorlands. Ignore the next turn right and continue to a crossroads at **High Needham**. Here turn right along an undulating road to reach the **Royal Oak** pub at **Hurdlow**, which is adjacent to the **High Peak Trail**. Pick up the Trail beyond the old **railway bridge** and head south to return the last 2 miles (3.2km) to **Parsley Hay**.

CYCLE

MAP: OS Explorer OL24 White Peak

START/FINISH: Parsley Hay on the High Peak Trail, grid ref SK147637

TRAILS/TRACKS: partly along the High Peak, then Tissington trails and along usually quiet minor roads.

LANDSCAPE: the route winds across the limestone plateau of the White Peak and includes an easy ride up a superb, shallow limestone dry-valley.

PUBLIC TOILETS: at Parsley Hay

TOURIST INFORMATION: Bakewell, tel 01629 813227

CYCLE HIRE: Derbyshire County Council centre at Parsley Hay, tel 01298 84493 www.derbyshire.gov.uk/countryside

THE PUB: The Royal Oak, Hurdlow, see point 6 on route

❶ One crossing of the B5054 near Hartington requires particular care. Walkers and horse-riders also use the High Peak Trail. Suitable for family groups who have some experience with on-road cycling, best tackled by older children

Getting to the start

Parsley Hay Centre is on the High Peak Trail and is signposted off the A515 Buxton to Ashbourne road. There is a pay car park here.

Why do this cycle ride?

A good mix of railway trackbed and some quiet by-roads that thread between stone villages, make this an easy ride on the White Peak's limestone plateau. With glimpses into some of the deeper dales, your main preoccupation may be in identifying some of the knolls and hills that form a wide horizon, while Long Dale is an enchanting stretch up a valley with wild flowers in the summer.

Long Dale

DERBYSHIRE

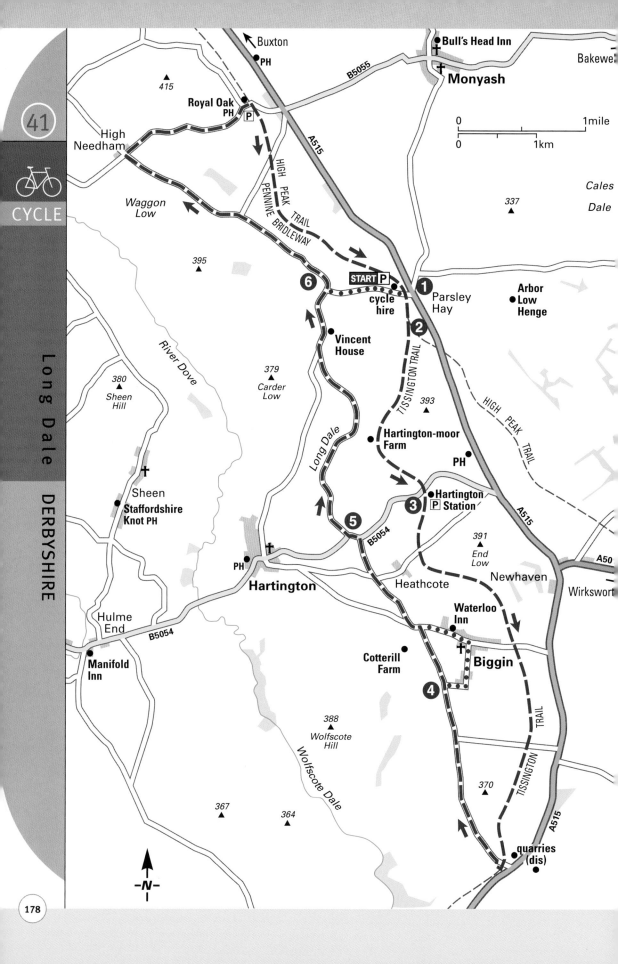

Buxton

PH

▲ 415

Royal Oak
PH
P

High
Needham

*Waggon
Low*

HIGH PEAK PENNINE BRIDLEWAY

TRAIL

A515

B5055

Bull's Head Inn

Monyash

Bakewe

*Cales
Dale*

▲ 337

0   1mile
0   1km

▲ 395

6

START P

1

*cycle
hire*

Parsley
Hay

**Arbor
Low
Henge**

2

River Dove

Vincent
House

379
▲
*Carder
Low*

380 ▲
*Sheen
Hill*

Long Dale

TISSINGTON TRAIL

393
▲

Hartington-moor
Farm

PH

HIGH PEAK TRAIL

A50

✝
Sheen
**Staffordshire
Knot PH**

5

✝
PH

Hartington

Hulme
End
B5054

▲
**Manifold
Inn**

B5054

3
P

Hartington
Station

Heathcote

391 ▲
*End
Low*

Newhaven

A515

Wirkswort

Waterloo
Inn

✝
Biggin

Cotterill
Farm

4

388
▲
*Wolfscote
Hill*

370 ▲

TISSINGTON   TRAIL

A515

Wolfscote Dale

367 ▲

364 ▲

quarries
(dis)

–N–

Royal Oak

about the pub

Royal Oak
Hurdlow, Buxton
Derbyshire SK17 9QJ
Tel 01298 83288

DIRECTIONS: from Parsley Hay car park turn left to the A515. Turn left towards Buxton. In about 1.75 miles (2.8km) turn left towards Longnor. The Royal Oak is just across the railway bridge next to the Hurdlow car park on the High Peak Trail

PARKING: 30

OPEN: daily, all day

FOOD: daily, all day

BREWERY/COMPANY: free house

REAL ALE: Bass, Marston's Pedigree, guest beer

Just as it did when it was built some 200 years ago, the Royal Oak continues to serve railway users, although today it provides welcome refreshment to weary walkers and cyclists tackling the High Peak Trail, a 17-mile (27km) route that follows the old trackbed. (There are cycle lock up and securing posts in the car park.) From the outside it may look a little time-worn but inside it's a fine place, with simply furnished rooms on several levels, two bars and a dining area, all with great views of the surrounding countryside. A blazing log fire in a grand stone fireplace warms the lounge bar in winter. Brass jugs, copper kettles and horsebrasses hang from the beams, while in the lounge the walls are decorated with old golf clubs and country paintings. There is a cellar pool room.

Food

From a standard menu you can order fresh cod and chips, loin of pork with apple sauce, beef and Stilton pie, salmon and broccoli pasta, curries, hot rolls and filled jacket potatoes. Blackboard daily specials favour fresh fish dishes.

Family facilities

Older children can make good use of the pool table in the cellar. Children of all ages are very welcome throughout the pub and younger ones have their own standard menu to choose from. Good summer alfresco seating on two grassy areas, both with country views.

Alternative refreshment stops

There are pubs at Biggin (Waterloo Inn), Sparklow (Royal Oak); snacks at Parsley Hay; several pubs and cafés in Hartington, just off the route.

☞ Where to go from here

Arbor Low Henge, a major Neolithic site near to Parsley Hay, is a significant stone circle although the stones are now lying flat. Small charge for entry.

Along the Tissington Trail

An easy ride from the Tissington estate village along an old railway line above the secluded valley of the Bletch Brook.

Dew Ponds

Once beyond the old station at Alsop, one feature of the landscape you'll notice along the route are the occasional small ponds in the pastures – these are dew ponds. The name comes from the belief that morning dew would provide sufficient water for cattle and sheep to drink. In days gone by these would be hollows dug out and lined with clay to stop the water from draining away. As this is an area where the rock is predominantly porous limestone, rainwater seeps away and surface water is very rare. The modern-day versions are watertight and they don't rely on dew, either, as they are regularly topped up by the farmers.

Summertime on the Tissington Trail sees a profusion of butterflies. The Common Blue is one of the most noticeable. This very small insect feeds largely on clover flowers and the bright yellow flowers of bird's foot trefoil, a low-growing plant that flourishes in limestone areas. Another butterfly to look out for is the colourful Red Admiral which lays its eggs on nettles, the food plant of the caterpillar.

the ride

1 The Tissington car park is at the site of the old railway station. Take time to find the information board which has a fine picture of the place in its heyday. There's also a village information board here; the village centre is only a short cycle away and it's well worth taking the loop before starting out. Turn left from the car park entrance, then right along **Chapel Lane**. This passes one of the five wells that are dressed in the village during the famous Well Dressing Ceremony held in May on Ascension Day. The lane rises gently to a junction at the top of the village. Turn left to drop down the main street, lined by greens and passing **Tissington Hall** and more wells. At the bottom keep left, passing the village pond before swinging right to return to the car park. Here turn left, passing beneath a bridge to join the old trackbed, which starts a long, easy climb.

2 This initial stretch is through a wooded cutting, soon shallowing to offer the occasional view through the trees across the glorious countryside here at the southern end of the National Park. The panorama sweeps across the peaceful valley of the **Bletch Brook** to take in the high ridge of rough pastures above **Ballidon** to the right.

3 The first natural place to turn around to return to Tissington is the car park and picnic area at the **former Alsop Station**. This would make a round trip of 6 miles (9.7km) and take perhaps 1.5 hours – and it's downhill virtually all the way back!

| 3h30 | 16 MILES | 25.7 KM | LEVEL 1 2 3 |

SHORTER ALTERNATIVE ROUTE

| 1h30 | 6 MILES | 9.7 KM | LEVEL 1 2 3 |

MAP: OS Explorer OL24 White Peak

START/FINISH POINT: Tissington Old Station, grid ref SK 177520

TRAILS/TRACKS: old railway trackbed, lanes in Tissington village

LANDSCAPE: limestone plateau of the White Peak, extensive views

PUBLIC TOILETS: Tissington and Hartington old stations

TOURIST INFORMATION: Ashbourne, tel 01335 343666

CYCLE HIRE: Peak Cycle Hire, Mapleton Lane, Ashbourne, Derbyshire, tel 01335 343156, www.peakdistrict.org

THE PUB: Bluebell Inn, Tissington, see Directions to the pub, page 119

Getting to the start

Tissington is signposted off the A515 Ashbourne to Buxton road, a few miles north of Ashbourne. Pass the pond in the village and bear right to find the gated entrance to the Tissington Trail car park.

Why do this cycle ride?

This is one of England's most famous cycling trails and, as it is an old railway line, you can simply choose just when and where to turn round and return to the start. We've suggested heading north, but you could as easily head south to the pleasant market town of Ashbourne, with its antique shops and bookshops. Going north offers a short option along a wooded route followed by a contrasting, airy route through cuttings and along embankments. It's your choice!

4 It's worth continuing north, however, as once the old railway passes beneath the main road, the character of the Trail changes, and a more open terrain offers different views and experiences. The track continues its gentle climb, soon crossing the first of many embankments. There are grand views left (west) across the rolling pastureland of the **White Peak** towards the higher, darker hills that characterise the Staffordshire moorlands, forming the western horizon. Closer to hand are round-topped hills capped by crowns of trees.

5 Off to your left, the village of **Biggin-by-Hartington** soon appears – notice the old **army huts** down to the left, still put to good use as storerooms. In the distance and looking north, you may pick out the distinctive knolls of limestone near Longnor, Chrome Hill and Parkhouse Hill. The strand of cuttings and embankments continues towards the next logical turning point, **Hartington Old Station**. Here, the former signal box has been preserved; climb the steps to view the old points and levers.

6 This is the ideal place to turn round and retrace the route back to the car park at **Tissington**.

Above: The valley of Bletch Brook

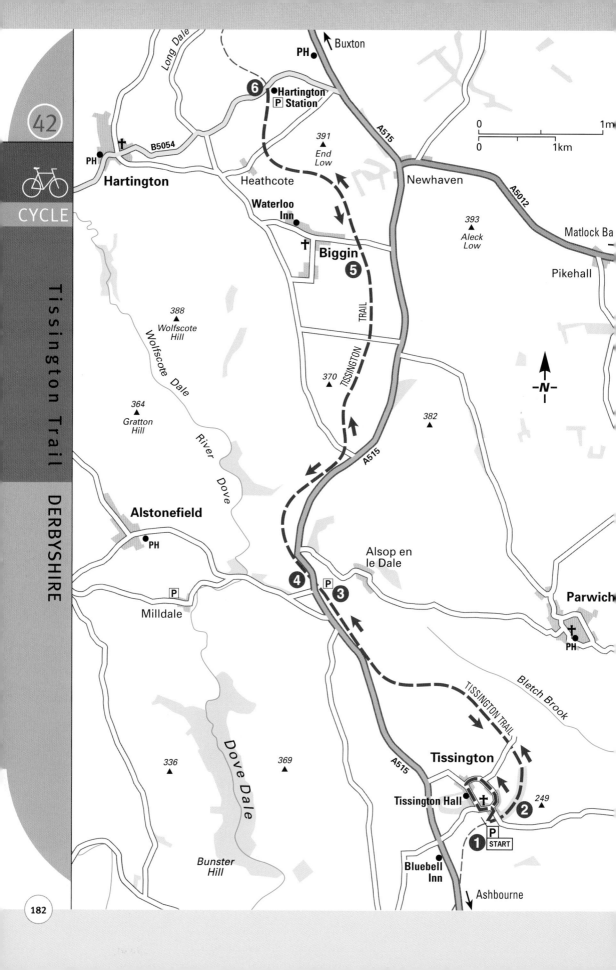

Tissington Trail DERBYSHIRE

Long Dale

PH ● ↑ Buxton

6 ● Hartington
P Station

A515

391
▲
End
Low

Newhaven

393
▲
Aleck
Low

Matlock Ba

PH ● ✝ B5054

Hartington

Heathcote

Waterloo
Inn ●

✝ Biggin
5

A5012

Pikehall

388
▲
Wolfscote
Hill

Wolfscote Dale

364
▲
Gratton
Hill

River Dove

370
▲

TISSINGTON TRAIL

382
▲

↑
A515
↓

←

Alstonefield

PH ●

P
Milldale

4

P 3

Alsop en
le Dale

Parwich

✝
PH ●

Bletch Brook

TISSINGTON TRAIL
↓

↗

336
▲

369
▲

A515

Tissington

Dove Dale

Tissington Hall ●✝

249
▲ 2

1 P
START

Bunster
Hill

Bluebell
Inn ●

↓ Ashbourne

0 ———————————— 1m
0 ———————————— 1km

-N-

Tissington Trail

Bluebell Inn

A favourite watering hole for walkers and cyclists following a day on the Tissington Trail, the stone-built Bluebell Inn dates from 1777. In the long, beamed bar you can rest weary legs and savour a reviving pint of Hardys & Hansons bitter. Fires at either end add welcome winter warmth, while in summer vases of flowers on each table add a splash of colour to the narrow room. Prints of local scenes, framed advertisements and old photographs of the pub adorn the walls and high shelves are lined with traditional pub memorabilia. There is a light and airy dining room.

about the pub

Bluebell Inn
Tissington, Ashbourne
Derbyshire DE6 1NH
Tel 01335 350317
www.bluebelltissington.co.uk

DIRECTIONS: from the Tissington Trail car park turn left back through the village to the A515 and turn right to locate the pub beside the main road

PARKING: 75

OPEN: daily, all day March–September

FOOD: daily, all day March–September

BREWERY/COMPANY: Hardys & Hansons Brewery

REAL ALE: Hardys & Hansons Best Bitter and Old Trip

Food

The bar menu is very extensive and lists traditional pub fare. Tuck into wild mushroom lasagne, beef in ale pie, Hartington chicken, a ploughman's lunch or a decent round of sandwiches. Limited daily specials may take in beef and tomato casserole, a giant Yorkshire pudding filled with scrumpy pork casserole, and local trout.

Family facilities

Familes are welcome inside only if they plan to eat. There's a standard selection of children's meals, in addition to portions of lasagne and Yorkshire pudding filled with beef stew. Unfortunately the large garden is next to the busy road so keep an eye on children.

Alternative refreshment stops

There are two village tea rooms in Tissington, the Old Coach House and Bassett Wood Farm.

☛ Where to go from here

Ilam Country Park is a National Trust estate just west of Tissington. Ten miles (16.1km) south of Ashbourne is Sudbury Hall, home to the National Trust's Museum of Childhood (www.nationaltrust.org.uk).

CYCLE

Tissington Trail

DERBYSHIRE

The Heights of Abraham

Matlock DERBYSHIRE

A steady climb raises you above the hurley burley of Matlock Bath to a more familiar Peakland landscape.

Matlock Bath and the Derwent Valley

Between Matlock and Cromford the River Derwent forges its way through a spectacular, thickly wooded limestone gorge. At Matlock Bath it jostles for space with the bustling A6 highway, the railway to Derby and a string of three-storey houses, shops and amusement parlours, built by the Victorians, who flocked here to take in the healing spa waters. On the hillside to the east lies the gaunt castle of Riber, while Alpine-type cable cars glide up the Heights of Abraham, above cliff tops to the west. The original Heights of Abraham rise above Quebec and the St Lawrence River in Canada. There, in 1759, British troops under General Wolfe fought a victorious battle with the French under General Montcalm.

Matlock Bath is Derbyshire's mini-Blackpool, yet there are peaceful corners, and this fine walk seeks them out. It climbs through the woods and out on to the hillside

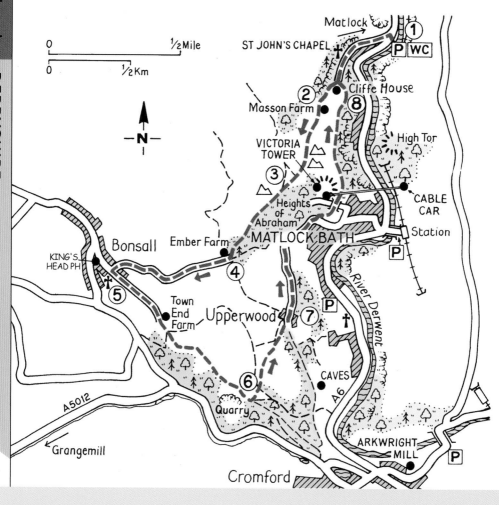

2h30	4.5 MILES	7 KM	LEVEL 2

MAP: OS Explorer OL24 White Peak

START/FINISH: Matlock: pay car park at Artists Corner, grid ref SK 297595

PATHS: narrow woodland paths, field paths and unsurfaced lanes, 10 stiles and gates

LANDSCAPE: fields and wooded hillsides

PUBLIC TOILETS: at car park

TOURIST INFORMATION: Matlock Bath, tel 01629 55082

THE PUB: King's Head, Bonsall, see Point 4 on route

❶ This walk has a long, and in some places, steep opening section before levelling out beside the Heights of Abraham leisure park

Getting to the start

Matlock is on the A6 between Buxton and Matlock. The car park at Artists Corner is well signed.

Top: The River Derwent running through Matlock Bath
Page 186: Looking across the Heights of Abraham to Riber Castle

above the town. The Victoria Prospect Tower peeps over the trees. Built by unemployed miners a century ago it's now part of the Heights of Abraham complex. Above the complex, a little path leads you through woodland. In spring it's heavy with the scent of wild garlic and coloured by a carpet of bluebells. Out of the woods, an attractive hedge-lined unsurfaced lane weaves its way through high pastures, giving distant views of the White Peak plateau, Black Rocks and the cliffs of Crich Stand.

At the end of the lane is Bonsall, whose perpendicular church tower and spire has been beckoning you for some time. In the centre of this old lead mining village is a market square with a 17th-century cross. The lane out of Bonsall takes you to the edge of an area of old mine shafts and modern-day quarries. The route goes north, back into the woods of the Derwent Valley, passing the high hamlet of Upperwood, where fleeting views of Matlock and Matlock Bath appear through the trees.

Right: Cable cars heading up to the Heights of Abraham

the walk

1 Cross the A6, then take **St John's Road** up the wooded slopes opposite. It passes beneath **St John's Chapel** to reach the gates of **Cliffe House**. Take the path on the right signed **'To the Heights of Abraham'**. The path climbs steeply beside the estate wall through the woodland edge; scramble over a high, broken stone step stile and veer left to another stile into the rough fields above **Masson Farm**.

2 The footpath continues to an old gateway and waymark post, with **Victoria Prospect Tower** directly ahead.
Turn right beyond the gateway, and rise to a stile at the top of the field. Beyond this the footpath threads through hawthorn thickets before passing a small gated entry (left) into the **Heights of Abraham** complex.

3 Ignore this and continue uphill for about 30yds (27m), then turn left over a stile (waymarked **Derwent Valley Walk**). After crossing a tarred access road, the narrow footpath re-enters woodland.

4 At the far side of the woods turn right along a farm lane, passing well below **Ember Farm**. This pleasant walled lane winds down pastured hillslopes into Bonsall village. To find the **King's Head** turn right at the lane; it's about 200yds (183m) along here. Then return to this spot.

what to look for

St John's Chapel, seen early in the walk, was designed and built in 1897 by Sir Guy Dauber for Mrs Harris, who lived at Rock House, a short way down the hill. It was meant to serve the parishioners who found it difficult to reach St Giles at Matlock, but it was also a place for those who preferred a High Church service.

5 Turn left past the school along a lane that becomes unsurfaced when you get beyond **Town End Farm**. This track climbs gently as a wide track around the fenced perimeter of the quarry to reach an old gateway across the narrowing track at the edge of woods; there's also a waymark arrow ahead and an old stone gatepost here.

6 Don't go ahead, but look left for a squeeze stile into pasture. Follow the path straight across to another stile into woods. Drop down to an old lane at a ruinous barn. Take the lower track, past a rusty gate, and walk through to the stub-end of a tarred lane.

7 This is the hamlet of **Upperwood**. Walk ahead across the turning area and around the left bend, remaining with this narrow tarred lane between cottages for nearly 0.5 mile (800m) to pass the lodge-house entrance to the **Heights of Abraham** showcave. Just around the next bend, leave the lane for a stepped path through the woods on the left, signposted **'Public Footpath to Matlock'**. Climb some steps to a high wooden footbridge over the **Heights of Abraham** approach road, and then continue on the woodland path. You'll pass under the Heights of Abraham cable cars (not easily seen) before eventually joining a track that has come in from the left.

8 This track joins **St John's Lane** and the outward route at **Cliffe House**. Retrace your steps back to the start.

King's Head

Tiny, diamond-leaded windows, thick, weathered stone mullions and the mellowed stone structure to the cosy and homely King's Head indicate the pub's great age. Local word says that it was opened on the day King Charles I was executed in January 1649, although a more reliable date is the 1677 included in the structure. Outside, it is awash with colourful hanging baskets and flower tubs; inside are the Yeoman's Bar and the King's Lounge, both full of atmosphere. Expect darkwood panelling, glowing wood-burning stoves in winter, old benches and pews, a wealth of porcelain and china, and scrubbed tables topped with candles and fresh flowers. Don't forget tip-top ales from Bateman's and a good blackboard menu. It stands in the tiny market square next to the remarkable stepped Market Cross.

Food

Look to the chalkboard for steak and kidney pudding, parsnip and sweet potato bake, Caribbean lamb, Barnsley lamb chop, and a choice of fresh fish, perhaps including trout with prawn and garlic sauce. At lunchtime expect sandwiches and lighter meals.

Family facilities

Children will enjoy the pub's characterful interior – they are welcome throughout. They can choose from their own menu and eat al fresco in the sheltered courtyard on sunny days.

Alternative refreshment stops

The Barley Mow in the Dale just off the Via Gellia offers real ale and has a reputation for excellent food.

☞ Where to go from here

The Peak District Mining Museum at Matlock Bath Pavilion on the A6 alongside the River Derwent has reconstructed mines to explore and crawl through (www.peakmines.co.uk).

about the pub

King's Head
62 Yeoman Street, Bonsall
Derbyshire DE4 2AA
Tel 01629 822703

DIRECTIONS: in Bonsall village, near Point 5 on the route	
PARKING: 10	
OPEN: closed Monday lunch	
FOOD: daily	
BREWERY/COMPANY: Bateman's	
REAL ALE: Bateman's XB, Dark Mild, seasonal beers	
DOGS: welcome throughout	

Douglas Valley delights

WALK

Douglas Valley   LANCASHIRE

A gentle yet surprising corner of Lancashire, and it saves the best until last.

Moor and valley

West Lancashire is full of surprises. The walk starts with a slight ascent on to High Moor. The 'high' part creeps up on you, unsuspected until you start down an enclosed track and then out into a field. The spire of Parbold church is below and, to its right, the land falls away to the lowlands around Ormskirk and away to the sea. Inland you look across the Douglas Valley to the ridge of Ashurst's Beacon, which is another grand viewpoint.

Now you amble down into the valley. Once this was a major communications corridor. First the river itself was improved for navigation in 1742, then came the Leeds and Liverpool Canal – the longest single canal in Britain. It carried stone from local quarries and coal.

The canal declined and fell into dereliction but the growth of leisure boating has brought a revival. Having climbed up a little from the canal, and crossed a few fields, you come to the Fairy Glen. Its origins are largely natural, rather than supernatural, and there are some traces of small-scale quarrying, but there is a kind of magic about the place. Dappled sunlight gilds the rocks and waterfalls. The ground under the trees may show wood anemones and celandines, wood sorrel, or carpets of bluebells and wild garlic. Between June and September, especially in the lower reaches, there are great drifts of white flowers on loose spikes. This plant is appropriately named for Fairy Glen: it is enchanter's nightshade. The walk is over too soon and the busy road brings a rude awakening but you could always go round again.

the walk

1 In the middle of the lay-by there's a **stile and gate** into the corner of a field. Go up the side of the field and left along the top, then into a wood. Cross a small footbridge and continue up the footpath, then alongside a tiny **stream**. Follow the side of a **conifer plantation** until it bends away,

An overgrown woodland path at Fairy Glen

2h00 — **4 MILES** — **6.4 KM** — **LEVEL 123**

then bear right to the left-hand side of a clump of trees enclosing a **pool**. Continue up to the right into an enclosed track below **power lines** and on up to a junction with a tarmac track.

2 Go left, then bear left again down an **earthy track**. (To visit the Rigbye Arms first, go right at this point, then left along High Moor Lane. Retrace the route.) At the end of the earthy track go slightly right, across a field, to the corner of a **wood** then down its left-hand edge. Keep following this, which eventually becomes a narrow strip of **woodland**, to a stile in the bottom corner of the field. Follow a footpath down through the wood and then up to the A5209.

3 Cross the road and go left to a stile where the pavement ends. Go straight down a field and over another stile into a lane. Go right on this then immediately left down another lane. Cross the railway at a level crossing and continue until you reach a bridge. Drop down to the **tow path** and follow it eastwards for about a 0.5 mile (800m) to the next canal bridge (**No 40**).

MAP: OS Explorer 285 Southport & Chorley

START/FINISH: Large lay-by on A5209 west of Parbold; grid ref: SD 517109

PATHS: field paths and canal tow path, 11 stiles

LANDSCAPE: open fields, enclosed valley and wooded dell

PUBLIC TOILETS: none on route

TOURIST INFORMATION: Preston, tel 01772 253731

THE PUB: The Rigbye Arms, Wrightington

Getting to the start

This walk is equidistant from Wrightington and Parbold, about 3 miles (5km) west of Standish. The start of the walk is also accessible by public transport, which operates along the A5209.

View from Parbold Hill

what to look for

A conspicuous plant, of the canal banks in particular, is Indian (or Himalayan) balsam. It has reddish stems and, from July to October, showy white to pink flowers. Even more conspicuous, in a few places, is giant hogweed. It can grow anywhere up to 15ft (5m) tall and touching its hairy stems or leaves can lead to a severe skin irritation. Both species were introduced to Britain in the 19th century.

4 Cross this bridge and follow an obvious track, taking you back over the **railway** and up to a gate. Turn right on another track. In two places there's a separate footpath alongside, but it's always obvious. Where the track finally parts company go over a stile and along the bottom of a field. Cross the next field to a post and then a stile.

5 Descend the steep steps down into a wood and bear left into **Fairy Glen**. Cross a footbridge, climb some steps, then go left along a good track. Cross another footbridge below a **waterfall** and ascend more steps. Keep to the principal footpath, straight on up the glen as it becomes much shallower, until the path crosses a tiny **footbridge**. Soon after this the footpath leaves the side of the brook and briefly joins a track before it emerges on to the **A5209**. Cross and go right, back to the lay-by.

The Rigbye Arms

A perennial favourite among local ramblers, this 16th-century inn enjoys a remote moorland setting and provides a relaxed atmosphere and a warming open fire in the rambling, traditionally furnished interior. Muddy boots will be most at home in the Fox Hole Bar at the back. Here you'll find hand-pumped ales and popular, generously served food, ranging from pub favourites to more imaginative specials. Good outdoor seating for fine weather drinking, the garden features a barbeque and a Crown Bowling Green!

Food

Tuck into hearty sandwiches and traditional pub dishes, or look to the specials board for 'man-sized' steak and kidney pudding, freshly battered cod, chips and mushy peas, or braised lamb served with huge portions of vegetables.

Family facilities

Families are genuinely welcomed and there are family dining areas, a children's menu and a play area in the garden.

Alternative refreshment stops

On High Moor Lane you'll find the High Moor Inn, while near by you could seek out the Eagle & Child at Bispham Green or the Mulberry Tree at Wrightington Bar as both offer excellent food.

☛ Where to go from here

Visit Martin Mere, one of Britain's most important wetland sites, and get really close to a variety of ducks, geese and swans (www.wwt.org.uk). Take a look at Rufford Old Hall, built in 1530 and containing a fine collection of tapestries, arms, armour, and Tudor and Jacobean furniture (www.nationaltrust.org.uk). Children will love the Camelot Theme Park with its thrilling rides and spectacular shows (www.camelotthemepark.co.uk).

about the pub

The Rigbye Arms

2 Whittle Lane, Wrightington
Wigan, Lancashire WN6 9QB
Tel: 01257 462354

DIRECTIONS: off A5209 between Parbold and the M6 (J27) via Robin Hood Lane and High Moor Lane; see Point 2	
PARKING: 40	
OPEN: daily; all day Sunday	
FOOD: daily	
BREWERY/COMPANY: Tetley	
REAL ALE: Timothy Taylor Landlord, Tetley, Marston's Pedigree, guest beer	
DOGS: allowed in the Fox Hole Bar	

Rocks and water at Anglezarke

A landscape shaped by quarries and reservoirs, full of both historical and natural interest.

Anglezarke Quarry

A string of reservoirs moats the western side of the high moors of Anglezarke and Rivington and quarries scar their flanks. This is not a pristine landscape by any stretch of the imagination, yet today it is seen by many as an oasis of tranquillity close to busy towns and a motorway.

A gentle start just above the shores of Anglezarke Reservoir leads to Lester Mill Quarry, which was worked until the 1930s. The quarry wall is imposing, but somewhat vegetated, and the rock is loose in places. It is much less popular with climbers than Anglezarke Quarry.

The route continues through a mix of woodland and pasture to the head of the lake, then heads up the valley below steep, bouldery Stronstrey Bank. There's another quarry high on the right near the end of the bank, seemingly guarded by a number of gaunt, dead trees. Just beyond is another, set further back. Just beyond this, an impressive spillway testifies to the potential power of Dean Black Brook.

Now you cross The Goit, a canal that feeds the reservoir, to White Coppice cricket ground. There's a small reservoir just above and you pass others on the way down to the present-day hamlet. These served the mills that flourished here for well over a century. Along with the quarries at Stronstrey Bank these made White Coppice a busy industrial village with a population that may have approached 200. The mill closed in 1914 and little remains.

After White Coppice you climb to Healey Nab. Trees obscure what must have been a fine all-round view from the highest point, but there's a good southward prospect from the large cairn on Grey Heights. Winter Hill is the highest of the moors, unmistakable with its TV towers. The main mast is just over 1,000ft (305m) tall, so you could argue that its tip is the highest point in Lancashire. The string of reservoirs is also well displayed and you get a bird's-eye view of Chorley.

the walk

1 Leave the car park and go back down the **access road** to a kissing gate on the right and follow a track near the water. Fork right, on a side path that leads through **Lester Mill Quarry**. On rejoining the original path, turn right. The track soon begins to climb along the edge of **woodland**.

2 As the track bends right, go through a gap on the left. The path traverses a **wooded slope**. Descend steps, join a wider track and go left. Beyond a kissing gate follow a narrower path until it meets a road.

3 Go left 25yds (20m) to a kissing gate. Follow a track up the valley below **Stronstrey Bank**. Cross a bridge then go through a kissing gate and over another bridge to **White Coppice cricket ground**.

Looking across Rivington reservoirs from Anglezarke

2h30 · **7 MILES** · **11.3 KM** · **LEVEL 1 2 3**

WALK

Anglezarke LANCASHIRE

4 Bear left up a lane, then follow tarmac into **White Coppice** hamlet. Cross a bridge by the postbox. Follow a stream, then go up left by a **reservoir**. Bear left to a stile. Cross the next field to its top right corner and go right on a lane. Where it bends right go left up a track.

5 Skirt **Higher Healey**, follow hedged track, then angle up left into **dark plantations**. Fork left just inside, and ascend to an **old quarry** and follow its rim to enter a larch plantation.

6 Go forward to meet a clear path on the far side of the **plantation**. Turn left and immediately right to the large cairn on **Grey Heights**. Descend slightly right, winding down through gorse and past a **small plantation**. Below the plantation, bear left between hedgerows, cross two fences then follow a rough field track to a lane by **White House Farm**.

MAP: OS Explorer 287 West Pennine Moors

START/FINISH: Large car park at Anglezarke; grid ref: SD 621161

PATHS: mostly good tracks with some field paths, 10 stiles

LANDSCAPE: woodland, reservoirs, open valleys and farmland

PUBLIC TOILETS: none on route

TOURIST INFORMATION: Preston, tel 01772 253731

THE PUB: The Yew Tree, Dill Hall Brow

Getting to the start

Anglezarke and its reservoirs lie in the shadow of Winter Hill just 2 miles (3.2km) to the east of Chorley and reached via minor roads from the A6 in Chorley or the A673 at Adlington.

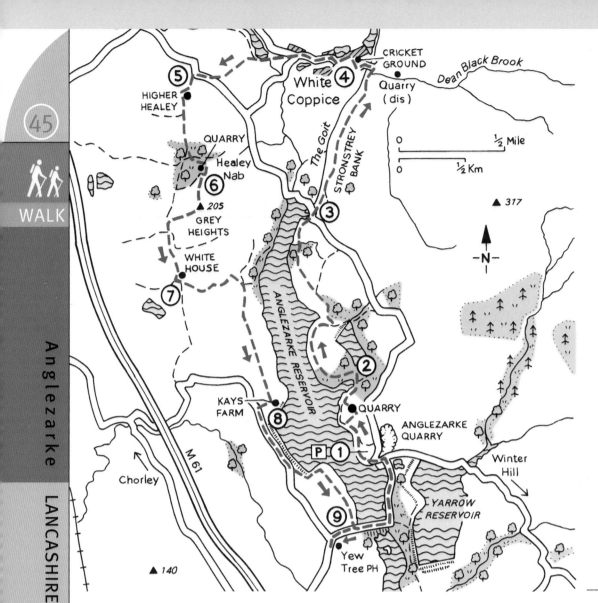

7 Cross a stile on the left below the **farmyard wall**, then bear left to the corner of the field. Cross the stile on the left, then along the field edge to stile on right, and join a confined path to a stile on the right. Follow trees along the field edge to a rough track. Go right and straight on to **Kays Farm**.

8 Go right down a track then left on a lane below the **reservoir wall**. As the lane angles away, go left over a stile then skirt the reservoir until pushed away from the water by a wood. Join the road across the **dam**.

9 To visit **The Yew Tree**, turn right and follow the road. Retrace your steps, and continue across the dam, following the road back to the car park.

what to look for

Subtle differences in the nature of the rock can be seen in the different quarries. These were significant for the uses to which the stone could be put. Parts of Anglezarke Quarry are 'massive' – there are very few cracks. Some of the rock here is especially pure and was used to line blast furnaces.

The Yew Tree

The Yew Tree, at Lane Ends, 250yds (229m) from the Anglezarke dam, may lack cask beer but offers a lovely moorland location on the edge of the West Pennine Moors, extensive views and a cosy atmosphere. Although very much a pub-restaurant, with a big emphasis on food, it does have a bar, serves light bar meals and, more importantly, welcomes walkers. Benches in the garden make the most of the views.

Food

Lunchtime bar meals may include roast ham, beef, or tuna mayonnaise sandwiches, Spanish omelette, grilled gammon, pasta bake, fresh haddock and plaice, steak pie and liver, onions and mash. The restaurant menu takes in halibut Breton, whole plaice and rack of lamb.

about the pub

The Yew Tree

Dill Hall Brow, Heath
Charnock, Chorley,
Lancashire PR6 9HA
Tel: 01257 480344

DIRECTIONS: see Getting to the start; pub at the southern end of Anglezarke Reservoir and best accessed from the A673 at Adlington south of Chorley; see Point 9.

PARKING: 75

OPEN: daily; all day Sunday

FOOD: daily; all day Sunday

BREWERY/COMPANY: Free House

REAL ALE: none served

DOGS: allowed in the garden only

Family facilities

Families are welcome inside but there are no special facilities for children.

Alternative refreshment stops

North of White Coppice just off the A674 at Wheelton (Briers Brow) is the Dressers Arms (excellent beer and locally sourced food), and beside the canal at Heapey is the Top Lock offering traditional pub food.

☞ Where to go from here

Enter King Arthur's Kingdom at the Camelot Theme Park for a magical day out watching spectacular shows, including a jousting tournament, and enjoy some of the thrilling rides (www.camelotthemepark.co.uk). Visit Astley Hall, a 400-year-old mansion with fine architecture and ornate furnishings, set in a scenic country park south of Chorley (www.lancashiretourism.com).

High around Loweswater Fell

A circuit from Low Lorton
to Loweswater and back
through Lorton Vale.

Alien invaders

Signs on this route draw attention to the
peril of red squirrels in the area. The red
squirrel is native to Britain but over the last
century or so has been widely displaced by
the grey squirrel, introduced from North
America. Red squirrels have longer bodies
and tails than the greys but a much more
slender build and are considerably lighter.
Today there are an estimated 2.5 million
greys to just 160,000 reds, and most of
those are found in Scotland. Around 30,000
red squirrels survive in England and Wales,
mainly in Cumbria and Northumberland.

The rhododendrons which make such
a splash on the fellside above Loweswater
are also an introduced species, this time
from the Himalayas. Spectacular in bloom,
they are tough, hardy mountain plants and
thrive in the acid soils and cool, moist
climate of the Lake District. The snag is that,
rather like the grey squirrel, they tend to
compete all too well with native plant
species and if left unchecked can displace
native shrubs and flowering plants over
large areas. In some areas you may see
conservation volunteers working to cut them
back – but it is a mammoth task.

the ride

1 Follow the road down to the bridge over
the **River Cocker** and round to the right.
Shortly after, turn left on a road marked
'Unsuitable for motor vehicles'. This begins
to climb almost at once and goes on for
about 0.5 mile (800m). The steepest section
goes through a tunnel of trees between **Low
Bank Farm** and **High Bank**.

*View towards Crummock Water from the lane
above Thackthwaite*

The beautiful view from the shores of Loweswater

2 Above this the gradient gradually eases. At the same time the surface becomes progressively rougher. This shouldn't pose any problems as long as you keep an eye on the track ahead and pick your moments to look round at the views. And these are great, over **Cockermouth** to the **Solway Firth** and the Galloway hills. There's one more short climb before the lane starts to dip downhill. The descent never gets too steep or too difficult, as long as you keep a good lookout for potholes. This run down levels out over tiny **Catgill Bridge** and brings you to a T-junction onto a road.

3 Turn left and wind past the fine buildings of **Mosser Mains**, just beyond which the road forks. Take the left branch that climbs gradually up the valley of **Mosser Beck**. There's a steeper section just before **Mossergate Farm**. Once you are past High Mossergate, the surface again gets rougher as the gradient eases. As the track levels out, the high Lakeland fells begin to appear ahead. Pass the narrow **Graythwaite Wood** (mostly rhododendrons, which gives an outlandish splash of colour in early summer) at the start of another swooping descent.

4 The track swings left, traversing a steep hillside above **Loweswater**. The surface is generally better on the steepest part of the descent, although there are still a few potholes. Continue along a rougher section, at a gentler gradient, through a **plantation** and finally down to meet the road just above the lake.

2h00 — **9.75 MILES** — **15.7 KM** — **LEVEL 1 2 3**

MAP: OS Explorer OL 4 The English Lakes (NW)

START/FINISH: outskirts of Low Lorton; grid ref: NY 1532577

TRAILS/TRACKS: quiet lanes, moderately rough tracks with some potholes

LANDSCAPE: woodland, waterside, gentle valley, rough grazing land and moorland

PUBLIC TOILETS: none on route

TOURIST INFORMATION: Cockermouth, tel 01900 822634

CYCLE HIRE: Keswick Mountain Bikes, tel 017687 75202; Grin Up North, Cockermouth, tel 01900 829600

THE PUB: Wheatsheaf Inn, Low Lorton, see Point **1** on route

❶ One very steep climb. Lengthy off-road descents, but not too difficult. Suitability: children 11+

Getting to the start
Low Lorton lies bewteen Cockermouth and Keswick, off the B5292. Park on wide verges near a phone-box on the B5289, just south of Lorton Hall.

Why do this cycle ride?
This ride has its challenges, including a tough climb early on, but you are repaid. There are fine views, first out over the Cumbrian lowlands to the Solway Firth and the hills of Galloway, in Scotland, then over Loweswater and its encircling fells, and finally up into the heart of the Lake District. There is some wonderful traffic-free riding on good tracks, and two exhilarating descents. These are never difficult, but to enjoy them fully you do need confidence in yourself and your bike.

CYCLE

Low Lorton

CUMBRIA

5 Bear left along the road. There's a short climb as the road veers away from the lake, followed by a slight descent and then a more level section. Crest another slight rise and there's a view of **Crummock Water** and the high fells, with **Great Gable** a prominent rounded peak in the distance. Just a short way down the other side is a turning on the left, signposted to Thackthwaite, and also a **C2C sign**.

6 Turn here and follow this narrow lane through the tiny hamlet of Thackthwaite, where a sign says, 'Red Squirrels Please drive slowly'. The lane is undulating but predominantly downhill, bringing you gradually down to the valley floor alongside the beck, past the caravan park at Whin Fell and on to a T-junction. Turn right over the bridge to return to the start point.

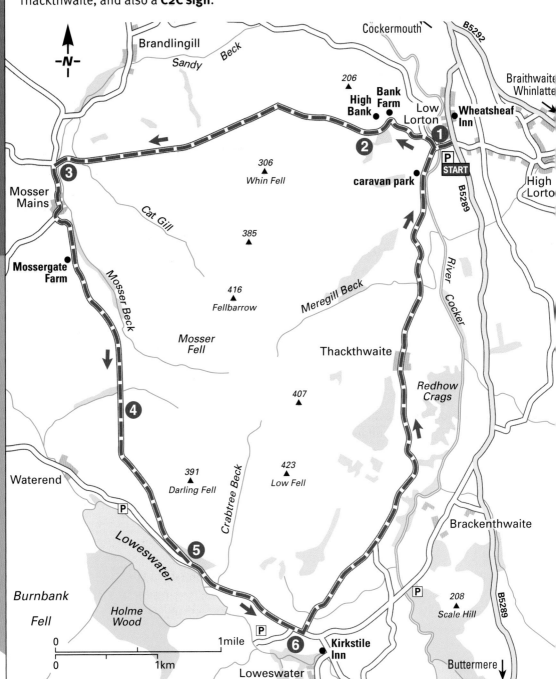

Wheatsheaf Inn

Long, low and white, this 17th-century inn sits squarely along the main road through Low Lorton, just a short way from the start and finish of the ride. The bar, with beams and log fire, is decorated with books and memorabilia to resemble a gamekeeper's lodge. There's another open fire in the non-smoking restaurant. To the rear is a large, safe garden with fine views to the fells, and the pub has a caravan site. There's a selection of beer from the Jennings brewery in nearby Cockermouth, and good food is a high priority, sourced locally if possible.

Food

A typical menu may include mussels in white wine and garlic sauce or home-made soup to start, followed by beef and beer pie, duck breast with orange marmalade, half shoulder of lamb with Cumberland sauce, or a large Yorkshire pudding filled with roast beef. Good fish specials and lighter lunchtime snacks.

Family facilities

Families are welcome inside and there are specific menus for younger children and for teenagers. Extensive rear garden for summer eating and drinking.

about the pub

Wheatsheaf Inn
Low Lorton, Cockermouth
Cumbria CA13 9UW
Tel 01900 85199
www.wheatsheafinnlorton.co.uk

DIRECTIONS: on the B5289, between Low Lorton and Lorton Hall

PARKING: 40

OPEN: daily in summer, closed Monday lunch October to May

FOOD: daily

BREWERY/COMPANY: Jennings Brewery

REAL ALE: Jennings Bitter, Cumberland Ale and seasonal beers

Alternative refreshment stops

Close to Point 6, in Loweswater village, you'll find the Kirkstile Inn (good food and home-brewed beer).

☞ Where to go from here

Wordworth's childhood home in the riverside town of Cockermouth is well worth a visit. Next door there is a working printing museum, The Printing House, with an interesting range of historic presses and equipment. At the Lakeland Sheep and Wool Centre children can see 19 different breeds of sheep, as well as shearing demonstrations and sheepdog trials. Alternatively, enjoy a tour of the Jennings Brewery.

Around Buttermere

A relaxing walk in one of Lakeland's most attractive valleys.

Buttermere

CUMBRIA

Buttermere

Much has been written about lovely Buttermere – the dale, the village and the lake. The area achieved considerable notoriety at the pen of Joseph Budworth, who stayed here in 1792 and encountered Mary, the daughter of the landlord of the Fish Inn. In his guidebook *Fortnight's Ramble to the Lakes*, he described Mary as 'the reigning Lily of the Valley', and the unfortunate woman became a tourist attraction.

In 1802 the tale brought to Buttermere one John Hadfield, a man posing as the Honourable Anthony Augustus Hope, MP. Hadfield wooed and won Mary, and they were married at Lorton church on 2 October 1802 (coincidentally just two days before William Wordsworth married Mary Hutchinson). With the honeymoon scarcely begun, however, Hadfield was exposed as an impostor and arrested on a charge of forgery – a more serious offence than that of bigamy, of which he was also guilty.

He was later tried and hanged at Carlisle. The whole saga was dramatised and found its way on to the stages of some London theatres. Accounts of the episode are given by Thomas de Quincey in *Recollections of the Lakes and the Lake Poets* and by Melvyn Bragg in his 1987 novel *The Maid of Buttermere*, and a description used by Wordsworth in 'The Prelude'. As for Mary, she later remarried, had a large family and by all accounts a subsequently happy life.

the walk

1 Leave the car park and turn right, passing the **Fish Hotel** to follow a broad track through gates. Ignore the signposted route to Scale Force and continue along the track towards the edge of the lake. Then follow the line of a hedgerow to a bridge at **Buttermere Dubs**. Cross over and bear left, passing just below the foot of the cascade of **Sourmilk Gill**. Cross a smaller footbridge and go through a gate into **Burtness Wood**. Bear left on a track through the woods that roughly parallels the lakeshore, finally emerging from the trees near **Horse Close**, where a bridge spans **Comb Beck**.

2 Follow the path to reach a wall leading to a sheepfold and a gate. Go left through the gate, cross **Warnscale Beck** and walk out to **Gatesgarth Farm**. At the farm, follow signs

Left: Hikers gazing across Buttermere
Below: Ducks on the shore of Crummock Water

to reach the valley road (the **B5289**). Turn left on the road for about 500yds (457m) until it meets the **lakeshore**. For much of this distance there are no pathways: take care against approaching traffic.

3 As the road leaves the lakeshore again, leave it for a **footpath** on the left signposted 'Buttermere via Lakeshore Path'. The path leads into a field, beyond which it never strays far from the shoreline and continues to a stand of Scots pine, near **Crag Wood**.

4 Beyond **Hassnesshow Beck bridge**, the path enters the grounds of Hassness, where a rocky path, enclosed by trees, leads to a gate. Here a path has been cut across a crag dropping into the lake below, and shortly disappears into a brief, low and damp **tunnel**, unique in the Lake District. The tunnel was cut by employees of George Benson, a 19th-century Manchester mill owner who then owned the Hassness Estate, to enable him to walk around the lake without straying too far from its shore. After you emerge from the tunnel a gate gives access to a gravel path across the wooded pasture of **Pike Rigg**. Where a permitted path goes left to stay by the lakeshore, the main path keeps straight ahead, crossing a traditional Lakeland bridge of slate slabs.

MAP: OS Explorer OL 4 The English Lakes (NW)

START/FINISH: Buttermere, National Park car park beyond Fish Hotel (fee); grid ref: NY 173169

PATHS: good paths, some road walking, 2 stiles

LANDSCAPE: lakeside, fells, woodland and farmland

PUBLIC TOILETS: at start

TOURIST INFORMATION: Keswick, tel 017687 72645

THE PUB: Bridge Hotel, Buttermere, see Point 5 on route

🅛 Suitability: children 5+

Getting to the start

Buttermere village lies between the lakes of Buttermere and Crummock Water, on the B5289. Approaching from the south, pass Buttermere church and turn left before the Bridge Hotel. The car park is to the right of the Fish Hotel.

5 A short way on, through another gate, the path leads on to **Wilkinsyke Farm**, and an easy walk out to the road, just a short way above the **Bridge Hotel**. Turn left to return to the car park.

what to look for

While walking out to Gatesgarth Farm, have a look at the craggy sides of Fleetwith Pike. On the lower slopes a white cross can be seen clearly. This was erected by the friends of Fanny Mercer, a luckless visitor to Lakeland who, in 1887, while out walking, tripped over her long walking pole and fell to her death.

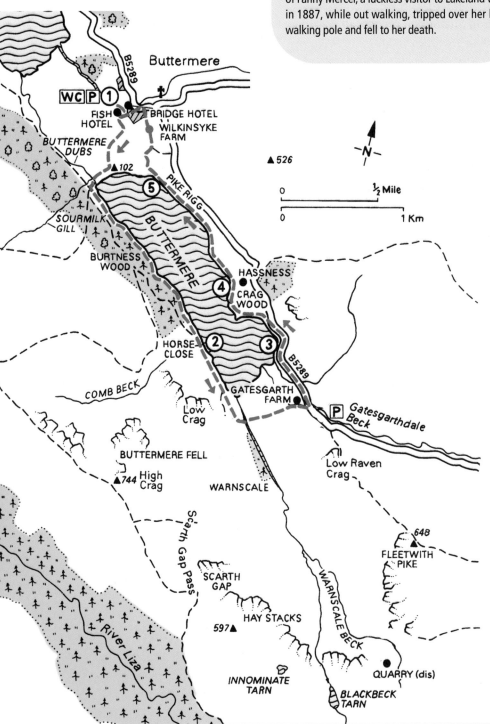

Bridge Hotel

Spend a weekend at this 18th-century former coaching inn and enjoy its stunning location in an area of outstanding natural beauty between Buttermere and Crummock Water. You can round off spectacular walks with afternoon tea, excellent ales or a hearty meal. On a fine day there can be fierce competition for tables in the small garden, a sheltered suntrap surrounded by climbing roses, with jaw-dropping views to High Crag, High Stile and Red Pike. What better place to enjoy a pint of Old Faithful from the (Cumbrian) Tirril Brewery? If the seats are all taken or the weather forces you indoors, there are two bar areas, one with oak beams, a flagstone floor and traditional Lakeland character. There's also a plush lounge with deep sofas and an open fire. Individually designed bedrooms.

Food

Main courses include Cumberland hotpot, home-made steak and kidney pie, vegetable stirfry, and deep-fried haddock in crisp beer batter. For smaller appetites there's a good selection of salads, sandwiches and toasties. Separate five-course dinner menu in the restaurant.

Family facilities

Children are welcome in the eating area of the bar; children's menu.

Alternative refreshment stops

There is a café at Buttermere and, like the Bridge Hotel, the Fish Inn serves teas, coffee, snacks and bar meals throughout the day. Wilkinsyke Farm does home-made ice cream and there's often a tea-wagon at Gatescarth.

☛ Where to go from here

Buttermere's attractive church of 1841 is in a superb position on a rocky knoll. It is tiny, with a bellcote and a lower chancel. From it there is a lovely view of the valley and the high fells on the south side, all the way to Hay Stacks.

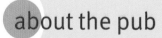

about the pub

Bridge Hotel
Buttermere
Cumbria CA13 9UZ
Tel 017687 70252
www.bridge-hotel.com

DIRECTIONS: in the centre of Buttermere village

PARKING: 26

OPEN: daily, all day

FOOD: daily, all day (restaurant evenings only)

BREWERY/COMPANY: free house

REAL ALE: Black Sheep Bitter, Theakston Old Peculier, Tirril Old Faithful

DOGS: welcome in garden only

ROOMS: 21 en suite

Keswick's Walla Crag above Derwent Water

Wonderful panoramas to the surrounding fells, a jewelled lake and sylvan splendour are the delights of this walk.

Derwent Water and Walla Crag

At the foot of Borrowdale – often referred to as the most beautiful valley in England – the northern head of Derwent Water opens to Keswick and the northern fells with dramatic effect. The highlight of this walk is undeniably the staggering view from the heights of Walla Crag. West across Derwent Water, beyond Cat Bells, Maiden Moor and the secretive Newland Valley stand the striking north western fells of Causey Pike, Sail, Crag Hill and Grisedale Pike. To the south west rise Glaramara and Great Gable. To the north, Skiddaw and Blencathra.

The lake is 3 miles (4.8km) long and 72ft (22m) deep and is fed by the River Derwent. A speed limit ensures that motor-powered boats do not ply its waters. Seasonal salmon, brown trout, Arctic char, perch and the predatory pike swim beneath the surface. There are four islands on the lake, all owned by the National Trust. The largest

and most northerly of the four is Derwent Isle. Once owned by Fountains Abbey it was bought by German miners from the Company of Mines Royal in 1569. The island and part of its grand 18th-century house are open to visitors on a handful of days during the year. St Herbert's Island was reputedly home to a Christian missionary in the 10th century, and monks remained in residence after his departure. A ruined summer house is all that stands there today. By the path, just above Derwent Bay, is an inscribed slate plaque in honour of Canon H D Rawnsley who did much to keep the lake as it remains today. He was vicar of Crosthwaite, the parish church of Keswick, from 1883 to 1917, and was one of Lakeland's greatest conservationists. In 1895 he became a co-founder of the National Trust. He was a campaigner against rude postcards and also encouraged children's author Beatrix Potter to publish her first book, *The Tale of Peter Rabbit*, in 1900.

Top: Small boats between wooden jetties, seen from Friars Crag on the edge of Derwent Water
Right: Friars Crag across Derwent Water

the walk

1 Proceed down the road to **Derwent Bay**. Go left opposite the landing stages, past a toilet block, on the track through **Cockshot Wood**. At a fork take the higher left-hand path. Exit the wood on to a fenced path across a field to the **Borrowdale road**. Cross, and climb stone steps into **Castlehead Wood**. Turn left, then bear right and climb steeply, levelling off at a shoulder. In a little way a steeper path climbs to the right, to **Castle Head**'s rocky summit – a great viewpoint.

2 Return to the shoulder, then turn right, downhill, curving right but keeping left at a fork, until rough steps lead down to a kissing gate. Take a path between fields to a road and houses. Go right and follow the road to its end at **Springs Farm**. Bear left on a track climbing through **Springs Wood**. Bear right at a fork, then follow the edge of the wood, passing a **TV mast**. At a kissing gate, dip back into the wood, cross a footbridge and go up rough steps to a lane. Turn right and follow the lane to its end below **Rakefoot**.

3 Cross the footbridge and ascend the rough track by the stone wall. Go through a gate to open fell and follow the wall up right. At a dip the main path cuts off the corner of the wall and rises to a kissing gate. The path beyond this runs close to steep, unfenced drops in places. (To avoid these simply follow the wall left to a stile near the summit cairn.) Follow the path, crossing the head of a gully (**Lady's Rake**), and climb to the polished rock cap of **Walla Crag** and superb views.

PATHS: OS Explorer OL 4 The English Lakes (NW)

START/FINISH: Lakeside car park, Keswick; grid ref: NY 265229

PATHS: good paths and tracks, steep ascent and descent, 3 stiles

LANDSCAPE: woods, open fell and lakeside

PUBLIC TOILETS: at the car park and above the landing stages

TOURIST INFORMATION: Keswick, tel 017687 72645

THE PUB: Lake Road Inn, Keswick, near start of route

❶ Paths run close to steep, unfenced drops on Walla Crag (an alternative route avoiding these is suggested). Suitability: children 10+, avoiding route 7+

Getting to the start

From central Keswick, take the B5289 Borrowdale road at the western end of the town. Follow it for 600yds (549m) and turn right to reach the Lakeside car park.

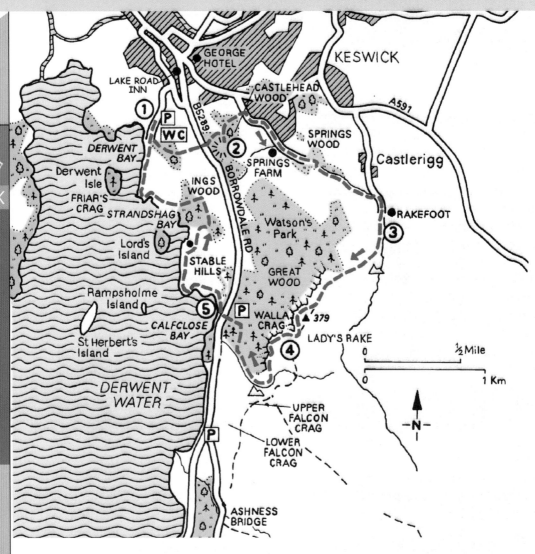

4 Continue in the same line to a stile and cross back over the wall. A grassy path descends parallel to the wall, becoming steeper as it drops towards **Cat Gill**. Keep descending steeply, with stone steps and slippery rock, until a track bears right near a footbridge, descending more easily through **Great Wood**. At a junction of tracks, drop down left to a tarmac track and straight across down a path to a gap in the wall by the **Borrowdale road**. Another gap in the wall opposite and a short path lead to the **lake shore**.

5 Go right, following the shore around **Calfclose Bay**. Leave the shore to skirt round **Stable Hills**, following its drive until a

what to look for

The rocky knoll of Friar's Crag, with its stand of Scots pine, is one of the most famous lakeside viewpoints. It is said to take its name from the monks who once lived on St Herbert's Island. At the foot of the crag, attached to the rocks which are often submerged when the lake level is high, memorial plaques detail all the former mayors of Keswick.

gate on the left leads to a path through damp **Ings Wood**. The path continues round **Strandshag Bay** to **Friar's Crag**. Go right and easily back via **Derwent Bay** to the **car park**.

Lake Road Inn

There's a bewildering choice of pubs in Keswick, most of them serving decent beer and regular pub food. But if you walk up from the Lakeside car park and through the little underpass, one of the first pubs you come to is the Lake Road Inn, and it turns out to be a good choice. The interior has some fine panelling and comfortable seating, giving it a cosy feel that's matched by one of the friendliest welcomes in the district. It also serves its range of robust, well-priced food throughout the day.

Food

From the printed menu you can choose filled jacket potatoes, roast ham salad, Cumberland sausage and onion baguettes, and main courses such as steak pie, lasagne, chilli, and chicken Kiev. Puddings include sticky toffee pudding with ice cream.

Family facilities

Families are welcome indoors and young children have a selection of standard children's meals to choose from. Enclosed patio garden away from the road.

Alternative refreshment stops

There are cafés and tea-gardens in Keswick near the start of the walk.

☞ Where to go from here

The Derwentwater Motor Launch Company runs regular sailings both clockwise and anticlockwise around the lake. Landing stages en route include Ashness Gate, Lodore, High Brandlehow, Low Brandlehow, Hawes End and Nichol End. It makes for a good walk to take the boat out and return by foot to Keswick. Family tickets offer good value.

Boats moored at Derwent Water

about the pub

Lake Road Inn
Lake Road, Keswick
Cumbria CA12 5BT
Tel 017687 72404

DIRECTIONS:	near the Lakeside car park
PARKING:	use town car parks
OPEN:	daily, all day
FOOD:	daily, all day
BREWERY/COMPANY:	Jennings Brewery
REAL ALE:	full range of Jennings beers
DOGS:	welcome in the old barn and garden only

Woods and water by Windermere

Along the peaceful western shore of England's largest lake.

Windermere

A 10mph (16.1km) speed limit for powered craft on the lake comes into force in 2005, and should make this ride much more peaceful than previously. However, the limit has been controversial and may yet be defied. Other water traffic includes yachts of all sizes, windsurfers, canoes, rowing boats and the traditional launches and steamers which ply up and down throughout the year.

An attractive feature, the privately owned Belle Isle is said to have been used since Roman times. Today it is supplied by a little boat, which serves the 38 acre (15ha) estate. Belle Isle's circular house, recently rebuilt after extensive fire damage, was originally built by a Mr English in 1774. Apparently William Wordsworth accredited Mr English with the honour of being the first man to settle in the Lake District for the sake of the scenery.

The woodland here is typical of the Lake District. Before clearances for agriculture, notably sheep-grazing, there were many more woods. The predominant species is the sessile oak, which in times past provided timber for local industry and bark for tanning. It is a close relative of the 'English' oak of more southern counties, and it is not easy to tell them apart, but on closer inspection you will see that the acorns have no stalks to speak of. These woods are also rich in mosses and ferns, and foxgloves, which fills the clearings.

the ride

1 Leave the **car park** and turn left on a surfaced lane. There are views along here of moored yachts, **Belle Isle** and the lake, with a backdrop of high fells. The shapely peak is **Ill Bell**. Follow the lane past lay-bys to reach a gate and cattle grid.

2 The road beyond is marked 'Unsuitable for Motor Vehicles'. Keep left past the entrance to **Strawberry Gardens**. Beyond this the track becomes considerably rougher, and soon begins to climb quite steeply. It's worth persevering!

3 Once over the crest and just as you begin to descend, look out on the left for a **wildlife viewing platform**. There are squirrel feeders scattered in the trees, and you may spot roe deer. Take great care on

MAP: OS Explorer OL 7 The English Lakes (SE)

START/FINISH: car park near Windermere Ferry; grid ref: SD 387958

TRAILS/TRACKS: mostly easy tracks, some stony sections

LANDSCAPE: rich woodland and lakeshore

PUBLIC TOILETS: none on route

TOURIST INFORMATION: Bowness-on-Windermere, tel 015394 42895

CYCLE HIRE: Wheelbase, Staveley, tel 01539 821443; Bike Treks, Ambleside, tel 01539 431245; Ghyllside Cycles, Ambleside, tel 01539 433592; Grizedale Mountain Bikes, Grizedale Forest, tel 01229 860369

THE PUB: Sawrey Hotel, Far Sawrey, near start of route

🛈 Mostly easy but one rough steep climb and descent. Suitability: children 8+. Mountain bike recommended, or walk some sections. Shorter ride from Red Nab, all ages

49

🚲 CYCLE

Windermere CUMBRIA

Getting to the start

Road access to Windermere's mid-western shore is via Far Sawrey or on minor roads from the south. Follow the B5285 towards the ferry terminal, turning left up a lane before the terminal itself, to reach a National Trust car park. Alternatively, you could bring your bikes over by ferry from Bowness-on-Windermere.

Why do this cycle ride?

This is a perfect ride for taking a picnic. The full ride is surprisingly challenging, with a steep, rocky climb and descent halfway, though elsewhere the going is easy. For a shorter ride, go from the car park at Red Nab. Then follow the bridleway to High Wray Bay.

the descent – there are loose stones and several rocky steps, and it may be safer to walk down. The track levels out for a short distance, then continues its descent, finally levelling out just above the lakeshore. The going is easier now, generally level. Pass several small **shingle beaches**. Keep left (almost straight ahead) at a fork and then, where a bridleway climbs off to the left, keep right (signed to **Red Nab** and **Wray**) along a smoother gravel track. At a gate, emerge onto a tarmac track but almost immediately fork right, signposted 'Bridleway Wray Castle'. Continue into the **Red Nab car park**.

Above: Windermere seen from Orrest Head

Tree-covered hills sloping down to Windermere from Gummers How

4 Go round a low barrier on to the bridleway. This is level, easy riding all the way along to a gate by a boathouse, beyond which you emerge to the curve of **High Wray Bay**. The bridleway now veers away from the lake. The bay is a popular picnic spot, with people arriving both by land and by water. Walk the bikes round to the grassy slope above the further shore.

5 Retrace your route to Point 2.

6 A bridleway rises off to the right here. It offers the option of a direct route to the pub at **Far Sawrey**, but the climb is longer, steeper and rougher than what you have encountered so far – so unless you found that all too easy, it's best to ignore it and simply return to the **car park**. The road route to the pub requires riding for 1 mile (1.6km) on the **B5285**, which can be busy at times, and also involves a steep climb midway.

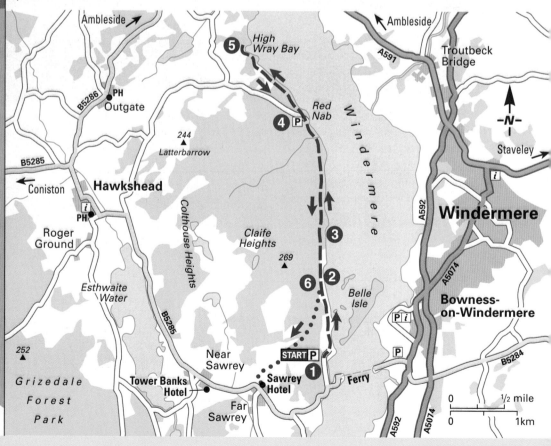

Sawrey Hotel

The Sawrey Hotel unites three original buildings into a remarkably harmonious whole. The oldest part, on the left of the current hotel entrance, dates back to around 1700. To the left again is the former stable block, altered in 1971 to form the Claife Crier Bar. This gets its name from a ghostly local legend, illustrated on the sign above the door. Some of the original stalls have been retained, making attractive and secluded seating areas, and the old beams are believed to have come from ships wrecked on the Cumbrian coast. Original horse-collars and other memorabilia decorate the walls. Outside is a pleasant garden, which keeps the sun until late in the evening and has views to Coniston Old Man and Swirl How.

 about the pub

Sawrey Hotel
Far Sawrey, Ambleside
Cumbria LA22 0LQ
Tel 015394 43425

DIRECTIONS:	on the B5285
PARKING:	30
OPEN:	daily, all day
FOOD:	daily lunchtime bar menu
BREWERY/COMPANY:	free house
REAL ALE:	Black Sheep Bitter, Theakston Best, Hawkshead Bitter, Jennings Cumberland Ale, guest beer
ROOMS:	18 en suite

Food
Bar lunches include smoked salmon sandwiches, a Hiker's lunch (cheddar cheese), smoked Esthwaite trout with salad, local venison sausage with tomato and apple chutney, and beef casserole. Set dinner menu only.

Family facilities
Children are welcome in the bar until 7pm, and allowed in the lounge at all times. At lunch, younger children have their own menu, and old children can chose smaller portions of some adult dishes. Safe garden.

Alternative refreshment stops
None along the route. The New Inn at Far Sawrey and Tower Banks Arms in Sawrey.

☛ Where to go from here
Hill Top is the 17th-century farmhouse at Near Sawrey where Beatrix Potter wrote and illustrated her tales of Peter Rabbit and his friends (tel 015394 36269; www.nationaltrust.org.uk).

Over Hampsfell from Grange-over-Sands

A walk through woods and over open fell above a charming seaside resort.

Grange-over-Sands
TAKE NOTICE
All persons visiting this Hospice by permission of the owner, are requested to respect private property, and not by acts of wanton mischief and destruction show that they possess more muscle than brain. I have no hope that this request will be attended to...
G Remington

So reads one of the panels inside the peculiar Hospice of Hampsfell at the high point of this walk. Its tone matches that of Grange-over-Sands, with its neat and tidy white limestone buildings, colourful gardens, sunny aspect and seaside disposition. It has long been a popular seaside resort, particularly since the Furness Railway reached the town in 1857. Day trippers also arrived by steamer across Morecambe Bay, disembarking at the Claire House Pier, which was dramatically blown away by a storm in 1928.

Today the sea is somewhat distanced from the sea wall, and the town, bypassed by mainstream holidaymakers, retains a refined air of quiet dignity. Grange has many splendid buildings and its ornamental gardens, complete with ponds, are a good place to relax and enjoy a picnic. The gardens rise to the open airy spaces of Hampsfell (Hampsfield Fell on the map) via the mixed woodland of Eggerslack.

The neat square tower, around 20ft (6m) high, which adorns the top of Hampsfield Fell, is known as the Hospice of Hampsfell.

It was apparently built by a minister from nearby Cartmel Priory over a century ago for 'the shelter and entertainment of travellers over the fell'. Enclosed by a fence of chains to keep cattle out, it provides a convenient shelter should the weather take a turn for the worse. On its north face stone steps give access to the top of the tower and a fabulous view. On the top, a novel direction indicator, which consists of a wooden sighting arrow mounted on a rotating circular table, lets you know which distant point of interest you are looking at. Simply align the arrow to the chosen subject, read the angle created by the arrow and locate it on the list on the east rail.

the walk

1 From the north end of the car park walk through the **ornamental gardens**. The most direct route keeps left, close to the main road. Exit to the mini-roundabout and take the road signed to Newby Bridge, Ulverston, Windermere. Go up and round the bend, and find steps up to a **squeeze stile** on the left, signed 'Routen Well and Hampsfield'.

2 Take the path rising through **Eggerslack Wood**. Cross directly over a surfaced track and continue, to pass a house on the left. Steps lead on to a track. Cross this diagonally to follow a track, signed **'Hampsfell'**. The track makes one zig-zag and then climbs directly through the woods, passing old reservoirs which once supplied water to one of the hotels. At the top is a wall and stile.

what to look for

Rising skyward above the main street and below the church, the clock tower is noted as one of the finest buildings in Grange. It was financed by Mrs Sophia Deardon and built in 1912 from local limestone (probably from the quarry at Eden Mount) and the chocolate-brown St Bees sandstone.

If you look up the Fell Road out of Grange you will see an impressive white limestone building. Hardcragg Hall is the oldest house in Grange and is dated 1563. John Wilkinson, ironmaster, once lived here. His first iron boat was launched some 2 miles (3.2km) away at Castlehead on the River Winster.

2h00 — **4 MILES** — **6.4 KM** — **LEVEL 1 2 3**

MAP: OS Explorer OL 7 The English Lakes (SE)

START/FINISH: car park below road and tourist office, central Grange; grid ref: SD 410780

PATHS: paths and tracks, can be muddy in places, 7 stiles

LANDSCAPE: town, woods and open fell, extensive seascapes

PUBLIC TOILETS: at Ornamental Gardens, north end of car park

TOURIST INFORMATION: Grange-over-Sands, tel 015395 34026

THE PUB: The Lancastrian, Grange-over-Sands, near the start of the route

❶ Care needed with traffic on busy streets at the start and finish. Suitability: children 6+

Getting to the start

Grange-over-Sands is on the coast, south of Newby Bridge. Take the B5277 into the town. Just after the railway station keep left and follow the main street until signs point to a parking area down a lane on the left, below the Commodore Inn.

3 Cross the stile and follow the signposted path up the open hillside, passing sections of limestone pavement and little craggy outcrops. Cross another stile and go right along the wall. Where it veers away, continue in the same direction, following a grassy track past ancient stone cairns to the tower landmark of the **Hospice of Hampsfell**.

4 Turn left at the tower and follow the path over the edge of a little limestone escarpment (slippery rock). Continue over another escarpment and gently down to a stile. Keep straight ahead through a dip and up the green hill beyond. Cross over the top and descend again to a gate and stile.

Gardens and ornamental lake at Grange-over-Sands, the start point of the walk

Although the path bears left here, it is usual to continue directly to the little cairn on **Fell End**, with fine views over **Morecambe Bay**. Go sharp left to rejoin the main path, which skirts to the left of a little valley of thorn bushes and descends to a gate and a road.

5 Cross the road, take the squeeze stile and descend diagonally left across the field to a gate on to a road by the front door of **Springbank Cottage**. Descend the surfaced track to enter a farmyard and bear right to a **stone stile**. Go over the hill, following the path parallel to the wall and

cross a stile into a narrow path. Follow this, with a high wall to the right, round the corner and down to a road junction. Go left on a private road/public footpath, and then bear right at the fork. At the next junction turn right to descend the track and at the following junction go left down **Charney Well Lane**. When you get to another junction, bear left below the woods of **Eden Mount**. Keep descending to a T-junction and go right. At the junction with a larger road go left (toilets to the right) and descend past the church and clock tower to a junction with the main road (**B5277**). Go left and then right to the **car park.**

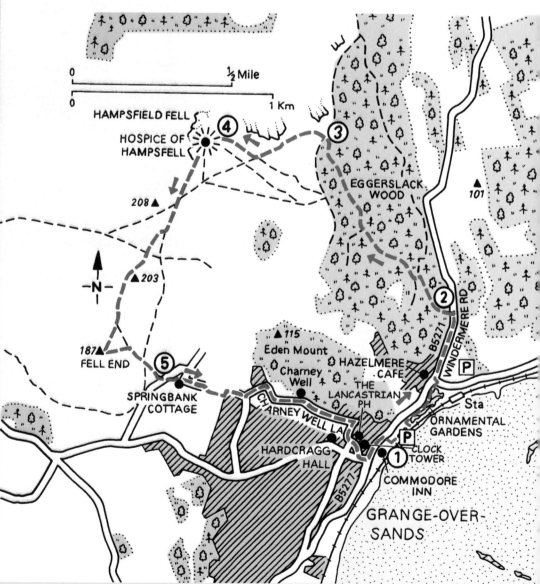

The Lancastrian

The Lancastrian is just a minute or two off the direct route of the walk, and occupies part of what used to be the town's cinema and dance hall. Inside the decor is, by and large, 'pubby' enough, but look for various literary quotations inscribed on the beams.

Food

Typical main dishes include chunky shepherd's pie, neck of lamb, scrumpy pork hock and duck breast in plum and ginger sauce. Lighter snacks include sandwiches and ploughman's lunches.

Family facilities

Children under supervision are welcome in the bars. Outdoor seating is limited to a couple of pavement tables.

about the pub

The Lancastrian
Main Street,
Grange-over-Sands
Cumbria LA11 6AB
Tel 015395 32455

DIRECTIONS: just off the walk – look up to the right from the mini-roundabout by the clock tower

PARKING: use walk car park

OPEN: daily, all day

FOOD: no food Tuesday

BREWERY/COMPANY: free house

REAL ALE: Boddingtons, Castle Eden Ale, guest beer

DOGS: welcome inside

Alternative refreshment stops

Grange-over-Sands has many excellent cafés and inns catering for a wide range of tastes. On the route, of particular merit are the Commodore Inn and Hazelmere Café.

☞ Where to go from here

North of Newby Bridge at Lakeside, on the southern tip of Windermere, is the Aquarium of the Lakes, home to the UK's largest collection of freshwater fish and with a series of themed natural habitats (www.aquariumofthelakes.co.uk).

From Garrigill to Ashgill Force

A broad valley hides exciting waterfalls and ravines.

Garrigill

As you approach the village, with the long ascent over Hartside, on one of the highest main roads in the country, you cross the main watershed of England. Below is the valley of the South Tyne, its waters feeding not west to the Irish Sea but east to the North Sea. The landscape is different from the Lake District, the hills big and bare.

It might appear that this landscape has changed little for centuries. The truth is, of course, that few English landscapes are static, and this is no exception. Today's generally pastoral scene conceals the scars of an industrial past. Garrigill's population in the mid-19th century was five or six times what it is today. Two main trends lie behind this decline, one being that fewer people work on the land today, while the second factor has been the disappearance of the once-dominant lead-mining industry. Mining

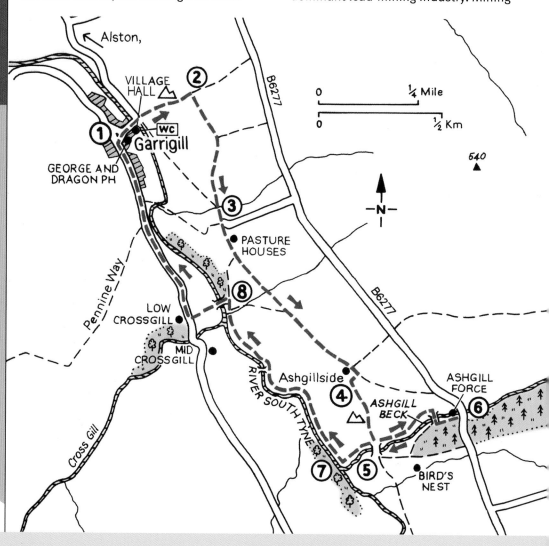

View across Garrigill and the South Tyne Valley

1h30 · **3 MILES** · **4.8 KM** · **LEVEL 123**

developed rapidly from the mid-18th century onwards, largely under the control of the Quaker-owned London Lead Mining Company, which built houses, schools and reading rooms for its workers and their families. Garrigill was virtually a 'company town'. Sharp eyes will be able to spot traces of this industry on the upper slopes. Look out, in particular, for sharp V-shaped valleys cut into the moorland, many of which are artificial. Known as hushes, they were created by damming a stream and then allowing the water to escape in a flash flood. This was a relatively quick and easy way of stripping off the topsoil to expose the rocks beneath.

the walk

1 Walk down the road in front of the **post office** and the **George & Dragon Inn** (signposted 'Alston, Nenthead') to a bridge high above the river **South Tyne**. The road bends left but a track continues straight ahead. Follow this track, very steep at first, to reach a tarmac lane at a bend.

2 Turn right immediately, signed to **Pasture Houses**, go through a gate and straight across a field. Cross a stile and continue to a gate below some new and restored buildings, and then to a stile. Bear right, descending slightly, towards a **farm** and trees. Go through a gate in the field corner and then along the left (upper) side of the **barn**. Cross the yard diagonally to a track which leads out to a road.

MAP: OS Explorer OL31 North Pennines

START/FINISH: parking on green in front of post office, Garrigill; grid ref: NY 7444150

PATHS: field paths, tracks and a quiet lane, 17 stiles

LANDSCAPE: open fields, wooded river valley with cascades and waterfalls

PUBLIC TOILETS: beside village hall, just before bridge at start of walk

TOURIST INFORMATION: Alston Moor, tel 01434 382244

THE PUB: George & Dragon Inn, Garrigill, see Point 1 on route

❶ Path runs above steep drops to river. Suitability: children 7+

Getting to the start

Garrigill lies south east of the village of Alston, which is at the junction of the A686 and the A689, due south of Haltwhistle. From Alston take the B6277 and turn off right. In Garrigill, park considerately around the village green.

3 Cross directly to a stile. Follow the wall below gardens on the left, then continue straight ahead to a stile. Keep straight ahead and level to another stile, then aim for another **farm** ahead. Go left of the first building and into the yard, then go left and right between the houses to a stile where the lane bends left again. Cross a short field and emerge onto a track. Cross this, and the **paddock** beyond, to a stile. Turn right, along the back of a house and through a gateway into a field.

4 Turn left and follow a green track, walking initially parallel to the wall and then descending to a **footbridge** and four-way fingerpost.

5 Don't cross the bridge but turn left (signposted 'Ashgill Force') and follow a path left of **Ashgill Beck**. Follow this, passing some small cataracts, to a footbridge with the main falls visible ahead. Cross the bridge and continue to the **falls**, passing **old mine workings** on the right. It's possible to walk right behind the falls, but be careful as the surface is loose, and often wet and slippery too.

6 Retrace your steps, crossing the first footbridge, to the lower footbridge by the four-way **fingerpost**. Now continue downhill, still following **Ashgill Beck**.

7 Where Ashgill Beck meets the River South Tyne, cross a stile on to the riverside path (**South Tyne Trail** waymarks). Follow the path, paved with flagstones in places, above a wooded gorge-like section. Where the river curves away to the left, it's possible to continue straight ahead across a rushy field. Go past a bridge (to **Mid Crossgill**) and continue along the river, under tall pines (watch for red squirrels here), to reach another four-way fingerpost.

Looking from behind Ashgill Force waterfall with the river running down the valley

8 Turn left across the **bridge**; walk up the track to a gate opposite **Low Crossgill** farm. Turn right along the road into **Garrigill**.

what to look for

Ashgill Force waterfall is the most striking sight on the walk. The stream has carved itself a significant gorge. A harder band of limestone has resisted its efforts while the softer shales below have been cut back, creating an overhang which allows you to walk right behind the fall, which is approximately 50ft (15m) high. There are several smaller but still lovely cascades lower down the course of the beck before it joins the South Tyne.

George & Dragon Inn

The 17th-century George & Dragon Inn occupies a unique position, where the best-known of Britain's long-distance walks, the Pennine Way, crosses perhaps its most popular major cycle route, the C2C. Needless to say, walkers and cyclists are big business here, and the owners know exactly what their priorities are. On bleak Pennine days, getting warm and dry is often the first priority and a blazing fire in the homely, stone-flagged bar helps. There's also an attractive stone and panelled dining room and four new bedrooms. Robust appetites and hearty thirsts are well looked after, the latter with foaming pints of Black Sheep or local micro-brewery ales. The pub is also a mini information centre with maps, leaflets and advice all on hand.

Food

The menu concentrates on traditional pub favourites, done well: the Cumberland sausage is from a butcher in nearby Alston, the game pie home-made. Non-carnivores are recommended to try the vegetarian moussaka. Snacks include sandwiches, filled jacket potatoes and a giant Yorkshire pudding filled with steak and gravy.

Family facilities

Children are welcome in the lounge and dining room until 9.30pm. In summer there's alfresco seating on the village green.

☛ Where to go from here

Visit Alston, England's highest market town, 1,000 feet (305m) above sea level, with steep cobbled streets and many 17th-century buildings. It's also home to the narrow-gauge South Tynedale Railway

about the pub

George & Dragon Inn
Garrigill, Alston
Cumbria CA9 3DS
Tel 01434 381293
www.garrigill-pub.com

DIRECTIONS: centre of Garrigill, at the start of the walk

PARKING: village green

OPEN: daily, and all day Saturday and Sunday from Easter to October. Closed Monday to Thursday lunchtime in winter

FOOD: daily

BREWERY/COMPANY: free house

REAL ALE: Black Sheep Bitter, 3 guest beers

DOGS: welcome inside

ROOMS: 4 bedrooms

running on part of the route of the (standard-gauge) Haltwhistle-to-Alston branch line. A few miles away, the Nenthead Mines Heritage Centre gives a real insight into the area's lead-mining past, and you can even venture underground to see exactly what a mine was like.

From West Burton to Aysgarth

From West Burton to Aysgarth
and back, via the famous
Aysgarth Falls.

Aysgarth Village and Falls

Many regard West Burton as the prettiest
village in the Dales. It is at the entrance to
Bishopdale, with its road link to Wharfedale.
South is the road to Walden Head, now a
dead end for motorists, but for walkers an
alternative route to Starbotton and Kettlewell.
At the end of the walk you'll travel for a short
time, near Flanders Hall, along Morpeth Gate,
the old packhorse route to Middleham.

After crossing the wide flood plain of
Bishopdale Beck, and crossing Eshington
Bridge, you climb across the hill to descend
into Aysgarth. A village of two halves, the
larger part – which you come to first – is set
along the A684 road. The walk takes you
along the field path to Aysgarth's other half,
around the church. Look inside at the
spectacular choir screen from Jervaulx Abbey.
Like the elaborate stall beside it, it was carved
by the renowned Ripon workshops.

Beyond the church, the path follows the
river beside Aysgarth's Middle and Lower
Falls. They have become one of the most
popular tourist sights in the Yorkshire Dales
National Park.

On your return, you pass two oddities
in the parkland behind the house at
Sorrellsykes Park. These two follies were
built in the 18th century by Mrs Sykes and
no one seems to know why.

the walk

1 With your back to the Fox and Hounds
turn left along the lane, past the Village
Shop. Opposite 'Meadowcroft' go left
through a ginnel, signed **'Eshington Bridge'**.
Cross the road, turn right then left, through
a gate and down steps. Pass the barn, go
through a gateway and across the field.
Go through a gap in the wall with a stile
beyond, then bend right to a stile on to
the road.

2 Turn left, go over the bridge and ahead
up the narrow lane. As it bends left go

The Aysgarth Falls are a major attraction in the Yorkshire Dales National Park

ahead through a stile, signed **'Aysgarth'**, then on through a gated stile. Go ahead to a gap in the fence near a **barn**, then through a gate. Bend left to a gate in the field corner, go through a gateway and on to a stile with a **footpath signpost**. Turn right and descend to another signpost, which points half right into a grassy hollow.

3 Go ahead to a stile in the field corner. Follow the signpost direction 'to Aysgarth' uphill to a gateway and go through a stile on the right. Cross the field half left to go through a gated stile on to a lane. Turn left, then almost immediately right through a stile, signed **'Aysgarth'**. Go through three stiles to a road.

4 Turn right into the village, past **The George & Dragon**. At the left bend, go ahead toward the Methodist church, then right at the green, and follow the lane. Go through a gate by **Field House** and to another stile, turning left along the track. Follow the path through eight stiles to the road.

5 Go ahead into the **churchyard**, pass right of the church and go through two stiles, through woodland, then over another stile. Follow the path downhill towards the river, descending steps to a gate, then a stile. When the footpath reaches the **river bank**, take a signed stile right.

6 Follow the path over two stiles to a signpost, bending right across the field to a road. Turn left over the bridge, turning right into **woodland** a few paces beyond, signed **'Edgley'**. Go over a stile and cross the field to a gate on to the road.

MAP: OS Explorer OL30 Yorkshire Dales – Northern & Central

START/FINISH: centre of West Burton, by (but not on) the Green; grid ref: SE 017867

PATHS: field and riverside paths and tracks, 35 stiles

LANDSCAPE: two typical Dales villages, fields and falls on the River Ure

PUBLIC TOILETS: none on route; Aysgarth Falls National Park visitor centre is close

TOURIST INFORMATION: Leyburn, tel 01969 623069

THE PUB: The George & Dragon, Aysgarth
🅛 The main road at Aysgarth can be very busy at the weekend.

Getting to the start

West Burton lies at the convergence of Bishopdale and the Walden Valley. It's a mile south of the A684 Wensleydale road and can be accessed by taking the B6160 between West Witton and Aysgarth. There's no car park but there's plenty of space around the huge village green.

Below: A rocket-shaped folly on grassy hills at Aysgarth

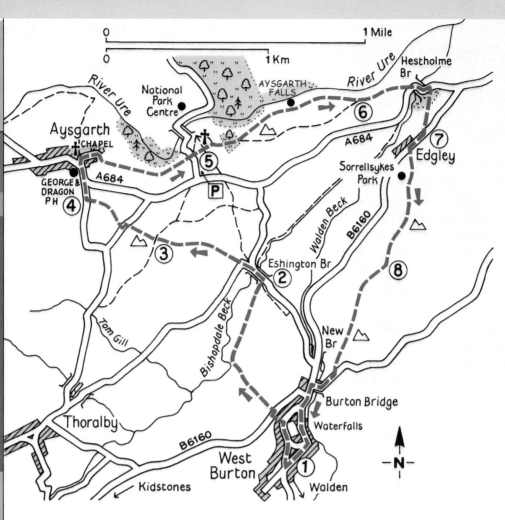

what to look for

The woods around Aysgarth have long been used for the production of hazel poles, and there is evidence of this trade on the walk, with the now-overgrown stumps of the hazel trees sprouting many branches, some of them of considerable age. In Freeholders' Wood beside the Middle and Lower Falls, on the opposite side of the River Ure from the route of the walk, the National Park Authority has restarted this ancient craft of coppicing. The name comes from the French *couper*, meaning 'to cut'. Each year the hazel trees are cut back to a stump – called a stool – from which new shoots are allowed to grow. As long as they are protected from grazing cattle, the shoots develop into poles, and can be harvested after around seven years' growth. Hazel poles are traditionally used for making woven hurdles, and the thinner stems for basket-weaving.

7 Turn right. About 150yds (137m) along, go left over a stile, signed '**Flanders Hall**'. Walk below the follies to a footpath sign, beyond which the route crosses two tracks from the farming complex of **Sorrellsykes Park**. Past the last house, waymarking posts highlight the route which crosses a dyke, then passes above a copse of trees.

8 Opposite a **stone barn** on the hillside to the left, go right, through a gate, and go downhill through two more gates, then over three stiles to a lane. Turn right and go over a bridge to join the village road. Turn left, back to the Green.

The George & Dragon

Beautifully situated near the Aysgarth Falls in the heart of Herriot country, this attractive and very popular 17th-century coaching inn has a long tradition of offering warm Yorkshire hospitality. The small and cosy bar sports beams hung with tankards, jugs and copper pots, wood-panelled walls, built-in cushioned wall seats, and a warming winter log fire. Separate, plush lounge filled with antique china, and seven comfortable en suite bedrooms. Paved beer garden with lovely views of Upper Wensleydale.

Food

On the light lunch menu you will find sandwiches, ploughman's and popular snacks. More substantial dishes take in lamb chump with fondant potato, spring greens and lamb jus, loin of pork with caramelised apple and black pudding with mash, steamed monkfish, and battered haddock. Fresh fish dishes and Sunday roast lunches.

Family facilities

Smaller portions of the main menu dishes can be ordered and youngsters have a children's menu to choose from. There are two family bedrooms upstairs.

Alternative refreshment stops

Up the road from the church in Aysgarth, just off the route of the walk, the Palmer Flatt Hotel has bar meals and a restaurant, as well as a beer garden with views. In West Burton, the Fox and Hounds is a traditional village pub serving meals. Aysgarth Falls National Park Centre, across the river from the church, has a good coffee shop.

about the pub

The George & Dragon

Aysgarth, Leyburn
North Yorkshire DL8 3AD
Tel: 01969 663358
www.georgeanddragonaysgarth.co.uk

DIRECTIONS: beside the A68 in the centre of the village
PARKING: 35
OPEN: daily; all day
FOOD: daily
BREWERY/COMPANY: free house
REAL ALE: Black Sheep Best & Special, John Smiths, Theakston Bitter
DOGS: allowed in the bar
ROOMS: 7 en suite

☛ Where to go from here

Visit the Yorkshire Carriage Museum by the bridge below the church in Aysgarth. Housed in a former cotton mill that wove cloth for Garibaldi's 'Red Shirts', the revolutionary army of 19th-century Italy, the museum has a fascinating display of old-time transport, from carriages and carts to hearses and fire engines. The Dales Countryside Museum in Hawes (www.destinationdales.org) tells the story of the landscape and people of the Dales past and present, with hands-on exhibits for children.

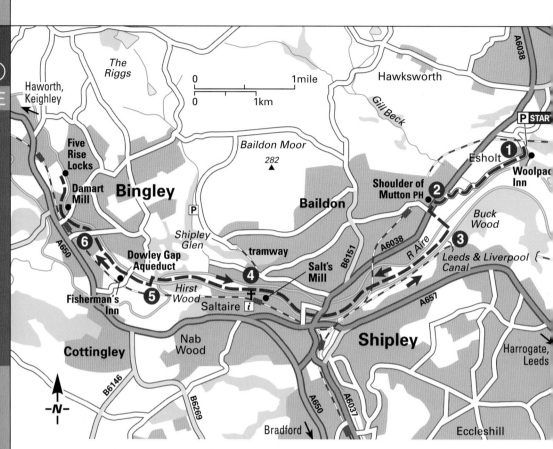

A slice of West Yorkshire from the rural environs of the TV series to the canalside mill towns of the Aire Valley.

Saltaire

Though the Industrial Revolution brought prosperity to the ruling classes, it also brought great inequalities. While the factory owners lived in their mansions in the country, their workers lived in overcrowded and unhygienic city streets. Wealthy Bradford mill owner Sir Titus Salt had been dismayed by this situation. He decided to move his mills into one unit, which would be built in a cleaner environment and would be part of a newly constructed model village. After finding his site at Shipley in the Aire Valley, Salt employed the best architects to design his project – Saltaire.

The village comprised 22 streets, all named after Salt's family, and, on its completion in 1876, there were over 800 beautifully constructed houses in an area of 25 acres (10ha). Particularly notable are the beautiful Venetian-style Congregational church and the six-storey mill. The mill closed down in 1892, following a recession, and Saltaire lay idle and degenerating. However, almost a hundred years later a Leeds millionaire, Jonathan Silver, restored the mill, which now houses the 1853 Gallery with hundreds of exhibits by local artist David Hockney. The village has been brought to life again with restaurants, a pub, antiques dealers and organised boat trips.

| 1h45 | 7 MILES | 11.3 KM | LEVEL 1 2 3 |

the ride

1 Turn left out of the car park on to the road (with care) and descend to the village. **The Woolpack**, post office and row of cottages, as featured for many years on the TV series *Emmerdale*, are on the left. Continue down the lane, passing the **Esholt Sports Club** and the campsite. The terraces of Bunker Hill on the right were *Emmerdale*'s Demdyke Row. Over a stone bridge and past a driving range the lane draws alongside the River Aire, then climbs right to meet the A6038 opposite the **Shoulder of Mutton pub**. It would be best to dismount here.

2 Turn left, following the footpath, then left again down **Buck Lane**. After a short way take the right fork, a mud and stone scrub-lined track that descends to the River Aire. Here a **steel bridge** built in 1889 takes you to the far bank, where the track climbs to the Leeds–Liverpool Canal at **Buck Wood**.

A visitors' farm at Esholt

MAP: OS Explorer 288 Bradford and Huddersfield

START/FINISH: Esholt; grid ref SE 182404

TRAILS/TRACKS: all quiet country lanes and tow path

LANDSCAPE: semi-rural and urban

PUBLIC TOILETS: Esholt car park and Five Rise Locks

TOURIST INFORMATION: Saltaire, tel 01274 774993

CYCLE HIRE: none locally

THE PUB: The Fisherman's Inn, Bingley

🛑 Busy road (A6038) at point 2; a steepish descent along the Buck Lane track to the river (point 2). Take care along the canal tow path

Getting to the start
Esholt lies on the north bank of the River Aire to the north east of Bradford. Follow the A650 trunk road to Shipley, then the A6038 through Baildon, before turning right for Esholt. The car park is on the hill, just to the north of the town and near the railway viaduct.

Why do this cycle ride?
This cycle ride visits some of the wonders of the Industrial Revolution, including Titus Salt's model village and the Bingley Five Rise Locks.

3 Turn right along the **tow path** here. After about 100yds (91m) you'll come across a **bench**, which some kind soul has sited right next to bushes that will in late August be endowed with some of the most luscious blackberries. We had a feast! The tow path is firm and wide at first, but beyond **bridge 209a**, carrying the railway to Baildon, it narrows considerably. If there are a lot of walkers about it would be best to follow the adjacent tarred lane and rejoin the tow path beyond the next bridge (209). Note: whichever way you choose, you'll be crossing traffic at this second bridge. At this point the canal is cutting through the industrial outskirts of Shipley, but soon things improve. Some smart **mill buildings** and a tower appear. You're entering the model mill town of Saltaire. Spend some time here; it's a fascinating place.

4 The tow path continues along a pleasing tree-lined section of the canal. Peeping through boughs on the left you'll see **Titus Salt's church**. At **Hirst Wood** beyond Saltaire, the River Aire and the canal draw close and the tow path continues on a narrow stretch of land between the two.

5 The canal finally crosses the river along the **Dowley Gap Aqueduct**. At bridge 206 the tow path on this side of the canal ends. Ride up the ramp, cross over the ridge, then descend to the tow path along the other side. At the next bridge **The Fisherman's Inn** has a beer garden.

6 The final stretch of the canal takes you through Bingley. There have been many changes here for the building of the Bingley Relief Road. After passing the huge **Damart Mill** and the three-rise staircase locks, you come to another tree-lined section before arriving at Bingley's famous **Five Rise Locks**. There's a steep but short climb to the top, but your reward is the fine view back to Bingley's woollen mills and chimneys and the chance of more refreshment at the lockside café. Retrace your route back along the canal to Esholt.

Five Rise Locks at Bingley

The Fisherman's Inn

Alternative refreshment stops
Before or after the ride you could try the Woolpack Inn at Esholt or, in Saltaire, there's Fanny's Café. In Bingley, there's the Five Rise Locks Café and Store.

☛ Where to go from here
You could take a walk along the signposted route from Saltaire to Shipley Glen, a popular picnic spot with a visitor centre and tramway up the hillside. For more information about the model mill town of Saltaire visit www.saltaire.yorks.com. Take a trip on the Keighley and Worth Valley Railway through the heart of Brontë country as it climbs to Haworth en route to Oxenhope. There are locomotive workshops at Haworth and an award-winning museum at Ingrow West (www.kwvr.co.uk).

An understated stone-built pub, conveniently sited right by the canal banks close to Bingley's famous Five Rise Locks. In summer there is a large attractive beer garden with wheelchair access and with pleasing views to the canal and across the Aire Valley. Very good standard of food, with a blackboard full of specials.

Food
Bar meals range from snacks and light bites to home-made pie of the day and sizzling steaks. Range of salads (chicken Caesar salad), ploughman's lunches, hot and cold sandwiches, filled jacket potatoes, gammon steak, and daily specials featuring fresh fish.

Family facilities
The pub has a children's certificate so they are very welcome throughout. There's a children's menu, smaller portions of main menu dishes and high chairs.

about the pub

The Fisherman's Inn
Wagon Lane, Dowley Gap,
Bingley, West Yorkshire BD16 1TB
Tel 01274 561697

DIRECTIONS: follow the A650 through Shipley. Just beyond where this crosses the River Aire at Cottingley, turn right along Wagon Lane towards Dowley Gap. The pub is on the right beyond the bridge over the railway

PARKING: 20

OPEN: daily; all day

FOOD: no food Sunday evening

BREWERY/COMPANY: Enterprise Inns

REAL ALE: Tetley, guest beers

Harewood House and estate

A stately home with parkland by 'Capability' Brown, a few miles from Leeds.

Harewood Estate

The Harewood Estate passed through a number of hands during the 16th and 17th centuries, eventually being bought by the Lascelles family, who still own the house. Edwin Lascelles left the 12th-century castle in its ruinous state but demolished the old hall. He wanted to create something special and hired the best architects and designers.

John Carr of York created a veritable palace of a house in an imposing neo-classical style, and laid out the estate village of Harewood too. The interior of the building was designed by Robert Adam. Thomas Chippendale made furniture for every room. The foundations were laid in 1759; 12 years later the house was finished. Inside are paintings by J M W Turner and Thomas Girtin. Turner was particularly taken with the area, producing pictures of many local landmarks. The sumptuous interior, full of portraits, ornate plasterwork and silk hangings, is in sharp contrast to life below stairs, in the kitchen and scullery.

The house sits in extensive grounds, which were groomed to be every bit as magnificent as the house. They were shaped by Lancelot 'Capability' Brown, renowned landscape designer. In addition to the formal gardens, he created the lake and woodland paths.

Harewood House has had to earn its keep in recent years. The bird garden was the first commercial venture, but now the house hosts many events.

the walk

1 From the lay-by walk 50yds (46m) away from the village of Harewood, cross the busy road with care, and walk right, down the access track to **New Laithe Farm**. Keep to the left of the farm buildings, on a rutted track heading into the valley bottom. Go through two gates and bear half left up a field, towards **Hollin Hall**. Keep left of the buildings to pass **Hollin Hall Pond**.

2 Beyond the pond take a gate and follow a track to the left, uphill, skirting **woodland** before climbing half right by **gorse bushes** to a gate in the top corner of the field. Beyond this an enclosed track now continues the climb to the top of the hill.

3 Here it is joined by a grass track from the left and bends right (you are now joining the **Leeds Country Way**). Keep straight ahead when the track forks, through a gate. Skirt woodland to emerge at a road; bear right here to arrive at the main **A61**.

54

WALK

Harewood Estate

WEST YORKSHIRE

3h00 — **6.5 MILES** — **10.5 KM** — **LEVEL 1** 2 3

MAP: OS Explorer 289 Leeds

START/FINISH: lay-by parking in Harewood; grid ref: SE 332450

PATHS: good paths and parkland tracks all the way, 2 stiles

LANDSCAPE: arable and parkland

PUBLIC TOILETS: none on route; in Harewood House if visiting

TOURIST INFORMATION: Wetherby, tel 01937 582151

THE PUB: The Harewood Arms, Harewood

❶ Path passes deep water at Hollin Hill Pond. Very busy and fast roads to cross (A61 and A659)

Getting to the start

Harewood is 8 miles (12.8km) due north of Leeds on the junction of the A61 and the A659. The lay-by car parking lies on the north side of the A659, about a mile (1.6km) to the east of the village. When arriving from the east, the lay-by is the same distance past the fourth and last turn-off to East Hardwick.

4 Cross the road to enter the **Harewood Estate** (via the right-hand gate, between imposing gate-posts). Follow the broad track ahead, through landscaped parkland, soon getting views of Harewood House to the right. Enter **woodland** through a gate, bearing immediately left after a stone bridge.

5 Bear right after 100yds (91m), as the track forks. At a crossing of tracks, bear half right, downhill on a track signed **Ebor Way**. Turn right at the next junction, then take a left fork to pass in front of **Carr House**. Follow a good track down towards the lake. Go through a gate, keep left of a high **brick wall** and walk uphill to join a metalled access road to the left. Walk down past a **house** and keep straight ahead at crossroads. Cross a bridge and follow the lane up to a gate, soon passing **Home Farm** (now converted to business units).

6 Follow the road through pastureland, turning right at the T-junction. Continue through woodland and pasture until you come to the few **houses** that comprise the estate village of Harewood.

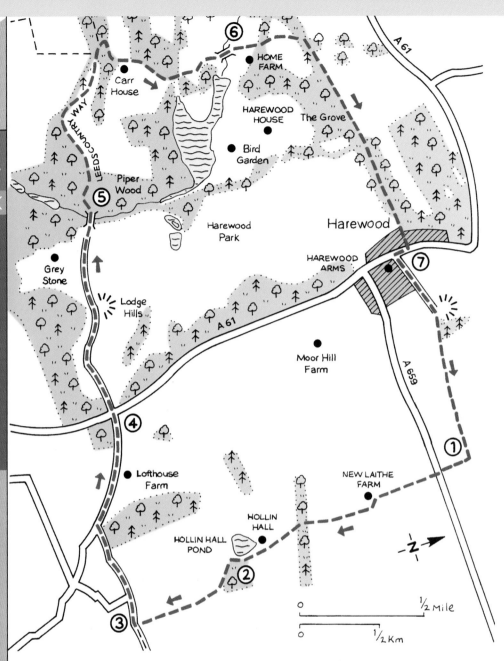

Harewood

7 Cross the main A61 road with care and walk right, for just 50yds (46m), to take a metalled drive immediately before the Harewood Arms. Pass **Maltkiln House,** keeping straight on, through a gate, as the road becomes a track. Enjoy great views over Lower Wharfedale. Ignore the stile in the fence to your right and and stay with the pleasant track to a junction south of **Stockton Grange Farm,** where you turn right. This permissive bridleway takes you back to the A659 a few paces away from the lay-by.

what to look for

The red kite, a beautiful fork-tailed bird of prey, used to be a familiar sight. But the numbers had dwindled to just a few pairs, mostly in Wales, due to centuries of persecution. There is now a new initiative to reintroduce the red kite to Yorkshire, and a number of birds have been released at Harewood House. You may be lucky enough to spot one.

The Harewood Arms

about the pub

The Harewood Arms
Harrogate Road, Harewood
Leeds, West Yorkshire LS17 9LH
Tel: 0113 288 6566
www.harewoodarms.co.uk

DIRECTIONS: opposite the main gates to
Harewood House in the village centre
PARKING: 100
OPEN: daily; all day
FOOD: daily; all day Saturday and Sunday
BREWERY/COMPANY: Samuel Smiths
REAL ALE: Samuel Smith's OBB
DOGS: allowed in the bar and garden
ROOMS: 23 en suite

*Built in 1815, this former coaching inn
stands opposite the gates to Harewood
House and provides a smart and
comfortable base for those visiting
Harrogate, Leeds, York and the Dales.
Behind the rather foreboding stone façade*
*of this Georgian hall lies a friendly pub
serving excellent food. The carpeted
lounge bar is extremely comfortable with
many easy chairs, and Sam Smith's Old
Brewery Bitter is hand-pulled from
wooden casks. The restaurant serves
à la carte and table d'hôte menus. Its
Georgian windows look out on to the
pleasant leafy back garden.*

Food
In the bar tuck into various salads,
sandwiches, filled baguettes, grilled
Yorkshire gammon, omelettes, and local
sausages and mash. In the restaurant, roast
rack of lamb with redcurrant jus and sea bass
with cream, white wine, prawn and fennel
sauce show the style of cooking. Afternoon
teas are also served.

Family facilties
Although there are no specific facilities for
children, there is a family area in the bar and
children are welcome overnight.

Alternative refreshment stops
If visiting Harewood House you will find
a licensed café/restaurant.

☛ Where to go from here
While the walk described here uses rights
of way through the grounds of Harewood
House, you need to pay if you want to
investigate the house itself, or the bird
gardens, or the many other attractions
that include an adventure playground. Make
a day of it: do the walk in the morning, have
lunch at the Harewood Arms and investigate
the unrivalled splendour of Harewood House
in the afternoon (www.harewood.org).

Kirkham Priory and the Derwent Valley

Derwent Valley

NORTH YORKSHIRE

A circular ride around the peaceful Derwent Valley.

Kirkham Priory

Sometime in the early 1120s, William L'Espec was riding by the banks of the Derwent when his horse threw him. He died instantly. Grief-stricken, his father, Lord Helmsley, founded an Augustinian monastery on the site of the accident.

The priory started as a small church in 1125, but by the middle of the 13th century fine western towers had been built and the eastern end extended. Later chapels were added, one abutting the north transept, and a second by the presbytery's south wall. The money ran out and the work was halted. Unfortunately, Kirkham's lack of size didn't save it from destruction during the Dissolution of the Monasteries, when it was laid to waste.

The main tower of the priory collapsed in 1784 during high winds, and locals took much of the masonry to build their own houses. However the remains that survive do much to stir the imagination. Today, it's a rather peaceful setting with lawns sloping down to the river and sylvan hillsides beyond.

The remains of Kirkham Priory

2h00 — 8 MILES — 12.9 KM — LEVEL 1

The wall of the 13th-century gatehouse is the centrepiece, with fine sculpted figures representing, among others, Christ, St George and the Dragon, St Bartholomew and David and Goliath. Also of note are the delicate arches of the lavatorium, set in the west wall of the cloister.

the ride

1 Westow is a pleasant little hillside village lying half a mile (800m) above the River Derwent. Strangely the name originates from Wifestowe, meaning a place of women. The pub, the Blacksmith's Inn, is the centrepiece of the village as the church lies in isolation a mile to the north. Head north from the village centre then go left at the first junction, signed Kirkham and York. Although there's a bridleway on the right, it's usually too choked with vegetation to be of any use. It would be better to stay with the lane, passing the solitary electricity-generating **windmill** to arrive at a T-junction at the northern extremities of Howsham Wood. Turn right here, tracing the brow of **Badger Bank** high above the River Derwent. After staying fairly level along the bank, the lane makes a steady descent to the **Stone Trough Inn** at Kirkham.

2 From the inn the road descends steadily downhill, around a left-hand bend and past a small **car park** by the entrance to the priory, which is well worth a visit before you continue the journey. The road continues over **Kirkham Bridge**, an elegant three-arched stone structure, rebuilt in the 18th century.

MAP: OS Explorer 300 Howardian Hills and Malton

START/FINISH: roadside parking in Westow; grid ref: SE 753653

TRAILS/TRACKS: all quiet country lanes

LANDSCAPE: rolling pastoral hills and a wooded valley

PUBLIC TOILETS: none on route

TOURIST INFORMATION: Malton, tel: 01653 600048

CYCLE HIRE: none locally

THE PUB: The Stone Trough Inn, Kirkham Abbey

🛈 Some of the hills are fairly steep and challenging and would be tiring for young children

Getting to the start
Westow lies just off the A64 York to Malton road. Leave the A64 near Whitwell-on-the-Hill, following signs for Kirkham. Descend into the Derwent Valley past the priory. Go straight on at the junction to pass The Stone Trough Inn, turn left at the next junction, then right to reach the village centre. Park at the roadside.

Why do this cycle ride?
Here you can see the Derwent Valley at its most attractive, with great loops in the lively river, wooded hillsides, great mansions and a fascinating ancient priory.

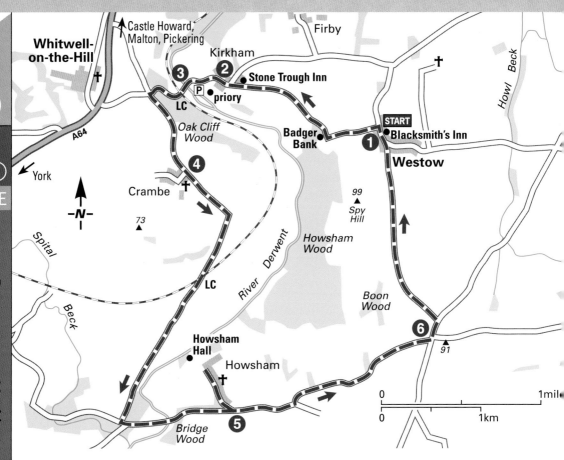

3 At the other side there's a level crossing followed by a short steep pull (you may need to dismount), as the road climbs through the dense conifers of **Oak Cliff Wood** to two closely spaced junctions. Ignore the right turns at both but instead follow signs to Crambe. The lane now follows the upper perimeter of the conifer wood before descending towards **Crambe** village.

4 This quiet backwater lies on a cul-de-sac to the right, so there's a there-and-back detour to this same spot to see the square-towered **St Michael's Church**. It's downhill from here, with a right-hand bend after 0.5 mile (800m). Beyond this you come to another **level crossing**. This one has a bell to ring to get the attention of the signalman, who will come to open it for you – it's all good 21st-century technology here in the Howardian Hills! The road descends further with the River Derwent clearly in view below left and the

grand mansion of **Howsham Hall** on the far bank. At the next T-junction turn left following the directions to 'Howsham and Leavening', but ignore the right turn shortly after. Your road crosses the Derwent at Howsham Bridge, before climbing steadily past **Bridge Wood**.

5 Howsham village lies on another cul-de-sac to the left. Its cottages have well-manicured greens; there's a small spired **church** on the right and the well-known and rather grand **Howsham Hall School** at the end of the road. Back on the main route, the lane climbs and winds over pastured knolls and after 3 miles (4.8km) comes to a high crossroads.

6 Turn left for Westow and Malton, then take the left fork for **Westow**. The road makes a gentle ascent to a rise east of **Spy Hill**. Now you descend back to Westow village.

The Stone Trough Inn

about the pub

The Stone Trough Inn
Kirkham Abbey,
Whitwell-on-the-Hill,
York, North Yorkshire YO60 7JS
Tel 01653 618713
www.stonetroughinn.co.uk

DIRECTIONS: see Getting to the start

PARKING: 100

OPEN: all day Sunday; closed Monday except
Bank Holidays

FOOD: no food Sunday evening

BREWERY/COMPANY: free house

REAL ALE: Tetley, Black Sheep, Timothy Taylor
Landlord, Malton Golden Chance, Theakston
Old Peculier, guest beer

---

*Restored in 1982 from the original Stone
Trough Cottage, the Stone Trough Inn
stands beside a narrow lane high above
Kirkham Abbey and the River Derwent.
Lots of oak beams, bare stone walls,
flagged floors and cosy rooms filled with
fresh flowers add colour and character,
and log fires and comfortable furnishings
draw a good crowd. Further attractions
include the super views across the
Derwent Valley and the impressive,
modern pub menus that make the most of
the abundant local produce available.
Good global list of wines and four tip-top
Yorkshire ales on tap.*

Food

In the bar you'll find excellent lunchtime
sandwiches (cheddar cheese and red
onion), starters of warm salad of crispy chilli
beef with honey and sesame seed dressing
and home-made soup, and main courses
such as local pork sausages on sage and
onion rosti with real ale gravy, creamy fish
pie, roast monkfish wrapped in Parma ham
with rosemary butter sauce, and whole roast
partridge with crab-apple jus. Puddings
include treacle tart with vanilla ice cream.
Separate restaurant menu.

Family facilities

Children of all ages are welcome. You will
find a children's menu and portions of
adult dishes, high chairs, small cutlery
and drawing materials to keep youngsters
amused.

Alternative refreshment stops

The Blacksmith's Arms, Westow.

☛ Where to go from here

The Cistercian Rievaulx Abbey, a short way
to the north, has connections with Kirkham,
and is well worth seeing (www.english-
heritage.org.uk). Castle Howard
(www.castlehoward.co.uk) is a short
drive away, as is Pickering and the North
Yorkshire Moors Railway, a fascinating
steam railway that travels through stunning
scenery into the heart of the moor
(www.northyorkshiremoorsrailway.com).

Moorland around Goathland and Mallyan Spout

From the popular moorland village with its television links, through woodland and over the moor.

Heartbeat country

Goathland is one of the most popular destinations for visitors to the North York Moors National Park. Its situation, around a large open common, criss-crossed by tracks and closely cropped by grazing sheep, has always been attractive. Today many tourists are drawn to Goathland because it is used as the fictitious village of Aidensfield for the popular television series *Heartbeat*. The Goathland Story exhibition tells the village's history from the time it was an Iron Age centre for making stone querns to grind corn, to today – and there's a special *Heartbeat* collection. The walk begins with a

visit to the 70ft (21m) Mallyan Spout waterfall into the West Beck. In dry weather only a trickle of water may fall from the side of the gorge into the stream below but after rain it can become an impressive torrent. Take care at all times: sometimes it may be impossible to pass the waterfall on the streamside path.

After you have crossed the ford and turned on to the moorland by Hunt House, you might find yourself accompanied by the sudden flutter of red grouse rising from their nest sites on the heather moorland.

If you visit in late summer, the moors will be clothed in the colours of heather. Sheep grazing has for centuries been the traditional way of managing the moors as the animals help keep the heather short and encourage the new shoots. To regenerate the heather, landowners regularly use carefully controlled burning in the early spring or the autumn when the ground is wet. The fire burns away the old heather stems, but does not damage the roots, nor the peat. New growth quickly springs up to feed the young grouse.

what to look for

In the valley of the West Beck, and especially near Mallyan Spout, you will see lots of ferns. Among the sorts you might spot are the male fern, with its pale green stems, the buckler fern, which has scales with a dark central stripe and paler edges, and the hartstongue fern, with its distinctive strap-like fronds. They are all typical of damp, humid areas, and like every fern, they are flowerless. Instead, they reproduce by means of spores – look under the leaves to find the characteristic dots that are the spore sacs or sporangia. The spores are dispersed by wind or by animals.

Mallyan Spout

WALK

2h00 — **4.5 MILES** — **7.2 KM** — **LEVEL 1 2 3**

MAP: OS Explorer OL27 North York Moors – Eastern

START/FINISH: west end of Goathland village, near church; grid ref: NZ 827007

PATHS: streamside tracks, field and moorland paths, 2 stiles

LANDSCAPE: deep, wooded valley, farmland and open moorland

PUBLIC TOILETS: Goathland village

TOURIST INFORMATION: Whitby, tel 01947 602674

THE PUB: The Goathland Hotel, Goathland

❗ The initial riverside path to Mallyan Spout is slippery

Getting to the start

Goathland is situated 8 miles (12.9km) southwest of Whitby. It lies just 2 miles (3.2km) west of the A169 Whitby to Malton road and can also be reached using the North Yorkshire Moors Railway from Grosmont or Pickering. The easiest parking is at the west end of the village near the church.

the walk

1 Opposite the church go through the kissing gate to the right of the **Mallyan Spout Hotel**, signed 'Mallyan Spout'. Follow the path to a streamside signpost and turn left. Continue past the waterfall (take care after heavy rain). Follow the footpath signs, over two footbridges, over a stile and up steps. Continue by the stream, then ascend to a stile on to a road beside a **bridge**.

2 Turn left along the road and climb the hill. Where the road bends left, go right along a **bridleway** through a gate. Turn left down a path to go over a bridge, then ahead by the **buildings**, through a gate and across the field.

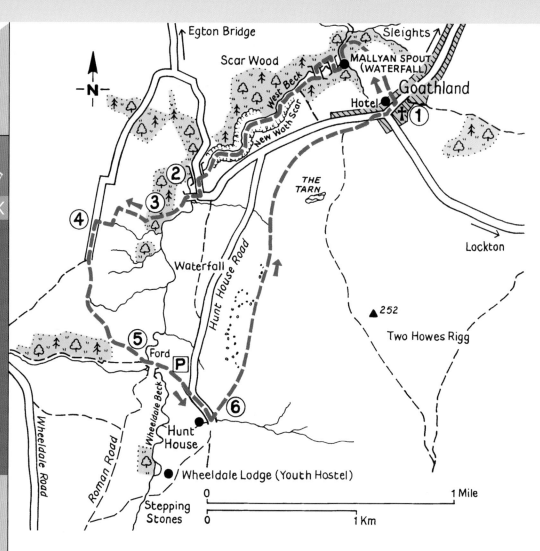

3 Part-way across the field, go through a gate to the right into **woodland**. Ascend a stony track, go through a wooden gate then left to another gate on the edge of the wood. Ignoring the gate, turn right up the field, before going left at the top through a **gateway**. Continue with a wall on your right and go through a waymarked gateway in the wall and up the field, to emerge through a gate on to a **metalled lane**.

4 Turn left along the lane, go through a gate and follow the '**Roman Road**' sign. Go through another gate, still following the public bridleway signs as you join a green lane. Continue through a small handgate, to descend to another gate and then on until you reach a **ford**.

5 Cross the ford and go straight ahead along the track, eventually to reach a road by a **bungalow**. Turn right up the road and left by a **wooden garage** to continue along a green track up the hillside.

6 Go straight ahead at a crossing track, passing a small **cairn** and bending left along the heathery ridge. The obvious path is marked by a series of **little cairns**. Eventually, take a left fork to go down a shallow gill and join a clear track. **Goathland church** soon comes into sight. Pass a bridleway sign and descend to the road near the church. The **Goathland Hotel** can be found on the right-hand side at the far end of the main street.

The Goathland Hotel

Conveniently sited on Goathland's main street, just 500 yards (457m) from the North Yorkshire Moors Railway, this stone-built Victorian building draws the crowds despite its off-the-beaten-track moorland village location. It is the Aidensfield Arms in the TV series Heartbeat and can get very busy with 'location' enthusiasts, so arrive early! Traditionally furnished, it has a spacious main bar with tiled floor, ceiling beams and winter log fires, a plush, carpeted lounge bar, and a wood-panelled restaurant. Comfortable bedrooms have moorland views.

about the pub

The Goathland Hotel
Goathland, Whitby
North Yorkshire YO22 5LY
Tel: 01947 896203

DIRECTIONS: on main village street
PARKING: 20
OPEN: daily; all day in high summer
FOOD: daily
BREWERY/COMPANY: Punch Taverns
REAL ALE: Flowers IPA, Camerons Strongarm
DOGS: welcome on leads
ROOMS: 9 bedrooms (8 en suite)

Food

Food is simple but well prepared. At lunchtime expect open sandwiches (home-cooked ham) and salads, ploughman's lunches and traditional bar meals like filled giant Yorkshire puddings (roast beef and onion gravy), home-made steak and kidney pie, and Whitby scampi and chips.

Family facilities

There are two family areas in the bars and smaller portions of adult dishes are available. Good-sized rear garden and three bedrooms with extra beds or cots available for families.

Alternative refreshment stops

As you would expect from a popular village, there are cafés and snack bars dotted around Goathland, as well as ice-cream vans on the green. The restaurant at the Mallyan Spout Hotel has a fine reputation.

☞ Where to go from here

Take a nostalgic trip on the North Yorkshire Moors Railway, which has a station in the valley below the village. It runs through Newtondale between Pickering and Grosmont and ran steam trains from 1847 until it was closed in 1957. It reopened in 1973 and most of its trains are steam-hauled (www.northyorkshiremoorsrailway .com).

WALK

Robin Hood's Bay

NORTH YORKSHIRE

Cleveland Way and Robin Hood's Bay

Through fields from this obscurely named village and back along part of the Cleveland Way.

Robin Hood's Bay

Walking the coastal path north of Robin Hood's Bay, you will notice how the sea is encroaching on the land. The route of the Cleveland Way has frequently to be redefined as sections slip into the sea. Around Robin Hood's Bay, the loss is said to be around 6 inches (15cm) every 2 years.

For countless visitors, Robin Hood's Bay is perhaps the most picturesque of the Yorkshire coast's fishing villages – a tumble of pantiled cottages that stagger down the narrow gully cut by the King's Beck. Narrow courtyards give access to tiny cottages, whose front doors look over their neighbours' roofs. Vertiginous stone steps link the different levels. Down at the shore, boats are still drawn up on the Landing, though they are more likely to be pleasure craft than working vessels.

There was a settlement where the King's Beck reaches the coast at least as far back as the 6th century. No one has yet put forward a convincing reason why this remote fishing village should bear Robin Hood's name – as it has since at least the start of the 16th century. Stories say that either Robin was offered a pardon by the Abbot of Whitby if he rid the east coast of pirates, or that, fleeing the authorities, he escaped arrest here disguised as a sailor.

the walk

1 From the lower car park opposite the **Victoria Hotel**, turn left up the hill and, where the road bends round to the left, take a signed footpath to the right over a stile. Walk up the fields over three stiles to a metalled lane.

2 Turn right. Go left through a **signed metal gate**. At the end of the field the path bends right to a gate in the hedge on your left. Continue down the next field with a stone wall on your left. Again, go right at the end of the field and over a stile into a green lane.

3 Cross to another waymarked stile and continue along the field edge with a wall on your right. At the field end go over a stile on your right, then make for a **waymarked gate** diagonally left.

Large stones are strewn across the beach around Robin Hood's Bay

| 2h30 | 5.5 MILES | 8.8 KM | LEVEL 1 2 3 |

MAP: OS Explorer OL27 North York Moors – Eastern

START/FINISH: Car park at top of hill by the old railway station, Robin Hood's Bay; grid ref: NZ 950055

PATHS: field and coastal paths, a little road walking, 14 stiles

LANDSCAPE: farmland and fine coastline

PUBLIC TOILETS: at car park

TOURIST INFORMATION: Whitby, tel 01947 602674

THE PUB: The Victoria Hotel, Robin Hood's Bay

❶ Take care on the road at the beginning of the walk. Keep well away from the friable cliff edges

Getting to the start

The old smugglers' village at Robin Hood's Bay huddles in a coastal hollow at the end of the B1447. It can be accessed from High Hawkser on the A171 Whitby to Scarborough road. There are two main car parks, both off to the right of the B road in the upper part of the village. The lower streets are access only.

4 Walk towards the **Bottom House Farm**, through a gate and take the waymarked track round the right of the buildings to another gate, then to a waymarked opening beside a metal gate. Continue with a stone wall on your right, through another gate and on to a track that eventually bends left to a **waymarked stile**.

5 Continue to another stile, which leads to a **derelict footbridge** over a narrow beck. At a T-junction by a wooden electricity pylon, veer right and take a path to the right of the bank. After 50yds (46m), look for a signpost for **Hawsker** in woodland. Walk to the signpost then follow it right. As the hedge to your right curves left, go through a gap on the right and over a **signed stile**, walking straight ahead through the field to an opening by the main road.

6 Go right and right again, following the footpath sign, up the metalled lane towards two holiday parks. Pass **Seaview Caravan Park**, cross the former railway track and continue along the metalled lane, which bends right, goes downhill, crosses a stream and ascends to the **Northcliffe holiday park**.

Far left: Narrow streets and alleys in Robin Hood's Bay are fronted by a jumble of houses

7 Follow the footpath sign right, then go left and follow the metalled track down through the **caravans**, eventually leaving the track to go left to a waymarked path. Follow the path towards the **coastline**, to reach a signpost.

8 Turn right along the **Cleveland Way** for 2.5 miles (4km) alongside eroded shaly cliffs. At **Rocket Post Field** there's a minor waymarked **diversion** across fields to the right, caused by the cliff path collapsing into the sea. On the approach to Robin Hood's Bay go left through a gate and past houses to reach the main road. Turn left for the lower car park and hotel.

what to look for

At low tide, the bay reveals concentric arcs of rocks, the remains of a large rock dome that has, over the millennia, been eroded by the action of the sea. The ridges are bands of hard limestone and ironstone that have eroded less quickly than the softer lias between them. Where the lias is exposed fossil hunters search for shells (among them the characteristic whirls of the ammonites) and larger sea creatures.

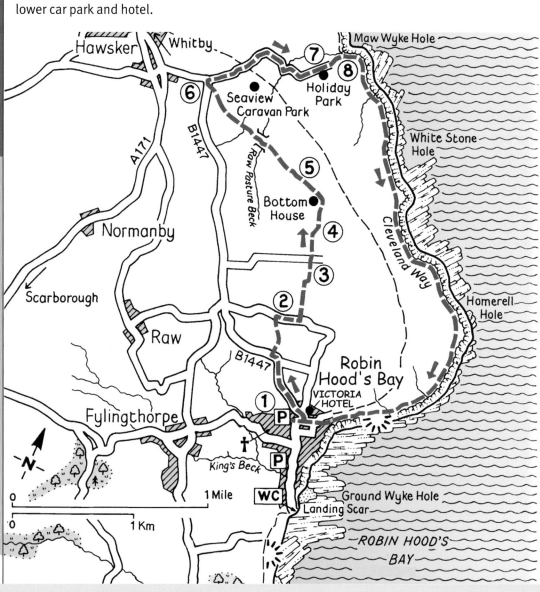

The Victoria Hotel

Sited at the top of the village with fine views over the bay, this Victorian 'Gothic-style' building delivers more than first impressions promise, with fine food, hand-pulled Camerons beers and helpful courteous service. There is a family 'no smoking' room, simply but attractively furnished with bright warm colours – also an airy dining room with wood-panelled floor and huge panoramic windows overlooking the bay. Add ten pine-furnished en suite bedrooms, most with sea views, and you have a comfortable coastal retreat.

Food
Traditional food ranges from cold platters (cheese ploughman's with salad and pickles) and burgers to freshly battered Whitby haddock and chips, sausages and mash, steak pie, garlic chicken, sirloin steak with Stilton and white sauce, and home-made curries.

Family facilities
Families are made very welcome at this friendly inn. There's a family area downstairs and children have a good menu to choose from. Bedrooms include en suite family rooms.

Alternative refreshment stops
Stoke up in Robin Hood's Bay before the walk, as there is nowhere else on the route. In the village there are several pubs and cafés, including the Laurel Inn on New Road.

☛ Where to go from here
Travel south along the coast to Ravenscar, a headland where the Romans built a signal station. Alum shale, used in fixing, was mined here in the 17th and 18th centuries; you can see the scars of the industry and the Peak Alum Works explains more about the activity. Head north to Whitby and visit the town's fascinating museum (www.whitby-museum.org.uk) or enjoy a trip around Whitby harbour on board an authentic replica of Captain Cook's HMS *Endeavour*.

about the pub

The Victoria Hotel
Robin Hood's Bay, Whitby
North Yorkshire YO22 4RL
Tel: 01947 880205

DIRECTIONS: see Getting to the Start; pub opposite the car park

PARKING: use village car park

OPEN: daily; all day July and August

FOOD: daily

BREWERY/COMPANY: free house

REAL ALE: Camerons Bitter & Strongarm, guest beer

DOGS: in garden only

ROOMS: 10 en suite

The Pentlands

A lovely, bracing walk across the hills.

Although this walk starts from Edinburgh's busy city bypass, you'll soon feel that you're miles from the city. The Pentlands are an uncompromising range of hills which clasp

the city in their craggy, green arms. Their peaks rise up to 1,898ft (579m) above sea level and offer many great walks.

This route takes you past several reservoirs, which keep Scotland's capital supplied with water. The first you pass is Torduff Reservoir, which was built in 1851 and is 72ft (22m) deep. Later on you come

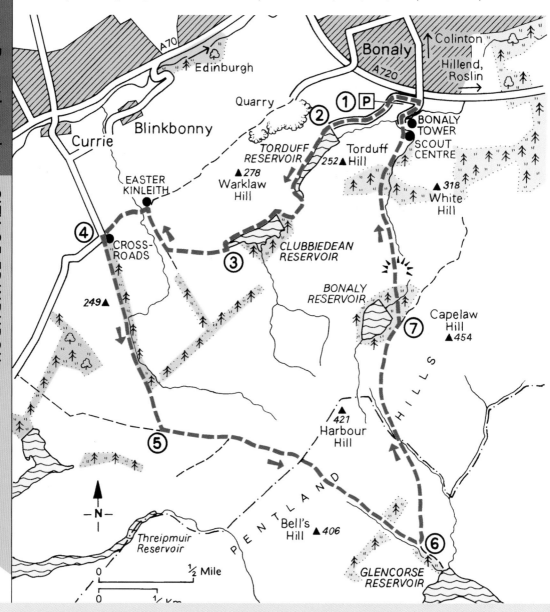

down to Glencorse Reservoir. Beneath its waters lie the remains of the Chapel of St Katherine's (or Catherine's) in the Hopes dating to the 13th century and the reign of Robert the Bruce. If it's been very dry (unlikely, I know) and the waters are shallow, you might just see it.

The Pentlands are full of such historic monuments and memories. In prehistoric times, the hills were far more populated than they are today. On a low hill above Flotterstone, Castlelaw is a well-preserved hill fort dating from around the time of the Roman invasions. Its most intriguing feature is a souterrain, a long underground passage with a small side-chamber. The purpose that such structures served remains unclear.

The hills are criss-crossed with ancient routes and, near Farmilehead, the Camus Stone commemorates a battle fought against the Danes. In 1666, General Dalyell of The Binns (an ancestor of the former MP, Tam Dalyell) beat a ragged army of insurgents fighting for the Covenant at Rullion Green. These days there are army firing ranges near Castlelaw, while recruits from barracks at Glencorse and Redford are put through their paces on the hills.

In the final stages of this walk you'll pass Bonaly Tower, once the home of Lord Cockburn (1779–1854), a writer and judge who is remembered for the sketches that he penned of Edinburgh society. He was a conservationist who loved traditional Scots architecture. Cockburn employed architect William Playfair to rebuild an old farmhouse as a castle. The tower, for all its battlements and turrets, is a fake. All the same, Cockburn loved the castle he created. 'Human nature is incapable of enjoying more happiness than has been my lot here,' he wrote.

4h00 — **10 MILES** — **16 KM** — **LEVEL 2**

MAP: aqua 3 OS Explorer 344 Pentland Hills

START/FINISH: Bonaly Tower, grid ref: NT 212679

PATHS: wide firm tracks, short stretches can be muddy, 3 stiles

LANDSCAPE: reservoirs, fields and hills

PUBLIC TOILETS: at Flotterstone Information Centre

TOURIST INFORMATION: Edinburgh, tel 0131 473 3800

THE PUB: The Flotterstone Inn, Milton Bridge

❶ Obey signs to keep dogs on leads near livestock

Getting to the start

Bonaly Country Park is 4 miles (6.4km) southwest of Edinburgh city centre and 1 mile (1.6km) south of Colinton. The car park is in Torduff Road, a turning to the right off Bonaly Road just across a bridge over the bypass.

Below: A peaceful woodland walk

Pentlands   CITY OF EDINBURGH

the walk

1 From the car park by the bypass, follow the signs pointing in the direction of Easter Kinleith and walk along the metalled track. You will reach the **water treatment works** on your left-hand side. Continue on past the works to reach the gate by the East of Scotland Water sign.

2 Go through the gate and continue walking ahead, keeping **Torduff Reservoir** on your left-hand side. When you reach the top of the reservoir, walk over the little bridge and follow the metalled track as it bends round to the right. Walk under a line of electricity pylons, and go over a small bridge, passing an artificial cataract on your left-hand side, and continue past **Clubbiedean Reservoir**.

3 Your path now bears left and then immediately right, with fields on either side. Pass under another line of pylons and walk to **Easter Kinleith farm**. Now follow the path as it bends back to the left to become a metalled track signposted 'Harlaw'. Pass a sign for Poets' Glen and continue ahead, over a bridge and on to a large white house on the left-hand side called **Crossroads**, where the track meets a public road.

Below: Glencorse Reservoir

4 Turn left and follow the sign for **Glencorse Reservoir**. Follow this track, past a conifer plantation on your left-hand side, then cross a stile next to a metal gate. Continue ahead until you reach a T junction. Turn left through a wooden gate next to larger metal gate.

5 Follow the track, which runs beside a dry stone wall before crossing open moorland. Continue in the same direction until you come to a copse of conifers on the right-hand side, with Glencorse Reservoir ahead. You will see a sign indicating the route by foot to **The Flotterstone Inn** (1 mile/1.6km). You could head for the inn now, or continue to the car park, and drive there later.

6 Turn left here and follow the sign to **Colinton by Bonaly**. Walk uphill and maintain direction to go through a gap in a wire fence. The track now narrows and takes you through the hills until it eventually opens out. Continue in the same direction to reach a fence encircling conifers. Keep the fence on your left and walk down to cross a stile on the left-hand side.

7 Walk past **Bonaly Reservoir**, then through a kissing gate and on downhill, getting good views over Edinburgh as you descend. When you reach a wooden gate, go through and continue ahead, walking downhill, with trees on either side. Go through another kissing gate and follow the tarmac path ahead, passing a **Scout Centre** on the right-hand side followed by **Bonaly Tower**. Turn left at the bridge over the bypass and return to the car park at the start of the walk.

The Flotterstone Inn

Just 7 miles (11.3km) from the city centre, yet backing onto wild, unspoilt countryside, The Flotterstone Inn has long been a draw both for hill-walkers and for families on weekend outings. The long established pub, which would once have been a farm, is an attractive whitewashed building several miles from the nearest village. Inside, there is a spacious bar with comfortable seating, whilst the garden is equally beguiling on hot summer afternoons, with a backdrop of trees and the gurgle of a woodland burn to complement the rustic ambience.

about the pub

The Flotterstone Inn
Milton Bridge
Near Penicuik
EH26 0RD
Tel: 01968 673717

DIRECTIONS: on A702 (Biggar Road) 2 miles (1.2km) south west of Easter Howgate. Go east from walk on A720 to reach A702	
PARKING: 30	
OPEN: daily, all day	
FOOD: daily, all day	
BREWERY: free house	
REAL ALES: varying selection of cask ales	
DOGS: allowed in bar	

Food
The food on offer will satisfy the most ravenous of appetites. Steaks – prime Scottish beef – have been properly hung and marinated before being chargrilled on hot coals, whilst the blackboard menu may include a 'roast trio' of beef, turkey and gammon. For those in search of lighter fare there are half a dozen different salads, Ploughman's lunch, club sandwiches or a range of vegetarian specialities. There is always a selection of real ales, although the choice varies week to week.

Family facilities
Children are permitted in the bar and high chairs are available.

Alternative refreshment stops
The Spylaw Tavern in Colinton serves light lunches, and it has a beer garden.

☞ Where to go from here
If you're feeling fit then make for Hillend Ski Centre on the Pentlands. This is a dry-ski slope, suitable for ski and snowboarding practice. A chairlift takes you to the top if you don't fancy the climb. You're also close to the Gilmerton Cove, a mysterious complex of underground chambers that have yet to be properly explained (for details of tours contact tourist information office).

Gifford to Haddington

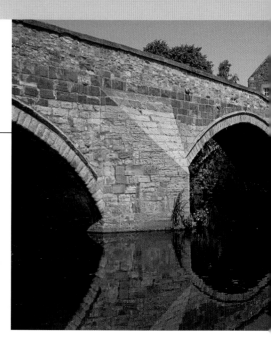

Between the coast and the hills of East Lothian.

Yester and Lennoxlove

The heartland of East Lothian consists largely of rolling countryside and gentle hills, ideal for cyclists. Set among an agricultural landscape is its most attractive feature, villages built from the local red and brown sandstone and characteristic pantiled roofs. One of these villages, Gifford, has grown up as a planned community, built to accommodate the estate workers associated with Yester Castle, now a ruin. Sir Hugo Giffard (sic) built the earliest castle in 1250 and, because of the sloping ground around its base, the Goblin Ha' lies partly underground and survives to this day. The attractive 17th and 18th century village lies on its northern edge, linked to the Yester estate by an impressive avenue of lime trees.

Although there are cycle paths on disused railway lines in the area and you can link up with the national cycle network at Haddington, this route takes you exclusively through quiet country roads offering lovely views towards the coast to the north and the Lammermuir Hills to the south.

Half way round is Lennoxlove, dating from the 14th century, which is now the home of the Duke of Hamilton, Scotland's premier peer. Two hundred years ago this was the work place of the poet Robert Burns' brother, who was the factor (agent) for the estate. His mother and sister also lived in a cottage nearby and you can follow some of their history around this route.

The ride

1 Turn right past the Goblin Ha', heading along Main Street (B6355) towards Yester Church, where you fork left onto the B6369 signed to Haddington. At this junction note the plaque (on the stone wall to your left) to the Rev John Witherspoon, the only clergyman to sign the American Declaration of Independence. The road rises gently, crossing a small stream, where herons and dippers can sometimes be seen, to Myreside.

2 You will have just passed a sign to the Chippendale International School of Furniture, which welcomes visitors. Looking back the way you have come you will see the Lammermuir Hills guarding East Lothian's southern flank. From here continue, mostly freewheeling, down the gentle incline. Ten miles (16km) ahead are the rocky tops, old volcanic plugs, of North Berwick Law and the Bass Rock, while 4 miles (6.4km) to the right is Traprain Law, site of a prehistoric hill fort where a spectacular hoard of Roman silver was found. At the next junction turn left, then right after 0.5 mile (0.8km).

Haddington's Nungate Bridge, a
16th-century construction altered in
the 18th century

1h45 — **10 MILES** — **16 KM** — **LEVEL 1**23

MAP: OS Landranger 66 Edinburgh
START/FINISH: The Square; Gifford,
grid ref: NT 533680
TRAILS/TRACKS: quiet B and minor roads
LANDSCAPE: woods and agricultural land
PUBLIC TOILETS: Gifford village
TOURIST INFORMATION: Haddington,
tel 01620 827422
CYCLE HIRE: none near by
THE PUB: The Goblin Ha', Gifford
❶ Watch out for occasional tractors and
other farm vehicles

Getting to the start

From Edinburgh take the A1 east towards
Berwick-on-Tweed, exiting on the B6471
into Haddington; turn right at the end of the
main street onto the B6369 to Gifford,
bearing left into Main Street to the car park
in the Square in front of the Village Hall on
the right.

Why do this cycle ride?

This gives an opportunity to experience
good roads, usually fairly quiet, with views
across rolling farmland and distant hills in
one of the more English looking parts of
Scotland. It also offers a chance to enjoy the
house and grounds of one of the stately
homes of Scotland.

3 In 200 yards you pass the estate wall
and woods of Lennoxlove, whose
entrance is in a further 0.9 mile (1.2km).
You may want to take a diversion into the
grounds to view the trees and herbaceous
borders or visit the house or Garden Café
(restricted opening times). From the
entrance gates continue for another 0.3 mile
(0.53km) to the junction with the B6368.

4 If you want to sample the charms of
Haddington, East Lothian's premier
market town, turn right here. Otherwise turn
left and in about 0.5 mile (0.8km) you will
reach a further section of estate walls, with
woods behind, on the left and views over
fields to Haddington on your right.

5 In another 0.5 mile (0.8km) on the right
is an off-road layby next to a monument
to the family of Robert (Rabbie) Burns,
Scotland's national poet. A hundred yards
before this is the well his mother drew water
from when she lived near here in the early
19th century. Continue along the road and
soon bear left towards Bolton (just over a
mile away). Along this section are mixed
woods in the estate and views ahead to the
Lammermuirs.

6 Bolton is a small mostly 18th century village of attractive brown stone houses with traditional pantiled roofs. Note the cylindrical doocot (dovecot) with its little lantern tower next to the farm opposite the church on your left. In the churchyard you will find the Burns family burial plot. Just after leaving the village bear left up a gentle incline and take the left turn ahead. For the next mile there are farms to your left and woods to the right. Eaglescairnie Mains Farm does B&B.

7 At the next junction bear left onto the B6355, passing a striking thatched house, Bolton Muir, with tall chimneys and a wooden facing. Follow this undulating road with a final descent back to Gifford over the Gifford Water to the car park in the Square.

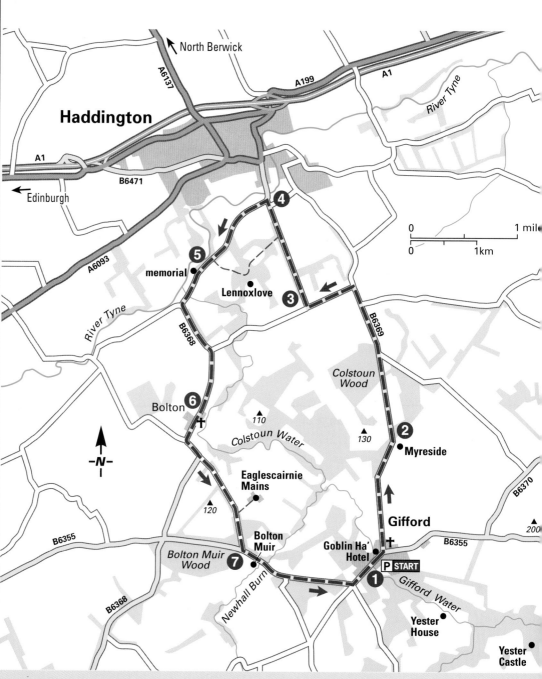

The Goblin Ha' Hotel

The Goblin Ha' has two bars: the public bar in a 17th-century pantiled building on the corner of the village square but the main lounge bar and dining areas only appeared in the attached 18th-century building on Main Street last century. The name derives from the partially underground Goblin Ha' (the Hall in nearby Yester Castle), dating from the 13th century. It is referred to in Sir Walter Scott's poem Marmion and earlier records state that 'ancient stories relate that it was built by magic arts'. The main bar and dining areas have recently been extensively modernised to create a conservatory and beer garden at the back. Beers from the local Belhaven Brewery are always on tap and it has a range of guest beers in both bars. In 2003 it won the CAMRA Best Pub of the Year award for Edinburgh and southeast Scotland.

Food
The food includes traditional bar snacks – haddock and chips, burgers, steak pie, curry – as well as a wider dining room menu using local produce, including venison casserole, rack of lamb, salmon steak and a range of salads. Sunday roast lunches.

Family facilities
Children are welcome in all areas. There are separate children's menus and play areas next to the beer garden.

Alternative Refreshment Stops
The Tweeddale Arms Hotel in Gifford, the Garden Café at Lennoxlove or Peter Potter Gallery in Haddington are all good alternatives.

☛ Where to go from here
Visit the Seabird Centre in North Berwick, featuring live camera links to the Bass Rock, which has the largest gannet colony in the northern hemisphere. (www.seabird.org)

about the pub

The Goblin Ha'
Main Street, Gifford, East Lothian
EH41 4QH
Tel: 01620 810244

DIRECTIONS: Gifford Village Square, see Getting to the start

PARKING: 10 spaces outside Village Hall or use Main Street

OPEN: daily, all day

FOOD: daily, 12-2, 6-9

BREWERY COMPANY: Belhaven

REAL ALE: Belhaven Best and guest beers

The Braes o' Killiecrankie

Pitlochry

PERTH & KINROSS

A lovely deeply wooded riverside leads from the famous battlefield to Loch Faskally

'If ye'd hae been where I hae been
Ye wouldna been sae swanky o
If ye'd hae seen where I hae seen
On the braes o Killiecrankie o'

The song commemorating the victory of the Battle of Killiecrankie in July 1689 is still sung wherever anyone with an accordion sits down in a pub full of patriotic tourists. In fact, both sides in the battle were Scots. When James II was ousted from England in a bloodless coup in 1688, the Scots Parliament (the Estates) voted to replace him with William of Orange.

John Claverhouse, 'Bonnie Dundee', raised a small army of Highlanders in support of King James. The Estates sent a larger army under another Highlander, General Hugh Mackay, to sort things out. Dundee, outnumbered two to one, was urged to ambush Mackay in the Pass of Killiecrankie. He refused, on the grounds of chivalry. The path above the river was steep, muddy and wide enough for only two soldiers; a surprise attack on such difficult ground would give his broadsword-wielding Highlanders too great an advantage. The battle actually took place on open ground, north of the pass.

Killiecrankie was the last time the claymore conquered the musket in open battle, due to a deficiency in the musket. Some 900 of the 2,500 Highlanders were shot down as they charged, but then the troopers had to stop to fix their bayonets, which plugged into the muzzle of the musket. The Highlanders were upon them, and they fled. The battle lasted just three minutes. Half of Mackay's army was killed, wounded, captured or drowned in the Garry. One escaped by leaping 18ft (5.5m) across the river; the 'Soldier's Leap'. Dundee died in battle.

Today, it is hard to believe that such bloody events occurred along the route of this peaceful riverside walk. Mature mixed

4h30 — 8.75 MILES — 14.1 KM — LEVEL 1 2 3

woodland cloaks the steep slopes of the pass above the tumbling waters of the River Garry, trout rise in the rock pools of the Linn of Tummel and red squirrels may sometimes be seen in the branches of old pines. Loch Dunmore is an idyllic spot: a placid pond with an oriental bridge set in the wooded grounds of Faskally House.

the walk

1 Cross the front of the visitor centre to steps, signed 'Soldier's Leap', leading down into the wooded gorge. A footbridge crosses the waterfall of Troopers' Den. At the next junction, turn left (**'Soldier's Leap'**). Ten steps down, a spur path on the right leads to the viewpoint above the Soldier's Leap.

2 Return to the main path, signed '**Linn of Tummel**', which runs down to join the River Garry below the railway viaduct. After a mile (1.6km) it reaches a footbridge.

3 Don't cross this footbridge, but continue ahead, signed 'Pitlochry', along the riverside under the tall **South Garry road bridge**. The path runs around a huge river pool to a tarred lane; turn right here, passing the **Fisheries Research laboratories**. The lane leaves the lochside, then passes a track on the right, blocked by a vehicle barrier. Ignore this; shortly turn right at a signpost, **'Pitlochry'**.

4 Immediately bear left to pass along the right-hand side of **Loch Dunmore**, following red-top posts. A footbridge crosses the loch, but turn away from it, half right, leaving the main path to follow a much fainter path across a grassy glade. The path

MAP: aqua3 OS Explorer 386 Pitlochry & Loch Tummel

START/FINISH: Killiecrankie visitor centre, grid ref: NN 917626

PATHS: wide riverside paths, minor road, no stiles

LANDSCAPE: oak woods on banks of two rivers

PUBLIC TOILETS: at start

TOURIST INFORMATION: Killiecrankie Visitor Centre, tel 01350 728641

THE PUB: The Old Mill Inn, Pitlochry

Getting to the start

Killiecrankie Visitor Centre is on the B8019, 3 miles (4.8km) north west of Pitlochry. Car parking is available at the visitor centre.

soon becomes more distinct and after 110yds (100m) it reaches a wider track. Turn left, with a white/yellow waymarker. After 220yds (201m) the track starts to climb; a short distance up the slope the white/yellow markers indicate a smaller path on the right, which follows the lochside. Where it rejoins the wider path, bear right at a **green waymarker** and cross a footbridge to the A9 road bridge.

5 Cross Loch Faskally on the **Clunie footbridge** below the road bridge, turn left up the path and then immediately right, on to a quiet road around the loch. In 1 mile (1.6km), at the top of the grass bank on the left, is the **Priest Stone**, an early Christian monolith. After the **Clunie power station**, you reach a car park on the left. Here a sign indicates a steep little path down to the **Linn of Tummel**.

6 Return to the road above for 0.5 mile (800m), to cross a grey suspension bridge on the right. Turn right, downstream, to pass above the Linn. A spur path back right returns to the falls at a lower level, but the main path continues along the riverside (signed 'Killiecrankie'). It bends left and goes down wooden steps to the Garry, then runs upstream and under the high road bridge. Take the side-path up on to the bridge for the view of the river, then return to follow the descending path signed **'Pitlochry via Faskally'**. This runs down to the bridge, Point 3. Return upstream to the start.

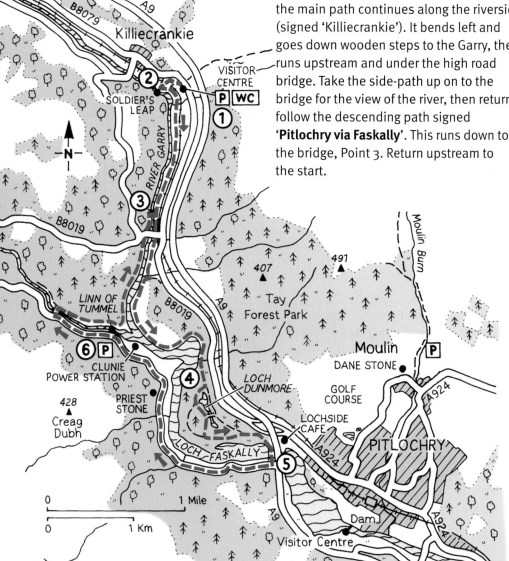

The Old Mill Inn

about the pub

The Old Mill Inn
Mill Lane
Pitlochry
Perthshire PH16 5BH
Tel: 01796 474020
www.old-mill-inn.com

DIRECTIONS: just off the north side of the High Street, behind the Royal Bank of Scotland

PARKING: 30

OPEN: daily, all day

FOOD: daily, all day

BREWERY: free house

REAL ALE: Jennings Cumberland Ale, Tetley Bitter and changing range of other beers.

DOGS:. only in garden

Family facilities
Children are welcome. The pub garden features an attractive play area beside the water-wheel.

Alternative refreshment stops
Pitlochry is well served with pubs, restaurants and cafés. Killiecrankie Visitor Centre has a small cafeteria for light snacks.

☛ Where to go from here
At the Pitlochry dam, which forms Loch Faskally, Scottish and Southern Energy has a small visitor centre celebrating its hydro-electric schemes. It also has a window into the salmon ladder beside the dam. From March to October you can watch the fish battle their way up towards Killiecrankie.

The building was a working watermill until the 1950s and still retains a fine undershot water-wheel and mill-stream flowing through its grounds, which include an outside seating area. A range of around 150 malt whiskies is on offer, including rarities such as a 1955 Strathisla at £30 a dram!

Food
The menu includes Aberdeen Angus steak and locally caught fresh fish. Barbecues are a regular feature in the summer, while the upstairs restaurant serves the best Scottish produce and dishes: the menu offers soups, haggis, venison casserole, black pudding and steak and ale pie.

Pitlochry

PERTH & KINROSS

Acknowledgements

The Automobile Association wishes to thank the following establishments for their assistance in the preparation of this publication.

The George & Dragon, Aysgarth 223; Glan-y-Mor Inn 115; The Royal Oak, Kingsbury 135; Sawrey Hotel, Far Sawrey 211; The Stone Trough Inn, Whitewell-on-the-Hill 235.

The remaining photographs are held in the Association's own photo library (AA World Travel Library) and were taken by the following photographers:
Pat Aithie 117; Adrian Baker 128/9; Peter Baker 37, 39, 41; Stewart Bates 112; Jeff Beazley 173b, 175b; Malc Birkitt 145t, 145b; E A Bowness 12, 203, 207t, 215; Peter Brown 80; Ian Burgum 116, 113t, 113b; John O'Carroll 32/3, 33, 35, 74; Nick Channer 120, 121, 123, 127; Neil Coates 171, 175t, 179, 180/1, 183, 187; Peter Davies 148; Steve Day 56, 61, 62, 160/1, 162, 201, 210, 252; Kenya Doran 57; John Gillham 226, 227, 231, 232, 243; Steve Gregory 236, 240/1; Paul Grogan 136, 140/1, 142, 143; David Halford 83, 85, 87, 91; David Hancock 17, 18, 19, 27, 119, 151, 251; Rebecca Harris 99, 111; James Hatts 100/1, 101, 103, 104/5, 107; Anthony Hopkins 173t, 185t, 186; Debbie Ireland 45; Richard Ireland 46, 48, 49, 51tl, 51tr, 176; Caroline Jones 21, 125; Max Jourdan 40; Dennis Kelsall 44, 55, 59, 63, 67, 131; Ian Knapp 139, 147; Andrew Lawson 24, 25; Tim Locke 95; Tom Mackie 4, 15, 149, 207b, 208/9; Terry Marsh 152/3, 154, 155, 156, 157, 159, 163, 188/9, 189, 191, 193, 195, 200; Simon McBride 106; S & O Mathews 76/7, 81; Andrew Midgely 167, 169, 170, 185b; John Miller 86, 88/9, 97; John Morrison 220, 239, 240; Robert Mort 96; David Noble 92; Ken Paterson 245, 246; Hamish Scott 247, 255; Peter Sharpe 204, 213; Tony Souter 14b, 64/5; John Sparks 196, 196/7, 199, 217, 218, 219; Richard Surman 129, 205; James Tims 109; Peter Toms 43, 79; Richard Turpin 108; Sue Viccars 20, 23, 28, 29, 31; Wyn Voysey 13, 14t, 68/9, 71, 75; Jonathan Welsh 133, 164, 165; Linda Whitwam 228/9; Harry Williams 38, 52/3; Peter Wilson 221, 225.